CAPTAINS WITHOUT EYES

A Westview Encore Edition

CAPTAINS WITHOUT EYES

INTELLIGENCE FAILURES IN WORLD WAR II

Lyman B. Kirkpatrick, Jr.

Westview Press / Boulder and London

This **Westview Encore Edition** is printed on acid-free paper and bound in softcovers that carry the highest rating of the National Association of State Textbook Administrators in consultation with the Association of American Publishers and the Book Manufacturers' Institute.

Published in 1987 in the United States of America by Westview Press, Inc.; Frederick A. Praeger, Publisher; 5500 Central Avenue, Boulder, Colorado 80301

First published in 1969 by The Macmillan Company

Library of Congress Catalog Card Number: 87-29599
ISBN: 0-8133-7493-6

Printed and bound in the United States of America

The paper used in this publication meets the requirements of the American National Standard for Permanence of Paper for Printed Library Materials Z39.48-1984.

6   5   4   3   2   1

This book is dedicated to my children—

TERRY,

BARCLAY,

TIMMY and

HELEN—

with the prayer that the captains
who direct their destinies
will have clarity of vision

Contents

LIST OF MAPS   ix

PREFACE   xi

1. The Problems of Foresight   1

2. Case *Barbarossa*: The German Attack on Russia, June 22, 1941   17

3. Pearl Harbor: A Lost Battle v. A National Disaster, December 7, 1941   75

4. Dieppe: Prelude to D-Day, August 19, 1942   159

5. Arnhem: A Viper in the Market, September 17, 1944   199

6. The Bulge in the Ardennes: Hitler's Last Threat, December 16, 1944   229

7. The Brilliance of Hindsight   267

REFERENCES   283

BIBLIOGRAPHY   291

INDEX   297

Maps

BY HOLLY HOWARD

Operation *Barbarossa*   69
The Empty Seas   145
The Battle of Dieppe   181
The Six Bridges to Arnhem   209
The Battle of the Bulge   251

Preface

Not LONG AGO at a dinner party a friend commented favorably on my first book, *The Real CIA*, in which in a semiautobiographical fashion I explained the origin, development and responsibilities of the Central Intelligence Agency —an organization with which I had the honor to serve during its first eighteen years of existence: 1947–65. I was asked if I was working on a new book and if so, what it was about. I explained that *Captains Without Eyes* was the story of how the failure of intelligence in five important battles in World War II had decisive results.

The lady on my left had an immediate comment. "Oh, you men! You are always fascinated with war. You find it exciting, and never can forget it. That's why you want to write about it!"

One cannot deny that there is a great deal of truth in what she said. War is exciting; just as the dangerous, the unknown and the speculative are always exciting. But having been through one war, having seen two others at too close hand and having had a son go to war, I would not recommend it for excitement seekers. It is too dangerous, but even more important, it is a stupid and senseless way for men to settle disputes.

Having said that, I hasten to add that I am not optimistic about the possibility that man will cease using force to settle disputes. The use of violence for this purpose is as old as recorded history. I regret to say that I do not see the nobler aspects of man emerging as dominant and do not believe he will stop using force until there is some overwhelming external compulsion which makes it necessary to be peaceful.

The reason I have written *Captains Without Eyes* is because I found the role of intelligence in battle a fascinating one. I had the great privilege of being the intelligence briefing officer at the Tactical Headquarters of General Omar N. Bradley's 12th U.S. Army Group during most of the campaign in Europe in 1944–45. This afforded me an opportunity as a very junior officer to observe at first hand— be a participant in—an intelligence failure in a major battle: The Bulge in the Ardennes.

Less than two years after the end of World War II, I wrote an analysis of the intelligence failure in the Ardennes. Then service with the CIA precluded any further study of or writing on the subject except for the preparation of a lecture on intelligence in that battle for presentation to a military reserve unit. In 1965 I was able to return to the general subject and found the raid on Dieppe in 1942 to be another battle where inadequate information led to major miscalculations. It was at that time that I realized the urgency of doing a book on the CIA to try to correct some of the misunderstanding of that important agency on the part of the American people. The project diverted me again from the subject of this book. Finally, in 1968 I was able to return to *Captains Without Eyes*.

Over the years since World War II, I have benefited from discussions about military intelligence with my former superiors—General Omar N. Bradley, Major General Edwin L. Sibert, General Walter Bedell Smith, Lieutenant General Marshall S. Carter, Colonel William H. Jackson (Deputy G-2 at 12th Army Group)—and many wartime friends and associates—Colonel William M. Weaver (G-2 at 12th Army Group), Alexander Standish (Chief of Intelligence Branch at 12th Army Group), Brigadier General Oscar Koch (G-2 of the Third U.S. Army), General William Quinn (G-2 of the Seventh U.S. Army), Major General James O. Curtis, Jr. (G-2 Staff at SHAEF), Major General Thomas Betts (Assistant G-2 at SHAEF), Colonel Matthew Baird (who served in the Pacific), Rear Admiral Marion Cheek (a naval intelligence officer in the Pacific), Captain Walter Pforzheimer (who served in Air Corps Intelligence in Europe) and many others. To them I am grateful. However, the views expressed in this book are mine alone, except where otherwise noted.

My wife, Rita, has greatly assisted in the writing of this book, acting as research assistant, editorial advisor and typist. My daughter Jeanne Barclay Kirkpatrick also assisted with some of the research. Doris Michel gave generous assistance on the Dieppe chapter. I am also indebted to my sister, Helen Kirkpatrick Milbank, whose experience as a war correspondent and skill as a writer provided a background for wise advice. Holly Howard of the Rhode Island School of Design produced the maps. I also want to acknowledge the advice of George A. Horkan, Jr., both on this book and *The Real CIA*. Richard Marek, my editor at The

Macmillan Company, provided constant encouragement and many valuable suggestions.

Finally, I am probably foolish to hope that *Captains Without Eyes* will make any contribution toward fewer intelligence failures by United States military forces in future wars. After all, these five battles are only some of those in World War II in which there was faulty intelligence. What is past may be prologue, but all too few read even the prologue, let alone the text. Men do not learn too much from past mistakes. Vanity assures them they could not be so stupid, so history repeats.

I do hope the book may in some small way help persuade Americans that adequate information is a vital necessity for victory in battle and that so long as there is any danger of future wars, the United States must have a strong intelligence service.

LYMAN B. KIRKPATRICK, JR.

Anawan Cliffs
Narragansett, Rhode Island
January 1969

CAPTAINS WITHOUT EYES

1.
The Problems of
Foresight

ONCE A BATTLE is fought it immediately becomes
the subject of study. After-action reports are written by the
staffs. Military academies analyze the action for possible use
as a case study. Historians relate its importance to the
course of human events. And it becomes a name and a date
in the chronicle of time.

The attention the battle may receive will depend on its
relative importance in the course of the war. If it is of any
consequence, military historians will review all of the plans
for the battle, the action and after-action reports of the participating units, and interview the survivors. Books and articles will be written, and the name of the battle will be
perpetuated: Cannae, Thermopylae, Waterloo, Gettysburg,
the Marne, Dunkirk and many others.

In all of the studies of battle one aspect looms large. Why was it fought? And why at that time and place? But this is one of the most elusive aspects of all battles, unless the commanders on both sides record in detail their reasoning. It is elusive because it also involves the least accurately recorded of all military activity: the information or intelligence on the enemy that was considered before opening the battle.

It is intelligence that provides the foresight, that gives the captains their vision. If the captain is provided with complete and accurate intelligence on the enemy and uses it properly, it can lead to victory. If the captain is not given adequate intelligence on the enemy, or disregards what intelligence is provided, it can lead to disaster.

It is intelligence that is the principal subject of this study. What intelligence was available to the captains who directed the forces in these battles?

This is the story of five battles from World War II— battles that ranged in size from a few thousand men on each side to seven million men. Two of the battles, the German attack on the Soviet Union and the Japanese attack on the United States, were of a decisive nature in that they brought into the conflict the world's two largest industrial powers, and because the attackers failed in their objective of a quick death blow it meant their own ultimate defeat. Two of the battles, the Allied airdrop at Arnhem and the German offensive in the Ardennes, both in the fall of 1944, could have had decisive results had the attacks succeeded, but both failed. And one battle, the nine-hour British-Canadian raid on the German-held port of Dieppe on the French coast, while a disaster, was to have an important effect on the future course of the war.

The five battles all had certain common military characteristics, but many differences. The German attack on Russia on June 22, 1941, was a massive air and ground assault along a 1,800-mile front. Its objective was to destroy the Russian military forces and topple the Communist government. It was designed to catch the Red armies by surprise and every effort was made to blind the Russian intelligence service and to mislead the Soviet leaders.

The Japanese attack on Pearl Harbor on December 7, 1941, was also a surprise attack without a declaration of war and had as its objective the destruction of the United States Pacific fleet. It was an attack by carrier-borne aircraft on a fleet at anchor. This, the Japanese hoped, would give them the time to conquer Asia.

The British-Canadian assault on Dieppe on August 19, 1942—described by some as too big for a raid and too small for an invasion—tested German defenses and provided invaluable information for the operations to liberate Europe from German occupation. It was an amphibious attack on a strongly defended port city carried out by commando, marine and ground troops supported by tanks and naval gunfire, with strong air support designed to entice the Germans into an air battle, which the R.A.F. expected to win decisively.

The British airdrop at Arnhem on September 17, 1944 —part of the larger *Market Garden* operation to seize the bridges across the Rhine and Waal—was to open a corridor across Holland to the Zuider Zee, to help liberate the country and to provide a base for a quick armored thrust to the heart of Germany in order to end the war before the Nazis could recover from their staggering defeats in France. *Market Garden* was an airborne assault by three divisions supported by a ground attack by three corps.

The German offensive into the Ardennes Forest in Belgium on December 16, 1944, aimed at cutting through the American First Army to reach the Channel Coast and split the armies of the western Allies. Hitler's tanks had knifed through the Ardennes in 1940 and had been a vital factor in the quick and decisive defeat of France. The battle in the Ardennes in 1944 was initially almost exclusively a ground battle, with the exception of a few parachutists put behind the American lines for harassment purposes. Air power played an important role when the weather cleared after the first eight days of the battle.

These battles were selected for analysis not so much for their differing characteristics, or for the varying mixture of forces used, but for the one important common characteristic. In each instance there was a vital intelligence failure on one or, in some cases, on both sides. In every case there were certainly intelligence gaps. It is very rare for any nation to have perfect intelligence coverage of another nation, and in wartime, intelligence coverage is invariably less precise, generally ranging from fair to non-existent. In each of these battles the intelligence on the side of either the attacker or defender, or both, was of such a quality that it is not unfair to say that the leaders were truly captains without eyes.

Intelligence is a difficult profession and an imperfect science at best. It should be noted that there were other factors that affected the vision of the leaders before blaming intelligence for the failure.

There are no absolutes and few precise means of measuring the intelligence available to the military leaders on the opposing sides in these battles. In no instance was there total blindness—no attacks through unknown territory, or against a people whose hostility was in doubt, nor were they fought against military forces of undetermined strength.

In most instances the nature of the terrain to be crossed by the attacking forces was well known: the progress made in aerial photography between World Wars I and II had assisted in this problem. But despite this there were still some unpleasant geographical surprises awaiting the attackers: the use of the headlands flanking Dieppe harbor for gun emplacements had not been anticipated; the difficulties of moving across the canal country of south Holland plagued the Allied armor racing toward Arnhem; and even that student of Napoleonic campaigns, Adolf Hitler, failed to appreciate the extent of the natural obstacles in Russia.

In four of the battles described there was little question about the attitude of the peoples in the area of battle. In one, the German attack on Russia, it could have been a factor that might have affected the outcome of the war, but the attitude of the Russian people was not even considered in German intelligence estimates because Adolf Hitler did not want it considered. If the local populace did not interfere with the German forces they could become servile serfs; if they did interfere they were to be exterminated. The possibility that the peoples of Russia might be turned against the Soviet regime—and might contribute to German victory—was ignored. Hitler was invincible: intelligence was useful only if it was in accord with his own beliefs.

Military intelligence must assess more than the disposition of enemy forces, the location of fortifications and defenses, or even the probable war plans of the other country. It must assess what the enemy will do under various circumstances. If we attack in the north, will the enemy fiercely resist in that area, counterattack in the south, try to turn our flank or fall back to reserve positions? If we try to take the enemy's principal cities, will those be defended in strength? Should our major effort be to destroy the enemy's armed forces, to capture or destroy his industrial facilities and transportation or to seize the political center of the country?

Thus in many respects military intelligence becomes a war game in which each player is trying to anticipate the other's move and in which the personality, experience and characteristics of the opposing leader or leaders become an important—and often an elusive—factor, as well as one too frequently neglected or dealt with superficially by intelligence.

There is more to preparing for battle—or war—than just having the information on the enemy available (even if that were complete, which it never is). There must be organization—a term frequently brought into disrepute by those who equate it with cumbersome procedures and inefficiency. But wars cannot be fought and certainly are seldom won without organization.

An organization to provide intelligence for a war or a battle must be developed well in advance. Such an organization must have information on everything that could conceivably affect the course of the battle. It must make sure that the information available on the enemy gets to the men who must fight the battle. And it must do what it can to make sure that the commanders know how to use that information.

Occasionally the organization will exist, but the captains will not use it; or they will use it but ignore its advice; or they will reshape it to their own will, thereby compounding their own errors rather than compensating for or correcting them. Adolf Hitler did exactly that when he assumed Supreme Command of the German armed forces in 1940. He failed to use the OKW (Oberkommando der Wehrmacht) as a joint military staff but made it his personal secretariat.

He browbeat his senior commanders to such a degree that few dared differ with him, and those who did were dismissed or ignored. Hitler, who came to power in Germany as an admirer of the military, lost a great deal of that admiration before the war because his boldness brought success and the military were timid and ineffective. He mistreated the military intelligence service primarily because he suspected it of treason.* Adolf Hitler was a man blinded by his own obsessions and ignorance.

But it is not the personality of the captain alone which becomes a factor in preparing for a battle. Wars are fought by men with strong convictions and determinations, and, usually, the higher the rank the more pronounced these traits. Thus the man who makes the ultimate decision is not alone in affecting the outcome. All too frequently the information he receives will have been influenced by the prejudices of subordinates. If the information is about the enemy, it is even more susceptible to the capricious factor of human evaluation, because knowledge about the enemy in wartime is an almost monopolistic possession of the intelligence corps.

The intelligence service of any nation is a unique collection of individuals, attracted to or recruited for that work because of individual interest, qualification or capability. Some are scholars selected solely for their analytical ability. There are those who are attracted to intelligence work because of its presumed conspiratorial nature. And there are the regular military personnel, too often viewing an intelli-

---

* Hitler's suspicions about the Abwehr were heightened by Heinrich Himmler and the other S. S. leaders who did their best to undermine his confidence in the military intelligence service. However, the suspicions apparently were well founded. There is evidence that Abwehr personnel warned Belgium and Holland of the impending German attack in May 1940 and tried to warn the Russians in June 1941.

gence assignment with disdain, preferring operations or command and regarding information about the enemy as a not too vital factor in the battle in which "there can be no question about victory."

Every intelligence officer can have some effect on the battle—by what he believes or does not believe; by what action he takes or neglects to take. The espionage agent operating alone and in great danger may decide in haste or ignorance which document to take from a safe and quickly photograph, or which conversation to report and which to ignore. His "case officer," whether meeting with him periodically to pick up reports and to give guidance as to additional information needed, or dealing with him by radio from thousands of miles away, can vitally affect the flow of information in both directions. The "desk analyst" in headquarters, the first person to receive the raw intelligence regardless of the source, has a life-or-death role in deciding whether the information should be filed and forgotten or should be passed on up the command ladder, and if the latter, with what comment, "Probably true." "From a highly reliable source." "From an unknown source." or "Highly suspect, probably an enemy fabrication or deception."? Each individual who must pass on the information until it ultimately reaches the Commander in Chief, the Fuehrer, the Premier or the President can have a pronounced effect on the information.

In each of the five battles studied the influence of non-scientific factors such as human prejudice, inefficiency and poor organization had an important effect in blinding the captains.

In the German attack on Russia there were few in that atmosphere of euphoria brought about by Hitler's unbroken string of victories who dared tell the Fuehrer that he was gravely underestimating Russian strength, and on the other side, Stalin refused to believe some of the most precise information ever presented to a head of state about an impending assault by another nation. Stalin's personal conviction that Germany would make impossible demands on Russia for territory before attacking contributed to his blindness.

Before Pearl Harbor, less than six months later, the leaders of the United States were well aware of the highly critical relations with Japan; they too had been alerted to the possibility of an attack on Pearl Harbor, but they relied on intelligence organizations, uncoordinated and independent, which dissipated the effectiveness of a relatively recently revived emphasis on intelligence by the U.S. government.

The Dieppe raid of August 1942 was gravely affected by many human considerations. The Royal Navy did not want to risk heavy ships close to an enemy-held coast where they would be under attack by aircraft—the loss of the *Prince of Wales* and *Repulse* off the coast of Malaya to Japanese aircraft was all too fresh a memory—and thus deprived the landing troops of fire support which might have neutralized the devastating guns in the cliffs and the shore pillboxes, the threat of which had not been covered adequately by intelligence.

At Arnhem in September 1944 the First British Parachute Division landed practically on top of two German S. S. panzer (armored) divisions whose presence had been suspected; even more serious was the underestimation of the recuperative ability of the Germans after the disaster in France.

Finally, in the Ardennes in December 1944—less than three months after Arnhem—a German counteroffensive caught the Americans by surprise. Many believed a German counterblow possible, if not probable, but American headquarters had few hard facts about the preparations for the attack.

In all of these battles the ability of the captains to achieve victory was affected by something which obscured their vision. While it should be assumed that in each instance the leaders did everything to insure that their knowledge about the enemy was complete, in at least the case of Adolf Hitler this was not true. He was so convinced of his own infallibility and Germany's invincibility that he was disdainful of most enemies—potential or actual.

Assuming however that the captains wanted the clearest vision for decision, what should the World War II intelligence system have been ideally?

Intelligence requirements differ at various levels of command. A chief of state, a Hitler, a Roosevelt or a Stalin must be aware of everything which could affect the security of his nation. A battle commander should be aware of every enemy potentiality which could affect the outcome of the battle in which the forces under his command are engaged.

Only in rare instances are these objectives achieved, for there are two major aspects of an enemy which must be known. In the first instance the enemy's capabilities must be known in complete detail. Capabilities include the total capacity of the enemy to wage war. This includes not only the strength of the armies, navies and air forces, but also the industrial might and the will of the people, vital in an age of total war. Failure to appreciate the capability of the Germans to recover from the defeat in France led to the Allied defeat at Arnhem.

The second aspect—enemy intentions—is perhaps

more important than the first, and nearly always more difficult to obtain. Will he resort to war to obtain his national objective? Will he declare war? Use a surprise attack? Engage in subversion? Or, once on the battlefield, will the enemy fight to defend his present position? Fall back to new defensive positions? Fight to the last man? Surrender after certain losses? Or will he resort to unorthodox warfare or secret weapons?

Intentions constitute the most closely guarded of national or battlefield secrets. Often they reside in the mind of one man alone—a Hitler in Nazi Germany—or are shared by only a few top leaders. To discover national intentions a foreign intelligence service may literally have to discover what is in the minds of certain men, and still more difficult, what they would do under a variety of different circumstances.

Concealment of true intentions is sometimes a major objective in the complex interchanges of international relations. Hitler went to great lengths to conceal his intention of attacking the Soviet Union in 1941. There are other times when it may be very important that actual intentions are clearly understood by all other nations concerned, especially a potential adversary. During the Cuban missile crisis of 1962 the United States made no effort to conceal from the Russians the military build-up being readied to move into Cuba and destroy the rocket sites. It was vital that the Soviet Union understand that President John F. Kennedy intended to remove the missiles if Nikita Khrushchev did not. In this instance, Soviet knowledge of American intentions may have helped avoid war.

Nearly every major power in the world had its intelligence services at work in the 1930's to learn the capabilities and intentions of potential enemies. The Russian services were by far the largest and covered most effectively the key areas of the world. The British, French and Japanese intelligence services concentrated on key targets of interest to their countries. The United States, "isolated" behind the presumed safety of two vast oceans, was a poor sixth among the major powers in the effort devoted to intelligence.

What these nations had to forewarn them on national danger was not just one omniscient organization, but several different departments and agencies all collecting bits and pieces of information which presumably was collated and analyzed before being presented to the top policy makers of the government. In no country was there what might be called the ideal intelligence organization. In several the collectors were feuding bitterly; in most instances the coordination was faulty; and in nearly all the quality of analysis left much to be desired.

The State Department or Foreign Ministry was the organization holding primary responsibility for knowledge of world affairs. The officially accredited representatives abroad were responsible for reporting fully what was going on in the country of their assignment. Diplomatic missions included military attachés—army and navy representatives —assigned to keep abreast of developments in a service against which they might be fighting at some time in the future. General Ernst Koestring, for example, the German Military Attaché in Moscow in 1941, probably knew more about the potentiality of the Red Army than any other German, but his reports to Hitler were ignored and his warnings of Russian strength believed to be inaccurate. Diplomatic couriers carrying confidential pouches of mail reported on all they saw in their travels. German couriers carrying pouches from Berlin to Tokyo via Russia were characterized by more than one German official as providing the only information about the Soviet Union beyond the confines of Moscow. (The German couriers also inadvertently provided the Russians with intelligence. Richard Sorge, a top Soviet spy, penetrated the German embassy in Tokyo. In the spring of 1941 he heard German diplomatic couriers describe troop movements toward the Russian frontier.)

Behind the official foreign service of each nation is an intelligence or espionage service, the organization which handles the spies. Its mission is to secure information which the diplomats could not: to ferret out the secrets. The effectiveness of the intelligence service varies widely from service to service and from country to country. Recruiting spies is a difficult and dangerous business—difficult because it means discovering those at a high level in a foreign government with access to national secrets willing to commit treason, and dangerous because both the recruiter and the traitor, if discovered, face anything from a lengthy prison term, at a minimum, to a firing squad, or worse—the worst being long, drawn-out interrogation sessions at the hands of the NKVD or Gestapo. Death is infinitely preferable.

It was not simply a matter of telling the intelligence service to get all of the top secrets of the Kremlin, or of the Reich's chancellery. It meant finding where the information was; who had access to it—clerk or colonel; who was approachable and whether ideology or money would persuade him to commit treason. It meant circumventing the security service charged with protecting the national secrets. And last but far from least, it meant getting the information back to headquarters where it could be considered by the government in making a decision.

In battle the military services have the benefit of the information provided by the diplomatic corps—and of course their own attachés—and of the intelligence services. From these sources information of a national or strategic nature is available, and sometimes information of value for battlefield purposes. But once the war begins, military intelligence becomes almost the complete monopoly of the combat army, and in battle areas the tactical intelligence has to be obtained by the military.

Before a battle the military depended on information collected in advance and prepared as an annex to the operation plan. It seems somewhat ironic that the classic method of most military services is first to present the operational plan of battle, and then almost as an afterthought, an analysis of the enemy to be encountered in accomplishing the outlined objectives.

The advance intelligence estimates would include a terrain study of the battlefield, covering all natural and manmade features, with special attention to the defenses, fortifications, gun emplacements or other difficult obstacles. There followed an order-of-battle section listing all enemy units known or suspected of being in the area, the strength and equipment of each unit, the names and qualities of the officers and the defensive positions each unit would occupy. The estimate would include an analysis of what the enemy might do under every conceivable contingency once the battle started.

Once a battle is under way, if the advance intelligence is wrong, there is little that can be done to change the situation. The Canadian and British took heavy casualties at Dieppe because of inadequate intelligence. Hitler completely underestimated the capabilities of Russia, resulting in four years of bloody warfare and the defeat of Germany. The United States failed to be fully alert and suffered a catastrophe at Pearl Harbor.

Yet in some of these instances the information was available. Either the organization failed or the leaders would not believe it or act upon it. For if there are many pitfalls or problems in developing an efficient and effective intelligence system, there are far more in educating those at the policy level on its use.

Captains fail to make proper use of intelligence for many reasons. In some cases they simply do not care what the enemy is doing or can do. They have decided on an objective and are determined to accomplish it, regardless of what others might do. Hitler was determined to dismember Russia, even though he may have belatedly realized the strength of the enemy. He told the Italian Foreign Minister, Count Galeazzo Ciano, in August 1941 that he might not have attacked had he known how many tanks the Red Army had. This is hard to believe. He had rejected reports of Russian tank strength—and at the time he talked to Ciano he was still confident of victory. On the opposite side, Stalin refused to accept reports giving the exact date of the German attack, believing he still had more time to prepare.

Too few leaders, military or otherwise, know enough about intelligence and they seldom take the time to find out. To most leaders an intelligence organization is often suspect. They usually assume that it uses exclusively untrustworthy types—sneaky spies, sexy women, traitors, conspirators, the dregs of the international milieu. Both Hitler and Stalin mistrusted their intelligence services and each had services which combined internal security and external espionage—a dangerous feature at best.

In Hitler's Germany and Stalin's Russia the most powerful services were the security organizations, the Sicherheitsdienst (SD) and the Narodnyi Komissariat Vnutrennikh Del (NKVD) respectively. In both countries these units were responsible for internal security. Their efforts were directed not only at foreign espionage and subversion, but even more at protecting the party against dissidents who did not like the regime. In each case the security organization concentrated on all individuals and organizations suspected of political opposition. It was only natural that sooner or later the rival German and Russian intelligence services should fall into the category of "opposition." Thus in Germany the SD devoted more and more effort to watching the Abwehr and the Foreign Office, and in Russia, still in the aftermath of the Great Purges, the NKVD maintained surveillance over the Army and Foreign Ministry. The rivalries were not conducive to good intelligence operations, and as the security services also engaged in collecting foreign intelligence, the reliability of the intelligence produced deteriorated.

Of course it is considerably easier after the event to analyze what should have been done on the basis of all discernible facts. But to assume that the principals involved at the time knew all of the facts, or even most of the facts, could be most dangerous. Even granting that most of the pertinent facts were available to a leader, it would be a risky business to assume that *the* correct decision would be made. So many other factors enter into each situation aside from what the enemy is going to do—the intelligence of the situation—that even one hundred per cent accuracy of information is no guarantee for success.

Thus the reader should be forewarned. Resist the temptation of saying, "How could they have been so wrong?" Put yourself in the position of the men involved. Recall their personalities, motivation and environment of the time—including on occasion even the loss of a rational thought process—and then, if you can, pass judgment on their actions.

2.

Case *Barbarossa*: The German Attack on Russia

JUNE 22, 1941

ON SEPTEMBER 1, 1939, Adolf Hitler started World War II. The facts of his career are widely known, but I will outline them briefly again here.

Hitler was the unchallenged ruler of Germany. Named to Chancellor by President Hindenburg in 1933, he succeeded to the presidency in 1934 when Hindenburg died, and named himself Fuehrer (leader) of the Germans.

Hitler had achieved total power in Germany partly as a result of his uncanny comprehension of psychological appeals to the German people. Once in control, he secured his position through force and terror. He was to rule the continent of Europe from Moscow to the Atlantic by December 1941. Again, Hitler's intuition concerning the reactions of the other leaders of Europe seemed to play a vital role in

German victories. Yet it was this same conviction of Hitler's —that he knew how people would react—that led to his fatal mistakes.

Hitler's initial successes, politically within Germany, diplomatically and militarily in Europe, led in turn to an obsessive belief in his own infallibility. Certainly after the bomb blast of July 20, 1944, which badly injured him and nearly took his life, Hitler's actions were governed by determination, not reason.

The rise to power of the man who started World War II can be described, even by one who lived through it, as hard to believe. A corporal in the German army in World War I, Hitler joined the Workers' Party in 1920, and in 1923 participated in the so-called Beer Hall Putsch, an attempt to overthrow the government of Bavaria, for which he was arrested and imprisoned for less than a year (of a five-year sentence). While in prison he dictated a book, his political philosophy, *Mein Kampf,* to Rudolf Hess, the man who was to become his deputy and remain by his side until Hess flew to England in 1941 in a personal effort to end the war.

Upon release from prison Hitler quickly gained complete control of the party, organized his private army of Storm Troopers—to protect party activities and suppress opposition—and attracted a large personal following. Adolf Hitler was an orator of considerable ability with charismatic appeal for the German people. He shrewdly concentrated on those issues that would gain him the greatest support.

Hitler concentrated on the Versailles Treaty and the "stab in the back," to which he attributed Germany's defeat in World War I. The Versailles Treaty was a ready-made issue. The Germans would ascribe all of their woes in the 1920's—occupation, starvation, civil unrest, unemployment, inflation, isolation and war guilt—to the harsh terms of the victors. To this Hitler added the argument that Germany had not really lost the war but had been deprived of victory. The "stab in the back" theory was molded to appeal to prejudices against the Jews, intellectuals, pacifists and communists.

By 1930 Hitler's National Socialist German Workers' Party had emerged as a major force in German politics, increasing its representatives in the Reichstag from 12 to 107. Two years later Hitler made a strong showing in the presidential elections against the incumbent General Paul von Hindenburg, and in July of that year the Nazis emerged as the strongest party in the Reichstag, with 230 seats against 133 for the socialists, 97 for the center and 90 for the communists. On August 13, 1932, Hitler refused to serve as Vice Chancellor under Franz von Papen, certain he did not have to be number two. Ironically, just a month later the communists moved "no confidence" in the Reichstag and the government fell 512 to 42, paving the way for Hitler to assume power. Following the new election on November 6, Hitler's terms for assuming the chancellorship were unacceptable to President Hindenburg, who appointed General Kurt von Schleicher to form a cabinet that lasted less than two months.

On January 30, 1933, Adolf Hitler was accepted by Hindenburg and became Chancellor. Eighteen months later Hindenburg died and Hitler assumed the presidency.

Hitler quickly revealed the shape of things to come. On June 30, 1934, the Nazis in a violent bloodbath purged their ranks of dissidents and others accused of plotting against Hitler. Included among those killed were General Kurt von Schleicher, Hitler's predecessor as Chancellor, and Ernst Roehm, the foremost party organizer. Hitler acknowledged to the Reichstag that seventy-seven had been executed. The majority of the Germans were shocked and appalled at this lawless purge—but apathetic.

His power consolidated within Germany, Hitler moved rapidly to build the Greater German Reich that he dreamed would last a thousand years. He set out to regain what had been lost at Versailles. The chronology is a list of victories.

January 13, 1935, a plebiscite in the Saar resulted in a vote of 90 per cent for return to Germany. The Nazis had waged a vigorous propaganda campaign in the area, but the vote was probably a reflection of the true desires of the people. It gave Hitler a tremendous psychological boost. The Saar was returned to Germany on March 1. Hitler moved rapidly thereafter to expand his empire.

March 16, 1935, Hitler denounced the disarmament clause of the Versailles Treaty and restored universal military service in Germany. Britain and France protested, but did nothing.

March 7, 1936, Hitler sent German troops into the Rhineland. His generals were apprehensive, convinced that France would not allow German reoccupation of the Rhineland without a violent reaction, perhaps even driving them out by force. Again protest by France and Britain, but no force.

March 12, 1938, Hitler moved against Austria and within forty-eight hours had incorporated it into the Reich.

September 1938, Germany annexed the Sudeten area of Czechoslovakia; six months later occupied Bohemia and Moravia and established a protectorate over Slovakia. Czechoslovakia was gone. Britain and France had in effect given Hitler a free hand in a pact at Munich.

March 21, 1939, Hitler occupied Memel (now Klaipeda) on the eastern borders of East Prussia, wrenching it from hapless Lithuania.

September 1, 1939, Germany attacked Poland. Two days later Britain and France declared war on the Reich.

As Hitler would have written the history of what took place, on the night of August 31 a unit of Polish troops attacked the German radio station at Steichlitz, giving the Germans the provocation they needed for the attack on Poland.

Actually the raid was staged by Germans in disguise. A group of Himmler's S. S. troops in Polish uniforms attacked the station. Later all the Germans who participated were slaughtered, as apparently were all in the S. S. below the top leaders who knew of the operation, in an apparent effort to leave no evidence. The Polish uniforms, however, as well as equipment and documents had been obtained by the Sicherheitsdienst (Himmler's intelligence service) from the Abwehr (the military intelligence service). The Abwehr was an anti-Nazi organization. Its director, Admiral Wilhelm Canaris, was executed later for participation in the July 20, 1944, plot against Hitler's life. Survivors of the Abwehr remember the request for Polish uniforms in August 1939 and conclude that the attack on the radio station was fabricated.

Hitler's attack on Poland was as successful as he had told the generals it would be. The Polish Army was crushed in twenty-seven days. The word *Blitzkrieg*—Lightning War —became part of the language of the time, and the myth of the invincibility of the German Army with its fast-moving panzer (armored) divisions making deep thrusts into enemy lines started to grow.

April 9, 1940, Hitler occupied Denmark and invaded Norway. By the end of April most of Norway was in German hands, despite valiant efforts by the Norwegians and an Anglo-French expeditionary force (which landed in southern Norway but was forced to withdraw in two weeks). The legend of German invincibility continued to grow; and it was Hitler's infallible intuition that nourished it.

May 10, 1940, German armies struck at France through Belgium, Holland and Luxembourg and the war in the west was opened in full fury. In forty-two days it was over. The French asked for and signed an armistice at Compiègne on June 22. Three-fifths of France was occupied. The British Expeditionary Force had been driven into the sea at Dunkirk, where only a miraculous rescue operation by the navy and the air force saved it from destruction.

As he had done in Poland, Hitler combined sheer power with psychology to enhance the aura of his victory and the myth of German invincibility. Warsaw had been damaged badly by Nazi dive bombers, a particularly frightening weapon to civilians with its screaming dive and complete accuracy against undefended buildings. In the west, the center of Rotterdam suffered a similar fate when it did not immediately surrender to the onrushing Germans. Aircraft strafed columns of fleeing refugees to increase the terror.

The collapse of France in six weeks staggered the world. Here was a country whose army was reputedly the world's finest; its system of fixed fortifications along its border with Germany—the Maginot Line—presumably impregnable. But the French were still fighting World War I, and were no match for blitzkrieg tactics. French generals, acclaimed for their valor and doggedness in the trench warfare of the first great twentieth-century war, were outgeneraled by a new generation of German panzer generals. An obscure French colonel of armor, Charles de Gaulle, had accurately forecast the new war, but his had been a voice in a parched wilderness of obsolescent military thinking. Even the seven months which had passed since the preview in Poland had been wasted by the French General Staff.

After the fall of France it was a foolish German officer who thought, let alone suggested, that the Fuehrer might ever err. The string of consecutive victories—the Saar, the Rhineland, Austria, Czechoslovakia, Memel, Poland, Denmark, Norway, Holland, Belgium and France—made it unthinkable. The General Staff no longer took the initiative in planning, but waited for the word from the leader. He would tell them what to do—and how and when to do it.

Now only an unarmed England stood between Hitler and victory in the west. It was true that the United States was supporting Great Britain in every manner possible short of war, but Hitler's representatives in America reported to him on the extent of anti-war sentiment in that country. Moreover, he was disdainful of the ability of the United States, still in the early stages of rearmament, to have a decisive effect on the war in Europe.

Hitler decided to force the British to terms by the use of air power. On August 8, 1940, the German Luftwaffe launched an offensive to destroy British airfields and industries. For three months the Germans tried to crack the British defense, but failed.

Hitler had already decided to drop *Operation Sea Lion* —the invasion of England by ground forces. The German Army was ready and willing. But the Navy lacked the landing craft necessary to carry sufficient troops to England, and was highly respectful of the power of the British Royal Navy. The Luftwaffe had failed to win control of the skies over the English Channel from the Royal Air Force.

On July 29, 1940, Hitler told General Alfred Jodl to draft plans for an attack on Russia.

Hitler gave the operation on Russia the code name *Barbarossa*—Red Beard—the nickname of Frederick I. In so doing, he was perhaps unconsciously prophesying his own fate. Frederick I was one of the Fuehrer's idols—the personification of a German king, a man determined to restore the Holy Roman Empire, a student of history, the self-appointed successor to Constantine, Justinian and Charlemagne. He certainly embodied the characteristics that Hitler believed himself to possess. What could be more appropriate for Hitler than to give his greatest crusade Frederick's nickname. Frederick led the Third Crusade to reclaim the Holy Land, a crusade which collapsed when Frederick was drowned. Hitler led the Third Reich into Russia on his crusade to free the world from the Bolsheviks and died with it in the pyre of the Reich's chancellery. Hitler was a superstitious man and to give his great crusade the name of an ill-fated expedition in which the leader perished might have worried him, but his comment might well have been, "I will succeed where Frederick failed!"

Hitler once confessed a dread of snow and winter. He is reported to have forbidden German officers to read Armand de Caulaincourt's diary, *With Napoleon in Russia*, because of its description of the death of the Grande Armée in the snows of Russia. Yet when faced with the same winter, he refused even to provide winter uniforms for the troops. Perhaps in his subconscious he knew he faced the same fate as Napoleon if he acknowledged any threat from the Russian winter. Only one-fifth of the German attacking force was to be provided with winter equipment,[1] indicative also of the supreme confidence of the Germans, who expected the Russians to collapse before the start of winter. General Walther von Brauchitsch, commander in chief of the Army, foresaw only three to four weeks of serious battles.

That Hitler would name his crusade against bolshevism *Barbarossa* and would refuse to take into consideration Russia's greatest ally, nature, were typical of the man. He had no place for doubt. If he ever had such a human trait in his character, by 1941 it had been banished.

A leader must possess self-confidence and ego. Without them he would not be a leader. One of Hitler's first acts was to designate himself Fuehrer (leader) of all the Germans. He then prescribed the national greeting to be, "Heil, Hitler." His was supreme ego; he believed only in himself. Indeed, if Adolf Hitler once gave serious consideration to the existence of a supreme being it was only to confirm his own destiny. The leader of all the Germans was convinced that he had been *chosen* to build a Greater Reich that would rule the world for a thousand years.

The conviction of his infallibility gave Hitler an audacity that more rational mortals could never have possessed. Each successfully exploited weakness of an opponent made him even bolder. He seized political opportunities with a cynicism and an uncanny intuition that made him even more awesome to his followers, who had already deified him far beyond the justified pretensions of any mere mortal.

Hitler, the war leader, was even more fearsome. The intensity of the man was so great as to be overwhelming. The physical energy which he expended in putting forth his views, whether at a Nazi party rally or a generals' conference, was exhausting to listeners and sapped any resistance or difference that might exist. The violence of his conviction and fury of his rage immobilized even the most determined. Of all the Germans, the Fuehrer was the most determined. It was his will power that was irresistible—in leading Germany from victory to victory and in carrying it from defeat after defeat to unconditional surrender.

In carrying Germany down to defeat, Hitler's ego and amorality played the key roles. If the Germans could not win the war when he had led them so brilliantly, then they deserved to be destroyed, just as he had planned to destroy the Russians and all others who stood in his way or whom he disliked. Every inhumanity which man could inflict on man had been used by Hitler and his Nazis. His crimes were so monstrous and on such a scale that even in an age which brought forth the "ultimate weapon" he was the ultimate evil. He had waged a total war with a totality that left no acceptable outcome but victory.

THE INEVITABLE PATH TO WAR

From the day that Adolf Hitler became the Fuehrer of all the Germans, war with the Soviet Union may well have become inevitable. Almost from the moment that he signed up as the seventh member of the German Workers' Party (later to have National Socialism added to its name) Hitler preached of the danger of Bolshevism, identified the Slavs with the Jews as an inferior race to be exterminated and spoke of German expansion in terms of territory in the east.

The Russian leaders did not recognize the ultimate danger. In 1934 Stalin gave orders to the Communist Party in Germany to support the right-wing Nazis in the election rather than the liberal Social Democrats, an action which led to the destruction of both the Communist and the Social Democratic parties. One cannot help but wonder whether Stalin thought the street-fighting between the Nazis and Communists in Germany was just boyish exuberance. He clearly thought Social Democrats more popular than the National Socialists whom he believed he could either defeat or live with and whom he regarded as the less dangerous of the two. True, this is part of the communist conviction that its most dangerous enemy is the liberal left, which has a competitive appeal, and not the right. In this instance Stalin was one hundred per cent wrong.

Joseph Stalin was not oblivious to what was happening

in Germany, though he misjudged which was the greater enemy, the National Socialist Party or the Social Democratic Party. At the Seventeenth Congress of the Communist Party of the Soviet Union in January 1934, Stalin noted that an anti-Russian trend in German policy was replacing the Bismarckian tradition of good relations with Moscow. The following month the Nazis picked the Communists as scapegoat for the Reichstag fire on February 27, arresting thousands of them that very night and banning the Communist and Socialist Party papers.

Stalin immediately launched an extensive armament program for the Soviet Union and opened an aggressive campaign for agreements which might deflect attacks from Russia. The 1932 non-aggression pacts with Poland, Estonia and Latvia were extended into ten-year agreements on April 4, 1934. On June 9, agreements were signed with Czechoslovakia and Rumania, and the Soviet Union officially accepted the World War I loss of Bessarabia to the latter. On September 18, Russia joined the League of Nations and supported France in attempting to develop an eastern Europe pact, along the lines of the Locarno Pact of 1925, to provide collective security. The refusal of Germany and Poland to participate ended that hope.

In 1935 Stalin appeared to move more and more into an anti-Nazi position. Anthony Eden, the British Foreign Minister, visited Moscow in March and Stalin presided over a reception at which "God Save the King" was played.[2] On May 2, Pierre Laval was in Moscow to sign a treaty of alliance with the Soviet Union for France; on the sixteenth, Eduard Beneš signed a pact for Czechoslovakia that committed Russia to come to Czechoslovakia's assistance in the event of attack—provided France acted first in honoring its treaty to defend the Czechs.

In July 1935 a month-long undeclared war with Japan broke out along the border of Siberia and Manchuria, increasing Russian apprehension over the dangers of attack from both west and east, an alarm not eased by Italian adherence to the Anti-Comintern Pact in November of the previous year.

With the outbreak of civil war in Spain in July 1936, the Soviet Union assisted the Loyalist forces while the Germans and Italians supported General Francisco Franco. Britain and France adopted a policy of "non-intervention." British and French generals attended maneuvers of the Russian Army and were reported to be impressed by its quality.[3] In speeches at the Nazi Party rally in Nuremberg in September 1936, Hitler violently denounced Bolshevism and spoke of the Ukraine and Siberia.

"If I had the Ural Mountains with their incalculable store of treasures in raw materials, Siberia with its vast forests, and the Ukraine with its tremendous wheat fields, Germany and the National Socialist leadership would swim in plenty!"[4] When Germany and Japan signed the Anti-Comintern Pact in 1937, the threat to Russia seemed even more ominous.

The following year the crisis for Stalin grew. On June 12, Marshal Mikhail Tukhachevsky and seven other Russian generals were accused of conspiring with the Germans and the Japanese, and were executed after a secret court martial. However, only a few then knew the extent of the purges in the defense system. Executed were: all 11 Deputy Commissars of Defense; 75 out of 80 of the members of the military-Soviet of 1934; every commander of a military district; 13 of the 15 army commanders; 57 of the 85 corps commanders; 110 of the 195 division commanders; 220 of 406 brigade commanders; and 24,000 other officers from the rank of colonel down.[5] If Stalin's objective was to turn the command of the military over to the younger generation, who had known nothing but communism, he succeeded admirably, but he deprived the military forces of most commanders who had handled units above regimental size.

Whatever confidence Stalin might have had in the western powers was shattered in 1938. Hitler's annexation of Austria in March advanced the German empire eastward and exposed Czechoslovakia, a Russian ally, to even greater danger. By September Hitler was ready to move against Czechoslovakia, and Stalin was ready to come to its defense. The first Russian setback occurred when Britain and France agreed to meet with Germany and Italy over the Czech question without inviting the Soviet Union to participate. Stalin instructed Foreign Minister Maxim Litvinov to tell the Czechs that Russia would go to war on their behalf if the French carried out their obligations to defend Czechoslovakia. But the Poles and Rumanians refused to agree in advance to the passage of Russian troops over their territory to assist Czechoslovakia. In return the Russians warned Poland not to press its claim for Czech territory.[6]

The British and French leaders were clearly unprepared to cope with Hitler in September 1938 and gave him what proved to be a free hand in Czechoslovakia. They were not convinced that Russia, despite its offer of assistance, would be of much help in defending the Czechs. Stalin, in turn, had remained skeptical about the intentions of the western powers despite seeking their assistance—and particularly mistrusting their intentions toward the Soviet Union—and was now convinced he had to cope with Germany on his own and needed to buy time while he continued to build his defenses, both political and military.

At the Eighteenth Congress of the Communist Party of

the Soviet Union in March 1939, Stalin told the members that there were no grounds for a conflict between Germany and Russia. He denounced the British and French for spreading the idea that the Russian Army was weak and that there were disorders inside the Soviet Union. He claimed that responsible Nazi leaders were not dreaming of the conquest of the Ukraine. It would seem that Stalin was not fully aware of the degree of Hitler's power, even though he should have known that the previous year Hitler had taken personal command of all the German armed forces and had established the Oberkommando der Wehrmacht as his personal military staff.

A week after the Party Congress, Russia proposed a conference of Britain, France, Rumania, Poland and Turkey to discuss problems of mutual defense. The British answered that they were not interested in such a conference. This may have been what decided Stalin to turn to the Germans. Two weeks later, on April 3, Stalin dismissed the Jewish Maxim Litvinov as Foreign Minister and replaced him with Vyacheslav M. Molotov, presumably on the basis that only a non-Jew could do business with Adolf Hitler.

On April 15, 1939, the British asked if the Russians would unconditionally guarantee the borders of Poland and Rumania and within forty-eight hours received a negative answer, along with Stalin's counterproposal of a Russian alliance with Britain and France. This reply was not encouraging to the western powers. The fact was that they regarded Poland as stronger than Russia and did not want to risk their close ties with Warsaw.

On the same day that Stalin proposed the alliance with the British and French, his ambassador in Berlin was sounding out the Germans on closer ties with the Soviet Union. The initial reaction was an interest in increased trade, but little else. On May 20, Foreign Minister Molotov told the German Ambassador in Moscow, Count Werner von der Schulenburg, that his government considered a political understanding necessary before trade relations could be expanded. Two days later the Germans signed a military alliance with Italy, an event which could not have encouraged Moscow.

Six days later, on May 28, 1939, the Japanese Kwangtung Army resumed their probes into the Soviet Far East. Stalin must indeed have felt the pressure of the Axis pincers, seriously pondered the probability of a two-front war and worried about the time remaining to prepare the Soviet Union for battle. By July 22, evidently still stalling for time, he had obtained an agreement from Germany to discuss an increased exchange of goods.

By the latter part of July 1939 Stalin was in the midst of intensive negotiations with the Germans as well as with Britain and France. The latter two offered to send a military mission to Moscow, but their lack of enthusiasm must have been apparent to the Russians, for after agreeing to send the mission, they delayed its departure for eleven days and then dispatched it by slow boat. Too, its composition was not very flattering to the Russians; the officers were of lower rank than those sent on similar missions to Poland and Turkey. There was no assurance that the mission had the authority to reach an agreement with the Soviet Union. If these were not sufficient obstacles to any agreement, a complete impasse was soon reached over the Russian insistence that Britain and France cooperate in Russia's demand for the right of passage of its troops through Poland in the event of hostilities. This was a concession which the British and French refused to press on their Polish ally. On August 5, the mission left Moscow.

On August 19, Russian forces in the Far East launched a counteroffensive against the Japanese, and by the end of the month had driven them out of Outer Mongolia with heavy casualties. An armistice with the Japanese was reached on September 16.

Exactly two weeks after the British-French military mission left Moscow, Molotov handed Schulenburg the draft of a Soviet-German pact. Only two days were needed to reach agreement on trade and another four to complete the details of a "non-aggression pact." There was reason for haste on both sides. Russia desperately needed to buy time, and Hitler's attack on Poland was just a week away. The pact called for dividing Poland between them, the western part and Lithuania to go to Germany. In addition to eastern Poland, Russia was to receive a free hand in Latvia, Estonia and Finland, as well as the right to take Bessarabia back from Rumania. The Germans professed a lack of interest in southeastern Europe.

Hitler attacked Poland on September 1, with an overwhelming force of more than a million and a half, crushing the brave but poorly armed Polish force of 600,000 in twenty-seven days. Stalin was surprised and alarmed at the speed of the Polish collapse and on September 17 he moved Russian troops into eastern Poland. He took immediate steps to secure the Baltic States, including Lithuania, and within a month the Soviets had established air and naval bases in all three countries.

The Bulgarians and Finns were not so cooperative. Bulgaria refused a Russian offer of alliance in October 1939 and demands for base rights in Finland were rejected. On November 30, Russia attacked Finland. It was a war in which the Russians gained strategic territory but lost what little prestige they might have possessed as a military power. The Finns fought bravely and ably and for three months the world was treated to the spectacle of a tiny nation holding one of the largest nations in the world at bay. Russian generalship was poor; Finnish leadership was excellent. The Finns fought well in the field, showed clear superiority in winter warfare and stubbornly held the Mannerheim Line defending Helsinki. The Soviet Union asked Germany to accelerate the shipment of machine tools needed to produce siege guns. By March 1940 sheer Russian weight had worn down the valiant Finns and they reached terms, ceding the Karelian Isthmus, the city of Viipuri and the naval base at Hanko.

At last, Russia had prepared for the defense of Leningrad in the war that its leaders must have regarded as inevitable. It had acquired territory to the northwest of the city by pushing the Finnish border back from twenty-five miles away to nearly three times that distance.

Despite the Russian victory in the winter war, it served mainly to confirm the estimates of German, British and American intelligence that the armies of the Soviet Union were not of high quality.

Stalin took advantage of German preoccupation in western Europe to consolidate his position in the east. On June 15, 1940, an estimated eighteen to twenty Soviet divisions moved into the Baltic States. Two days later Molotov advised German Ambassador Schulenburg of the Russian action. On July 14 the Russians incorporated these states into the Soviet Union, and on August 11 the Germans were told to close their consulates in Kaunas, Riga and Tallin.

On June 23, Molotov advised Schulenburg that Russia planned to take Bessarabia back and would use force if Rumania resisted. There was an added demand over and above that included in the Soviet-German pact of 1939. The

Russians wanted northern Bukovina too. The Germans pointed out that Bukovina was not part of the 1939 agreement, but the Russians seized both on June 28.

The next move was up to Hitler, and he made it with reasonable dispatch. Hungary was about to go to war with Rumania to get back Transylvania, which it had lost at the end of World War I. Hitler wanted no interference with the shipment of oil from the Ploesti oilfields in Rumania. He ordered Foreign Minister Joachim von Ribbentrop to meet with the Hungarians and Rumanians in Vienna and direct a settlement. On August 30, Rumania was forced by German pressure to yield 16,642 square miles of Transylvania to Hungary (and on September 8, 3,000 square miles of southern Dobruja to Bulgaria). The territorial concession did not disturb the Russians as much as the German and Italian promise to guarantee the new boundaries of Rumania, the small reward for the loss of territory. On September 1, Molotov accused the Germans of violating Article III of their pact—a provision for mutual consultation—and was immediately faced by Foreign Minister Joachim von Ribbentrop's counteraccusation of the same violation over the Russian seizure of northern Bukovina. On September 23, the Russians delivered to the Germans an aide-mémoire noting that they had interests in both Hungary and Rumania and should have been consulted before the territorial awards. The Germans quickly followed the diplomatic move on Rumania by sending troops to that country, and on October 9 the German chargé d'affaires in Moscow informed Molotov that the German troops were necessary to protect the Ploesti oilfields against a British attack.

The Germans were moving in the north too. On September 22 they signed an agreement with Finland permitting the transit of German troops across that country. The

Russians were advised that this was solely to facilitate the movement of soldiers back and forth to German-occupied Norway.

By that time the Nazi-Soviet maneuvering had reached a new intensity. Even though the Russians made diplomatic and military moves for their own defense which annoyed and alarmed the Germans, they were careful to maintain every pretense of friendly relations. During August 1940 Russian deliveries to Germany under the trade agreement were three times those coming from the Reich.

In September the Germans informed the Russians that they were about to sign a Tripartite Pact in Tokyo with Italy and Japan, but assured them that this was directed exclusively against the British. On the twenty-sixth Molotov asked to be shown the secret clauses of the agreement, but his request was ignored. Russian intelligence informed Moscow that the new military alliance provided for mutual assistance in the event that any party became involved in war with a power not then a belligerent. The Soviet Union was not then a belligerent, and neither was the United States. Great Britain was already fighting, so the German explanation was not convincing.

Foreign Minister Molotov went to Berlin in November 1940 for personal discussions with Hitler. The Russians must not have been aware then that planning for the German attack on the Soviet Union had already been under way for more than three months. The German Fuehrer tried to beguile the Russian with talk of dividing the British Empire and suggested that the Soviet Union join the Tripartite Pact for that purpose. Molotov's principal effort was to turn German attention from eastern Europe to the Middle East. The meetings concluded with mutual dissatisfaction with the results.

In the two weeks that elapsed between the Soviet Foreign Minister's departure from Berlin and his presentation of Russia's conditions for closer collaboration, the Germans moved rapidly to strengthen their position in eastern Europe. On November 20, Hungary joined the Tripartite Pact, and was followed on the twenty-third by Rumania. On the twenty-sixth, Molotov apprised the Germans of the Soviet Union's conditions: (1) all German troops should be removed from Finland; (2) Bulgaria should sign a mutual-assistance agreement with Russia; (3) the Soviet Union should be granted land and sea bases in the Bosporus and Dardanelles, the straits leading from the Black Sea to the Mediterranean; (4) if Turkey would not agree to this the Germans must join with the Russians in forcing Turkey to agree; (5) Germany should recognize the area south of the Persian Gulf as a Russian sphere of influence.

This time, (December 1940) Hitler had no intention of making any further concession to the Russians. He was about to set the precise date for an attack on the Soviet Union. He would continue trade as usual in order not to excite the Russians and would put into effect a massive deception operation in order to mislead them as to his true intentions. On January 10, 1941, a new Soviet-German trade agreement was signed, providing for continued shipment of Russian grain and oil in exchange for German machinery. The Russians, however, were slow to implement the agreement and the Germans became concerned over Moscow's true intentions.

By January the Italians were in trouble in their war against Greece, which they had invaded from Albania on October 28, 1940, after a demand for bases had been rejected. It was becoming increasingly apparent that Hitler would have to go to the rescue of Mussolini's Balkan adventure. Moscow, informed in advance of the German plan to move troops into Bulgaria, advised Berlin that this was contrary to Russian security interests. Ribbentrop replied that the troop movement was solely to aid the Italians in Greece.

At this juncture Hitler decided that the Russians would be more impressed with force than with diplomatic niceties; on February 22, Ambassador Schulenburg in Moscow was directed to advise the Russians that there were 600,000 German troops in Rumania. Five days later he advised Molotov that the Bulgarians would sign the Tripartite Pact on March 1. Molotov protested, to no avail. On April 1, Mr. S. Vinogradov, the Soviet Ambassador in Ankara, asked his diplomatic colleague, German Ambassador Franz von Papen, the meaning of Germany's declared intention to defend the Bulgarian and Rumanian Black Sea ports. Von Papen blandly replied that this was against a possible British attack from Greece but immediately informed Berlin that the Russians recognized that the declaration was intended for them.[7]

Meanwhile the Russians were tightening their controls over the Baltic States. All those suspected of hostility to the Soviet Union were forcibly shipped to the vast interior of Russia, where they would pose no threat in the event of hostilities.[8]

On March 25, Yugoslavia had agreed to the Tripartite Pact, but two days later a coup overthrew the government of Prince Paul and the new government denounced the pact. On April 5 the Soviet Union and the new Yugoslav government signed a treaty of friendship. The following day German forces swept into Yugoslavia and Greece from concentration points in Hungary, Rumania and Bulgaria. The Russians suffered a diplomatic setback, but Stalin was not ready for war, even though each move made German determination to control all of eastern Europe more obvious.

In March, Foreign Minister Yosuke Matsuoka of Japan was visiting Europe to build diplomatic fences. Hitler and Ribbentrop urged Matsuoka to persuade his government to attack Singapore. The Japanese official was noncommittal and, in turn, visited Moscow, where he tried to convince the Russians that Japan had no evil designs on the Far Eastern territory of the Soviet Union. His visit to Moscow did produce a neutrality pact which was signed on April 13. When Matsuoka left for Tokyo, Stalin not only went to the station to see him off, but took the occasion to be publicly cordial to the German delegation at the farewell ceremonies, undoubtedly hopeful that the news of this gesture would be relayed promptly to Berlin as indication of Russian friendship. On his return to Tokyo, Matsuoka informed the American diplomat Laurence Steinhardt that the Germans would not attack the Soviet Union unless the Russians reduced their shipments of supplies to Germany.[9] This was what Matsuoka had been led to believe in Berlin. Directive No. 24 of the Wehrmacht of March 5 had forbidden any mention of the true German plans against Russia to the Japanese.[10]

As it was, Ambassador Schulenburg had left his post in Moscow and was in Berlin at that time to report on Russian intentions. When he finally was received by Hitler, on April 28, he assured him that not only did the Russians not want war but that they would make additional concessions to avoid a fight and would supply up to five million tons of grain to Germany.

The strenuous Russian appeasement program continued through May 1941. On the third, Moscow recognized the pro-German Rashid Ali government in Iraq. If they expected Hitler's thanks they were disappointed. The next day in a speech to the Reichstag in which he reported on the progress of the war in southeastern Europe and on German relations in the Balkans, Hitler did not mention Russia. This alarmed Moscow. In each of his major speeches since the pact of August 1939 Hitler had mentioned the value of collaboration with the Soviet Union. The Soviet Ambassador, V. G. Dekanozov, was hurriedly summoned home to explain the omission. He could not.[11] On the fifth, Colonel Hans Krebs, the Assistant German Military Attaché in Moscow, returned to Berlin. He reiterated Schulenburg's earlier statement that the Russians wanted to avoid war, and while acknowledging that the Red Army was moving equipment to the west, assured the Wehrmacht that there were no troop concentrations that might indicate hostile intentions.[12] The following day Joseph Stalin became the Prime Minister of the Soviet Union, adding an official government position to his party role. While this could be viewed as a technicality, since as Party Secretary he had secured his position as absolute ruler of Russia, it was nevertheless immediately reported to Berlin as an important change in the power structure of the Soviet Union. On the seventh, in another effort to placate the Germans, the Russians expelled the Belgian, Norwegian and Yugoslav diplomatic missions from Moscow as no longer representative of those countries now under German occupation. Two days later *Pravda* published a lengthy denial that there were any significant troop movements taking place in the Soviet Union.

On May 10, 1941, Rudolf Hess, second to Hitler in the German hierarchy, flew to Scotland; he parachuted from his Messerschmitt 110 near the estate of Lord Hamilton, whom he had met at the Olympic Games in Berlin in 1936. Hess's personal mission, conceived and implemented entirely on his own, was to convince the British that they should make peace with Germany. The news of Hess's flight to Scotland

was as startling to Stalin as it was to Hitler, but Stalin refused to believe that the German Fuehrer was not party to the mission. Stalin was convinced that Hitler was attempting to reach terms with Great Britain in order to devote his full resources to an attack on the Soviet Union, hoping for the neutrality if not the actual collaboration of the British. If Stalin had been suspicious of both belligerents before, he was even more so after the Hess flight. Had the Germans been able to attack on Hitler's original target date, it would have been five days after Hess landed in Scotland. Had Stalin's intelligence service then been doing a better job in England, Stalin would have known immediately that the British were not impressed by the proposals of Rudolf Hess.

PREPARATIONS FOR THE ATTACK: GERMAN

In June 1940, having crushed France and driven the British Expeditionary Force into the sea at Dunkirk, Hitler was confident that it was only a matter of time before England would seek an end to the war. That month the OKW drafted an order reducing the army to 140 divisions in order to provide men for the navy and air force for the attack on the British Isles.

Hermann Goering was certain that his Luftwaffe would win air superiority over England, perhaps even force the British to complete capitulation. On July 10 the German flyers started the Battle of Britain that was to be fought over the British Isles for more than three and a half months and was to cost the attackers 1,733 planes without driving the Royal Air Force from the skies or breaking the will of the British.

The German Navy was not enthusiastic about an invasion of England. It had a healthy respect for the Royal Navy and was uncertain of its ability to protect German troop transports attempting to cross the English Channel. There was a shortage of landing craft. The Navy welcomed the cancellation of *Operation Sea Lion,* the operational name for the attack on England.

The German air attack against the British Isles had been in progress for less than three weeks when Hitler gave orders to begin planning for an attack on Russia. On July 29, Colonel-General Alfred Jodl, the operations chief of the OKW, informed four officers of his staff on the special command train "Atlas" then in the station at Bad Reichenall, not far from Hitler's villa on the Obersalzberg, that the Fuehrer had decided on a surprise attack for May 1941. They were told to draft a preparatory order moving the bulk of the army and the air force to western Poland.[13]

On August 9, 1940, Jodl signed the first directive for *Ostbau Ost,* the code name then given to preparations for the attack on Russia, implementing the orders given by Hitler. The Army was to be responsible for the preparation of the operational plan. That same month ten infantry and two panzer divisions were ordered to the east.[14] Some five divisions had remained in Poland during the attack in the west.[15]

In the meantime the Luftwaffe was hammering England. On August 1, Directive No. 17 ordered the German Air Force to overwhelm the R.A.F. and to destroy the British harbor facilities. During the next three weeks Hermann Goering's air squadrons were to lose 403 planes, and while the R.A.F. took staggering losses, it was assisted by the German propensity for switching priorities before accomplishing their objective. The initial attacks on radar stations were dropped as being unimportant, yet destruction of these stations would have deprived the British of the ability to anticipate the direction and objective of the German attacks and would have greatly hampered their defense. The Germans were aware of the excellent R.A.F. command system for controlling the battle, as they could hear the sector stations directing the fighter squadrons. So the Luftwaffe turned its attention to attacks on the sector stations, but again before achieving decisive results, switched to other targets. In the vast daylight battles in mid-September the Germans took such losses that they turned to night raids.

Hitler had been told that the earliest possible date for the invasion of England was September 15. He was warned by the unenthusiastic German Navy that the British Air Force and Navy would have to be neutralized or the invasion fleet could meet disaster. He was also told that the weather was so uncertain at that time of year that it could have a decisive effect on the outcome. When it became apparent that the Luftwaffe was not winning the Battle of Britain, he put off *Operation Sea Lion* on September 17, and on October 12 confirmed that he would not invade England but would continue to threaten Britain so as to deceive the Russians as to his true intentions.

On September 6, Jodl issued orders to Admiral Wilhelm Canaris, the chief of the military intelligence service (Abwehr), on the steps to be taken to conceal German intentions in the east. The Abwehr was to convince the Russians that only the German troop concentrations in the south of Poland were important, while those in the north were inconsequential.[16] The Abwehr would plant misleading reports and employ double agents to filter reports to the Russians that the troops in south Poland were eventually to be used for the attack on England and were being kept in the east in the event the British landed in the Balkans. The

German Military Attaché in Moscow was directed to explain troop movements in Poland as normal replacement of
older men by young recruits.[17] Every effort was to be made
to mislead the Russians on the buildup in the east so as to
achieve maximum surprise.

Plans for the attack on Russia progressed rapidly during the fall of 1940. By December 18 the directive for the
attack was ready and scheduled for May 15, 1941. The invasion of Yugoslavia and Greece in April and the exceptionally
late arrival of spring in Russia forced a postponement of the
attack.

Hitler also changed the basic plans for attack presented
by the army on December 17, to put the main weight initially against Leningrad rather than Moscow.[18] By February 3, 1941, the strategic deployment for the attack had
received the Fuehrer's approval and the engineers began to
strengthen and lengthen the airfields in Poland, an activity
quickly noted by British intelligence.[19] The OKW was
authorized to review plans for the attack with the Finns and
the Rumanians. General Heinrichs, the Chief of Staff of the
Finnish Army, had visited German headquarters in Zossen
in December and had received a preliminary briefing.[20] He
returned to Salzburg on May 25 and was advised of the final
details by Jodl. It was agreed that the Finns would mobilize
fully in the period from June 9 to June 17. On June 11,
General Ion Antonescu of Rumania was briefed about the
plan but was not told of the date of attack until a week
later. The Hungarians were not advised until the day before
the attack took place. The Italians were the last to know.
Hitler sent a long letter to Mussolini, which Il Duce received at 2:30 A.M., June 22. There could have been no better indication of the German evaluation of the security of
their allies. The Finns were rated the most secure—they had

just had a war with the Russians. The Rumanians were next —they had been forced to cede considerable territory to Russia. The Hungarians ranked third. And the Italians were not trusted at all.

Nor had the Italians confided in the Germans before their attack on Greece, which they had greatly underestimated. By December the Greeks had driven the Italians back, occupied a quarter of Albania, and forced the Germans to send troops to bolster their ally, which was also doing poorly fighting the British in Africa. Further, the Italian action against Greece had brought the British into the Aegean to pose a threat to the German flank in the Balkans.

When the Yugoslav regime of Prince Paul was overthrown on March 27 and the government of General Dušan Simović renounced its alliance with Germany, Hitler had to postpone the attack on Russia to clean up the Balkans. On April 6, German troops swept into Yugoslavia and Greece. By the end of the month it was obvious that the troops committed in southeastern Europe would not be ready for *Barbarossa* by May 15. On April 30, Hitler set the new date for the attack on Russia as June 22.

THE GERMAN INTELLIGENCE SERVICES

Repeated success soon creates a reputation of omniscience and invincibility, and such was the reputation of Nazi Germany in 1941. Hitler's unbroken string of victories gave the impression of vast intelligence networks providing the Fuehrer with all of the information necessary to direct Germany from one conquest to the next.

Nothing could have been further from the truth. While the German intelligence services undoubtedly had agents in many parts of the world, and while Nazi Bund organizations provided information of some value, the real situation was that this war lord had traveled a long way on bluff, boldness, intuition and luck. There were no vast intelligence networks. There was no great research organization analyzing volumes of incoming reports and presenting them to corps of advisors to prepare policy recommendations for serious top-level review and decision-making. In fact, the intelligence resources available to the man who at one point controlled most of continental Europe were unbelievably meager—and that was not all.

The German intelligence services were divided, competitive, feuding and in at least one instance treasonable. At no point below Adolf Hitler himself was all of the information on any one subject assembled and analyzed. In many instances Hitler was his own intelligence officer. The consequences of this alone could have defeated Germany, but it would be presumptive to suggest that inadequate intelligence service was the sole cause of Germany's downfall. It is possible to argue that even the best and most accurate intelligence system in the world would not have altered the course of history.

The top analysis of military information for the attack on the Soviet Union came from the *Fremde Heeres Ost* (Foreign Armies East), which purportedly received all available information from all sources on the Soviet Union and the eastern European countries and presented its reports to the Quartermaster General, who in turn forwarded the information to the staffs of the Army, Navy and Air Force and the Wehrmacht. But it is reasonably certain that *Fremde Heeres Ost* did not receive everything at all times. Certainly the party intelligence system did not feed into the military, nor would Ribbentrop's Foreign Ministry, which had certain antipathies to the military, always report in full detail. It is wrong to assume that because Germany was at war all intelligence services would cooperate, share their information and work together toward victory. In Hitler's Reich there was suspicion, fear and bitter rivalry.

Ostensibly *Fremde Heeres Ost* was dependent on the Abwehr for the bulk of its information from clandestine sources. The Abwehr was solely responsible for control of espionage and counterespionage, but it could not deal with secret political material from foreign sources. The collection of political intelligence incredibly enough was divided between the Foreign Ministry, which covered all areas where Germany had diplomatic representation, and the Sicherheitsdienst (SD), the security service of the Nazi Party.

Espionage itself is difficult enough to manage, but to divide the responsibility among Military Intelligence, the Foreign Office and the Party Security Service made the task impossible. The Abwehr tried to form a common front with the Foreign Ministry against the SD, but neither was very successful in its efforts to protect itself against party influence.

There must have been fantastic confusion as the three German services competed for that all too rare intelligence asset, the agent with access to vital information. Each was quick to denounce the loyalty of the other's agents and the validity of the information produced. In their eagerness to outproduce each other, and their unwillingness to share information about their sources, the feuding Germans were easy prey for double agents and deception.

The Auslandsorganisation (the group that attempted to organize Germans in other countries) maintained its own intelligence service and funneled what it collected into the party system.[21] Eberhard von Stohrer, the German Ambassador in Spain, complained about the frequent inaccuracies in information collected by the Auslandsorganisation.[22]

Hermann Goering had organized his own intelligence service in 1933. The Forschungsamt (Research Office) intercepted communications and tried to decrypt encoded telegrams, tapped telephones and opened letters. It fed the SD.

Each of the military services had its own cryptanalytic agency. These were ostensibly under the control of the Wehrmachtnachrichtenvergingungen (WNV) (Armed Forces Signal Communications), under Major General Fritz Thiele.[23] The Heeresnachrichten Wesens (Army Communications System) turned its intercepts over to army intelligence.[24] The Beobachtung-Dienst (Observation Service) of the navy was the most effective of the cryptanalytic agencies.[25] The Luftwaffe had its Funkaufklärungsdienst (Radio Reconnaissance Service).[26] The OKW had established its own communication and cryptanalytic service in 1937. As if four military services were not enough, the Foreign Office controlled Sonderdienst Dahlem (Special Services at Dahlem), which processed some of the raw material intercepted by the military services and the post office.[27]

With all of these collection agencies and their analytic counterparts, one would have assumed the German policy makers to have been well informed. But these were competitive and uncoordinated organizations. There was overlapping and wasteful duplication. They did not share the raw material they collected, and in many important instances their interpretation of the data was in sharp conflict. There was only one person in Germany who could have pulled these feuding agencies together. He was Adolf Hitler, and he was not interested.

There is ample evidence that Hitler did not want one coordinated intelligence report. He told Heinrich Himmler, "The Abwehr always sends me a batch of individual, undigested reports. Of course they are all of great importance and come from the most reliable sources, but it is left to me to sift the material. This is not right, and I want you to instruct *your* staff to carry out their work quite differently."[28] (Himmler headed the S. S. and the SD, the bitter rival of the Abwehr.) Actually Hitler preferred it this way —as his own intelligence officer he could interpret the information as he saw fit and never be in the position of taking a view contrary to the collective one of the intelligence services.

The only coordination that took place was of the most informal and unofficial nature. Walter Schellenberg of the SD's intelligence service had periodic social meetings with representatives of the other services. He also went horseback riding with Admiral Wilhelm Canaris of the Abwehr, but they did little more than compare opinions.

Why should Hitler have cared in 1941? He had so far won all of his wars. In victory, intelligence is a luxury which occasionally can lessen casualties, if one is interested in that, or can make the task easier, if consulted.

But why should Hitler have confidence in his intelligence services? Their reports had been as wrong as his military analysts were. The French Army was invincible. The Maginot Line was impregnable. The Czechs would resist. Britain and France would launch a massive assault to save Poland. Why should he believe their reports on the Soviet Union, when their information on all other areas had been persistently overly pessimistic? Intelligence services must consistently be credible to be effective, and this the German services were not. Perhaps if they had been consistent in their views they would have been more influential, but how could they, when their information was fragmentary and their analyses biased by firmly established prejudices about

Russia's strength? The *Fremde Heere Est* was excellent at correlating the information it received, but if the information did not fit into their basic concepts the analysts were inclined to discount or ignore it. Key members of the evaluation section of the Luftwaffe worked for Die Rote Kapelle, the Soviet espionage network, so their analysis must have been biased.[29]

Furthermore, the reports from the intelligence services in most instances had to pass through senior staff officers who were toadies and sycophants and told Hitler only what he wanted to hear. Field Marshal Wilhelm Keitel, the Chief of the High Command of the OKW, told Canaris, the head of the Military Intelligence, "My dear Canaris, you may have some understanding of the Abwehr, but you belong to the navy; you really should not try to give us lessons in strategic and political planning."[30]

Hitler only wanted his own convictions confirmed and he was convinced that Russia was weak. He believed that the great purges of the thirties had seriously damaged the command echelon of the Red Army. His henchmen may even have been involved in the purges, for the allegation against Marshal Mikhail Tukhachevsky, Chief of Staff of the Red Army, who was executed in 1937, was that he was conspiring with the Germans. Walter Schellenberg, a key official in the Sicherheitsdienst, said that Nikolai Yezhov of Stalin's NKVD paid three million rubles in 1937 for evidence of Russian collaboration with the Germans.[31]

Hitler's conviction of Russian military weakness was strengthened by the Red Army's poor showing in the winter war against Finland in 1940. If the Russians had trouble defeating Finland, they should pose no problem for the German Army. Hitler was also convinced that Communist Party control in Russia was insecure and that the Russian people would welcome the Germans as liberators. Yet he was so disdainful of the Slavs as people that he gave orders to immediately execute all political commissars, to liquidate the Jews, and to be ruthless in handling the population in the occupied areas. His orders repelled the decent officers in the German Army and quickly convinced any Russians who might not have been communists that life under the Nazis would be intolerable.

German intelligence on Russia prior to the attack was spotty indeed. There were some potentially good sources, but there is no evidence that they produced much of value, and if they did, that it was believed. The Sicherheitsdienst had officers in Sweden, Finland, Turkey and all of the countries of eastern Europe. They reportedly had two agents on the staff of Colonel-General Konstantin K. Rokossovsky.[32] In addition they employed hundreds of low-level agents, infiltrated across the Russian border on foot or dropped by parachute, all equipped with radio sets.[33] The SD complained about the limited number of aircraft available for dropping agents.[34]

The Abwehr had some agents on senior staffs of the Red Army.[35] The Russian Army radio security was poor and by the time of the attack in June the German intelligence services had a fairly complete order of battle of all of the units in the frontier area.[36] This was not a particularly impressive accomplishment, as military units in the field use either a low-level code or talk in the clear unless there are adequate land-lines available, which there were not in western Russia in 1941. The codes could easily be broken; that combined with traffic analysis could fairly quickly establish where units were located. Stalin did not wish to alarm or provoke the Germans and undoubtedly refrained from ordering radio silence, which might have been interpreted as the sign of an impending Russian attack.

German communications intelligence, however, could not pick up the Russian reserve units deep in the interior of the country, and this led to a gross miscalculation of Red Army strength. The Germans estimated Russian strength at 200 divisions. In the first six weeks of the war they had already encountered 360.[37]

The German Military Attaché's office in the Moscow embassy probably had the most realistic information about Russian strength and intentions, but its views were not given much weight. General Ernst Koestring warned not to underestimate the ability of the Russian military forces.[38] General Heinz Guderian, the foremost armored warfare expert in the German Army, had published a book in 1937, *Achtung, Panzer!* which estimated Russian tank strength at 10,000, a figure he altered from intelligence reports of that time, which gave the strength as 17,000.[39] He had even had difficulty in using the more conservative figure in his book, as the then Chief of Staff General Ludwig von Beck thought it vastly exaggerated. General Beck was completely wrong about the Russians; in an appreciation written in 1938 he said the Red Army was not a factor to be reckoned with.

Obviously Hitler was disdainful of both the numbers and the quality of Russian tanks because he launched the attack with only 3,200 tanks, while yearly production was only 1,000. In 1933 Guderian had visited a single tank factory in Russia that was producing 22 a day.[40] Eight years later Russian production of tanks was many times that of Germany.

Six weeks after the attack Hitler saw General Guderian in Novy Borissov and told him, "If I had known that the figures for Russian tank strength which you gave in your book were in fact the true ones, I would not—I believe—ever have started this war."[41]

There was one additional intelligence source which was

able to provide some accurate information. This was long-range aerial reconnaissance. The Germans based a squadron at Budapest to cover western Russia. Hitler would not permit the start of flights over Russia until 1941 in order not to alarm Stalin, and even then those flights were restricted to the border area. The army asked for aerial reconnaissance in the fall of 1940, when they began planning for the assault. From the air the Germans were able to locate troop concentrations, get a reasonably accurate impression of the progress on fortifications and obtain information about the terrain, roads, railroads and bridges. The overflights were frequent. On April 22 the Russians protested 80 border violations by German planes between March 27 to April 18. The photographs were analyzed by Abwehr I, Section Luft. Two weeks before the invasion Colonel Rowehl's squadron in Budapest commenced long-range flights deep into Russia.[42]

THE RUSSIAN INTELLIGENCE SERVICES

The Russian intelligence services were the children of conspiracy and terror and inherited many of the characteristics of their parents, some good but several bad. Of the many information-collecting organizations, there was only one internal security service, the NKVD, which also collected information on foreign developments. This automatically made it the superior service.

The NKVD was the direct lineal descendant of Feliks Dzerzhinsky's CHEKA, established by Lenin and Trotsky immediately following the revolution. Its original members had survived the revolution as underground conspirators. Its first mission was to protect the Red Revolution from the White Counter-Revolution. Success was the only quality tolerated. Few survived failures in the Soviet services.

Stalin used the NKVD in his great purges of the late thirties that decimated the senior ranks of the Red Army. But even in the NKVD itself purges were recurrent—it is indeed a vicious circle when all of the executioners and witnesses must be eliminated. By 1941 few of the original Chekists survived, but those who did remain within the NKVD, whether an original revolutionary or a latter-day recruit, were true experts in the art of conspiracy.

Their craft included everything from espionage to execution, and the capacity to carry out their missions without detection. The early CHEKA-NKVD generation was probably best in the basic mission of the organization—protecting the security of the U.S.S.R.—or to be more precise, the Communist Party of the Soviet Union. Their very existence in pre-revolutionary days had depended on their ability to avoid apprehension by the large and not inefficient secret police organization of the Tsar. Now they were the hunter and knew from personal experience all of the techniques and tricks of the hunted.

This Russian service was extraordinary in its capacity to recruit agents from target areas: prominent individuals in Russian exile organizations plotting counterrevolution, leaders of party dissidents within the U.S.S.R. or government officials in a country which might one day be an enemy of Russia.

The NKVD was everywhere, inside Russia and outside. While throughout its history its primary mission was the security of the state, this was interpreted to mean everything of interest to the Presidium.

In 1941 the NKVD had only two years before absorbed the last remnants of the Comintern intelligence system: the Third (or Communist) International organized by Vladimir Lenin in 1919 to direct a world revolution. The Comintern was a vast international bureaucracy with headquarters in

Moscow, dominated and run by the Russians but including representatives of many nationalities. Its alumni include Josip Tito of Yugoslavia, Palmiro Togliatti of Italy and Ho Chi Minh of Vietnam.

While the primary mission of the Comintern was direction and guidance to communist cadres throughout the world, it was by its very nature a vast intelligence collection organization. It had specific networks organized for that purpose, but in addition it had the resources of the communist parties of the world, many of which could produce information of considerable value from dedicated members in key governmental positions, executive as well as parliamentary.

The Comintern had never been one of Joseph Stalin's favorite organizations, and after Lenin's death in 1924 he allowed it to wither on the vine. It held its last congress in 1935. Stalin tolerated its existence during the thirties while he continued to build, purge and rebuild the Soviet party organization, but in 1943 Stalin announced the dissolution of the Comintern, without even bothering to notify the member parties of the other countries. His action was widely heralded as a renunciation of world revolution. Russia's allies, especially Great Britain and the United States were somewhat reassured. However, the Russian Communist Party organization had in fact taken over the worldwide espionage and revolutionary activities (as well as personnel) of the Comintern.

Intelligence from abroad was received in many places in Moscow, but ultimately it was all channeled to the Presidium, where it was tightly controlled by the Secretariat. The many sources and varied channels had their advantages. First, the multiplicity of sources obviously enhanced the possibility of securing information important to the Soviet Union. Second, the nature of the sources insured that the level and quality of the information was varied: some high-level, from penetrations of foreign governments; some run-of-the-mill, from party members and informants. Third, the different channels used for getting the information to Moscow both increased the security of the system and insured that if one channel was blocked one of the others was sure to get through.

The NKVD ran a multitude of espionage networks all over the world; each reported independently into the center in Moscow. By 1941 either it or the Military Intelligence Department of the General Staff had absorbed most of the foreign intelligence activities of the Comintern.

The Fourth Department of the General Staff was definitely secondary in importance as an intelligence source to state security, but through its clandestine networks as well as from the military attachés and liaison missions it received much information of value. It was responsible for analyzing the military significance of the reports and for reporting its conclusions to the General Staff and the Minister of Defense.

In addition to the NKVD and military intelligence, Stalin in 1941 had intelligence flowing into Moscow from every other Russian government department that had representatives abroad. Not spies in the ordinary sense of the word, these representatives were required to report all they heard or saw, and in certain instances they were coopted by the NKVD or military intelligence to organize intelligence networks.

If Stalin's intelligence services had worked as they should and the system had functioned efficiently, then all of the information collected, from any part of the world or any organization, would have ended up in the same office in

Moscow. This office, called Control, operated directly under Stalin in his role as First Secretary of the Communist Party, and from it the information ostensibly went to the Central Committee. In effect, Control was the vehicle of the Secretary himself—certainly in Stalin's case.

It was Control's responsibility to analyze all incoming information and to prepare reports for the Presidium, the General Staff and interested departments. Control was also responsible for guiding the collection of intelligence needed for the security of the U.S.S.R. Perhaps most important of all, it was required to evaluate the quality of the sources so that the party and government members would know whether the information came from a source of unquestioned reliability, of questionable accuracy or of unknown quality.

But Stalin's intelligence system had also inherited the bad qualities of its parent, conspiracy. It was paranoid. It was not only suspicious of everyone else in the world, it did not trust itself. The NKVD watched everyone else, and they all watched the NKVD. Surely there was almost as much energy expended on internal observation as on external collection.

What effect this atmosphere had on reporting from abroad, on the quality of analysis and interpretation in Moscow, or on the frankness of the material presented to the Soviet leaders is difficult to say. One can only draw reasoned conclusions. How would one handle a report from Switzerland which purported to be an exact copy or reproduction of a German High Command document analyzing the strength of the Red Army and commenting that the leadership was poor because most of the qualified generals had been killed in the purges, that Russian tanks were of inferior quality and that some of the Russian people would turn against the communists at the first opportunity?

Remembering that the NKVD was skilled at fabricating false documents and planting incriminating evidence, and was supersensitive to any criticism of the regime, would the Russian network chief in Bern forward the report?

What would Control in Moscow do with the report? Forward it? Bury it? Reprimand Switzerland for sending it and put the chief on the "Watch List"? Or place the source on the "Unreliable List"? If sent forward, what comment would Control put on it? Would it say that this was probably an exact reflection of the views of the German General Staff? Or would it call it German fabrication?

If Stalin did receive and read such a report, what would his reaction be? One of fury at the unfavorable reflection on his actions? One of sober acceptance that the Germans might be seriously underestimating Russian capabilities and therefore might be bolder than the situation warranted? Or one of wanting to get additional information that might serve to verify or disprove the accuracy of the report?

These are not mere idle hypotheses. In any intelligence system a report passes through many hands. In actual fact, a report collected by a Russian agent out of the German Wehrmacht would have to be handed to a Berlin contact who in turn would send it by courier to Switzerland where it would be sent either by another courier or by radio to Moscow where several would handle it before it reached the highest level. Any one of the persons handling the report could edit it or file it. One can only surmise what happened in Stalin's system, but based on the dictator's reaction to one report on the eve of battle, we can be reasonably sure that despite its vastness the Soviet system had many flaws.

The Soviet intelligence system in 1941 was, beyond question, the world's largest. British and French intelligence had been damaged badly by the military disasters in western Europe in 1940. The British had had two key men in their German operations, Major R. H. Stevens and S. Payne Best, abducted by the Germans from the Dutch town of Venlo. Japanese intelligence was almost exclusively oriented to Asia, and American intelligence (like the military services) was just mobilizing.

Yet the armies of the Soviet Union were unprepared for the attack by Germany on June 22, 1941. The leaders of Russia were surprised by the timing of the attack. This was either a colossal failure on the part of the Soviet intelligence services or a miscalculation of gigantic proportions on the part of the Kremlin.

It is inconceivable that the communist intelligence services should not have produced vast volumes of information on the size and quality of the German armed forces. There were so many potential sources of information in Germany that it must have required a sizable research staff to collate and analyze the information. While the Nazis had tried ruthlessly to eradicate the communists in Germany, there remained underground cells in many key areas: in the military services; in munitions factories; in the government bureaucracy.

Even if the communist espionage nets had not succeeded in penetrating the key centers of Germany where knowledge of the plan for attacking Russia was available from December 18, 1940, on—six months and four days before the actual attack—then the preparations and mobilization in the east must have attracted the attention of low-level agents and informers. Three million men cannot be assembled unnoticed, even in the considerable area of eastern Europe running from the Baltic to Rumania.

Indeed, had all communist sources in Germany and Poland failed to produce, something must have come out of the German satellites that were to participate in the attack and therefore had knowledge of the plan considerably in advance. Finland and Rumania were aware of the German plans, and Hungary and Italy, while not informed of the attack in advance, must have considered it highly probable.

One of the really great mysteries is why the Russians did not take even greater defensive measures if Stalin was aware of the German concentrations on the Soviet frontier. The explanation that Stalin did not want to give the Germans a pretext for attack is the one usually offered. But to make this explanation valid it must then be assumed that Moscow thought German intelligence so good that it would immediately identify and report any intensification in defense precautions. This is a strange assumption for the high command of a totalitarian power which had conducted extensive purges over the years to eliminate any elements of the population it suspected of disloyalty.

The basic question, then, from the Russian side is why Stalin allowed the Red Army to be caught in the frontier area, not fully on the alert and relatively unprepared?

The complete answer to this question may never be known unless the hidden recesses of the Kremlin yield personal notes of the late dictator, minutes of the Presidium, files of the Secretariat or deliberations of the War Council which indicate a true appreciation of the growing dangers of a German attack in the spring of 1941 and a reflection on Soviet preparations.

The odds against such documents ever being made available for historical analysis are great, if the documents indeed exist. For it is not in keeping with Stalin's personality to have kept personal notes. He had lived the life of a conspirator in tsarist days and knew the dangers of records that might be seen by unfriendly eyes. His own secret police used documents kept by other unfortunate Soviet citizens as state evidence in the purge trials, turning the slightest innuendo into criminal conspiracy. There is no hint in Stalin's character that he felt he might ever have to justify his actions in the eyes of history.

What of the state or party records? The communists are well aware of the value (as well as the burden) of records, and the Comintern (the Third International) was one of the greatest paper mills of all time, keeping voluminous files of the minutes of meetings of its Congresses, its Executive Committee sessions and reports from parties all over the world, ad infinitum.

The conduct of war requires records of high national deliberations be kept. Even the most secretive of modern states have discovered that certain government decisions, even vital statistics, cannot be handled clandestinely but must be given some public dissemination. So the records *may* exist.

Whether there are records or not, the central issue remains: what did Stalin and his colleagues know of German intentions and capabilities in June of 1941, and what, if anything, did they do about it?

Stalin was unquestionably aware of the possibility of a German attack. To him it was a matter of timing—when would it come? On this point the dictator of all the Russias was blind.

Of all the reports received in Moscow, the most precise and complete were provided by the Russian intelligence services. Western Europe was blanketed by the Rote Kapelle—the "Red Chapel"—which had networks of agents in Germany, France, Switzerland, Belgium, Holland and Italy. The most extensive of these networks was in Germany, where the Russians had agents in every important ministry in the government and industry.

If Joseph Stalin had had any idea of the brilliance of the Russian military intelligence networks in Germany and Japan, the opening battles of war might have been different.

There were at least five Soviet agents on the General Staff of Hermann Goering's Luftwaffe. Lieutenant Colonel Harry Schulze-Boysen was in the Forschungsamt, a key spot for the collection of vital military information. Oberregierungsrat Arvid Harnack was a Russian expert in the Ministry of Economics. Legionsrat von Schelia was First Secretary of the Foreign Office. Colonel von Bentivegni was in military counterintelligence. And there was Colonel of Engineers Becker. These were important agents, but others were all over Germany, men and women who hated the Nazis and Adolf Hitler. These included men holding such posts as the head of counterespionage in the Breslau area,[43] and many others.

The most effective Russian intelligence ring operated out of Switzerland. It was headed by Alexander Koulicheff, who worked under the name of Alexander Rado ostensibly as a cartographer for Swiss newspapers. His chief agent was Rudolf Roessler, a German publisher, who used the pseudonym of Lucy. Lucy's sources in the German High Command were impressive and included several generals who had been his colleagues in World War I.

The intelligence provided by Lucy was accurate and plentiful: reports of wholesale troop movements to the east in early June as the final preparations for the German attack were being made; a report in mid-June advising that the attack would take place on June 22 and giving the precise order of battle; the army groups and their objectives. At first, Control in Moscow was suspicious of the reports from Lucy. The precise identity of the original source was never revealed to them and the information was so factual and specific as to seem a German plant. But Control could not ignore the report on the date of attack. That had been received too frequently to be discounted. Rado worried about sending it in. He feared he would be reprimanded for passing on provocative information.[44]

The network in Japan was equally effective. Richard Sorge had developed sources with access to the top level of the Japanese government. Sorge had established himself so well with the German embassy, even though he was ostensibly a journalist, that he was considered a trusted member of the staff and not only was confided in by the ambassador and the military attaché, but was used by them as an analyst and occasionally as a courier. Thus Sorge knew what both Germany and Japan were going to do. While Stalin may not have recognized Sorge's value at the time, the Soviet Union did twenty-three years later. On November 5, 1964, Sorge was made a Hero of the Soviet Union, a street in Moscow was named for him, and the following year the four-kopeck stamp bore his likeness.

Sorge's coverage of information vital to Moscow was remarkable. On March 5 he sent Moscow a microfilm of cables from Foreign Minister Ribbentrop to General Ott, the ambassador in Tokyo, giving the date of the attack on Russia as the middle of June.[45] He had advised Control in April and May of the loose talk by German diplomatic couriers about German troop movements to the east. In May Sorge learned from Colonel Ritter von Niedermayer that the decision had already been made in Berlin to go to war against Russia.[46] Sorge cabled Moscow on May 15 that the attack would be June 22. In June, Major Scholl, the Assistant Military Attaché, told Sorge the attack would be on June 20 or within two or three days after that and that there would be no declaration of war or ultimatum. Sorge not only reported this to Moscow, but emphasized its importance.[47]

Control in Moscow thus had reports from opposite sides of the world giving the precise date of the attack. There was no danger here of false confirmation, rather the identical information came from independent sources and through two different channels. These reports and warnings validated one another.

The Fourth Department of the General Staff received a report from a Russian military commission which toured German tank factories and schools in the spring of 1941 on Hitler's orders. German General Heinz Guderian commented, "The Russian officers in question firmly refused to believe that the Panzer IV was in fact our heaviest tank. They said repeatedly that we must be hiding our newest models from them, and complained that we were not carrying out Hitler's order to show them everything. The military commission was so insistent on this point that eventually our manufacturers and Ordnance Office officials concluded, 'It seems that the Russians must already possess better and heavier tanks than we do.' "[48]

Here was intelligence for both sides. The Germans undoubtedly reported to Hitler the doubts of their Russian guests as to whether they were being shown everything as he had ordered. Whether they also reported that the persistent Russian questioning led them to conclude that the Soviet Union had bigger and better tanks is not so certain. Hitler was disdainful of the quality of Russian equipment and annoyed by the constant reports on the large number of tanks available to the Red armies. Whether any of his underlings would have had the temerity in the spring of 1941 to challenge him is doubtful. Even more questionable is whether Hitler would have paid any attention or done anything about it.

If German intelligence had been functioning effectively at this critical juncture a few weeks before one of the most massive battles in history, it should have launched a vigorous campaign to discover what the Russians meant by their questions as to whether the Germans did have a better tank. The lack of knowledge about the latest Russian tanks was to have an important effect on the outcome of the battle. There is no evidence that the Abwehr did anything about this intelligence gap or that the German General Staff was particularly concerned.

In Moscow the situation was different. The reports from the military mission inspecting German tank production and armored schools must have gone on from the General Staff to Stalin himself. Whether he believed—as obviously the Russian mission did—that the Germans were holding out their latest armor, or whether he was certain the Russian T-34 (first committed to battle in July 1941) was better than any German tank is uncertain. What is certain is that Stalin had many other sources of information.

Furthermore, Stalin was warned by others, particularly the United States and Great Britain, of the forthcoming German attack and its date. Beginning in January 1941, nearly six months before the attack, warnings began to reach Moscow. In January the Commercial Attaché in the United States Embassy in Berlin advised Washington that Hitler was planning to attack Russia in the spring.[49] If an American commercial attaché in Berlin could gather such information, the Soviet intelligence service must also have had it.

On March 20, Sumner Welles, the Under Secretary of State in Washington, advised Constantine Oumansky, the Soviet Ambassador (and an experienced intelligence officer), that the Germans were planning an attack.[50] On March 25 the Germans ordered the expulsion of all Russian boundary and repatriation missions from the German side of the Lithuanian border.[51] This was certainly not a friendly gesture and its implication must have been studied in Moscow. On April 3, Winston Churchill sent a message to Sir Stafford Cripps, the British Ambassador to the Soviet Union, directing him to advise Stalin that the Germans were planning an attack and that they were moving three armored divisions from Rumania to southern Poland for that purpose. (The move of these units north was cancelled, as they had to be used by the Germans for the attack on Yugoslavia of April 6.)[52] The Russians must have paid some heed to the warning, for on April 10 a secret alert was sent to the forces on the western border of the Soviet Union. The German Navy's official diary noted a state of emergency for all Russian units as of that date.[53]

On June 1, German technicians working on a Russian cruiser in Leningrad were recalled by Berlin.[54] About June 10, Victor Cavendish-Bentinck of the British Joint Intelligence Committee was asked by Foreign Minister Anthony Eden to meet with him and Soviet Ambassador Ivan Maisky. The two British officials spent half an hour trying to convince the Russian of the impending German attack, at that point less than two weeks away.[55] There were clear signs available in Moscow too. Laurence Steinhardt, the American Ambassador, cabled Washington of the recall of German and Italian diplomatic wives and, perhaps even more significant, that the Counsellor of the German embassy had sent his dog—from which he was inseparable—back to Berlin.[56] The most prosaic evidence is important. If

Stalin would not believe the word of other nations, of which he was perhaps justifiably suspicious, perhaps he should have been influenced by such extraordinary behavior.

The Legations of the United States in Bucharest and Stockholm reported to Washington in early June the probability of an attack; these messages were promptly relayed to Moscow for the Russians. The American Consul at Königsberg reported the same.[57] On June 13, *Tass* accused Sir Stafford Cripps of spreading provocative rumors about the possibility of war. He was doing more than spreading rumors, but the Russian leaders would not listen. The German Naval Attaché reported to Berlin that Cripps was saying the attack would be on June 22.[58]

The massing of the German armies in eastern Europe was obvious at that point to any reasonably alert observer. Richard Sorge reported from Tokyo that German diplomatic couriers arriving from Berlin talked openly of German Army units moving east.[59] Franz von Papen, German Ambassador to Turkey, had received reports of his country's massive military buildup on the Russian border and interpreted it exactly as Berlin wanted Moscow to read it—as a form of political pressure to compel Russia to maintain a benevolent neutrality in the event of a German attack on Turkey.[60]

Even the German Military Intelligence Service may have participated in the warnings. An Abwehr agent, Josef Mueller, advised a British contact in Vatican City of the planned date of the attack, and Nicholas von Halem, of Admiral Canaris' personal staff, warned a British resident in Moscow, according to author Ian Colvin.[61]

The warnings continued to arrive in the Russian capital until the very last minute. A Czech deserter from a German division in the Lvov region defected to the Russians at 10 P.M. on the night of June 21 and told army interrogators that the attack would take place at 3 A.M. the following morning. It took three hours for the message to reach Stalin, who did not believe it and ordered the man shot.[62]

A study of Hitler's writings and speeches contained ample evidence of his obsession with Bolshevism and the Drang Nach Osten. The men in the Kremlin may have regarded this as political verbiage, but they must have been impressed with the number of times over the years when Hitler did exactly what he said he would do.

In Hitler's *Mein Kampf* and in some 1,500 speeches there are few themes reiterated so frequently as Bolshevism and the "living room" available in Russia. In the book, with its blueprint for a greater Germany, Hitler stated that Russia afforded the primary area for new lands and colonies for Germany, and spoke bluntly of the destruction of communism: "The new Reich must follow the paths of the ancient Teutonic orders . . . The end of Bolshevik power will be the end of Russia as a state."[63] From his first speech in 1930 until June 22, 1941, an attack on Russia was implicit: recover the gains of Brest Litovsk; enslave half of the *Untermenschen*—the Slavs; confiscate the land and make the Ukraine an outpost of eastern Germany.[64] For Hitler it was a universal crusade to save Christianity and civilization!

It was not that Stalin and the Russians believed that the Germans would never attack the Soviet Union. In 1936 they started to build a series of fortifications known as the Stalin Line, strong points located in the area between the Baltic Sea and the Pripet Marshes. The defensive plan of the then chief of staff, Marshal Mikhail Tukhachevsky, was to hold the mass of the reserves on the Dnieper and draw the enemy into the desolate spaces between Leningrad and the Pripet Marshes. Tukhachevsky was purged by Stalin in 1937. Four years later Adolf Hitler concentrated a major portion of his initial attack on Leningrad, which he intended to level to the ground. If the Russian reserves had been where Tukhachevsky wanted them, the siege of Leningrad might have been averted.

We may never know the weight which the Russian leader gave to these various sources of intelligence. But we do know that it was his judgment that was decisive in the Kremlin, and that regardless of evaluation or assessment at lower levels in the hierarchy, the final view would be that of one man alone.

How much Stalin's experience colored his judgment may forever be an enigma. Having used the NKVD to purge his enemies, and being well aware of their capacity for deceit and fabrication, was he likely to rely on their reports? He had been a clandestine operator himself as a youth and was well aware of the pitfalls of espionage. Was he likely to have placed much credence in an agent's report? He had purged the Red Army only a little more than three years previously, but had his confidence in military personnel been sufficiently restored to give due weight to their intelligence? And did he trust reports and warnings from other governments enough to take any action based on their efforts to alert him?

The case can be made that just as Hitler's intelligence services were generally poor, failed to collect adequate information and did not work together, the situation in Russia was exactly the reverse. The Russian intelligence services were tightly controlled and coordinated. The Russians had superb intelligence networks in western Europe and in Japan, which produced not only detailed information on the strength and disposition of the German and Japanese military forces, but even more unusual, precisely what those government's intended to do and when. The information

OPERATION BARBAROSSA

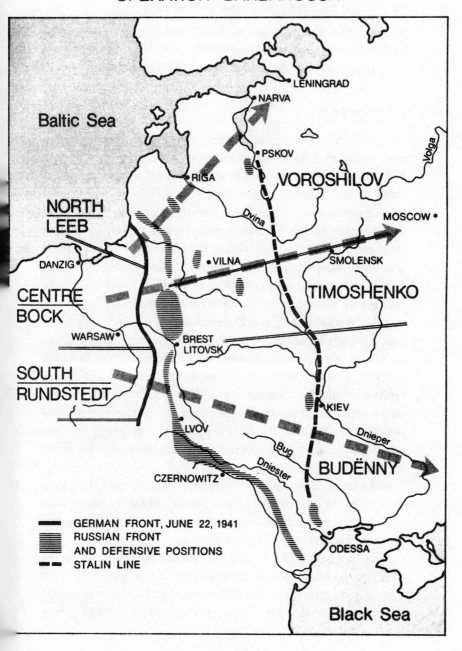

was not only accurate, it was timely and received in Moscow well before the event. Nevertheless, the Russians were not fully prepared for the attack when it came.

THE ATTACK

At 9:30 P.M. on the evening of June 21, Foreign Minister Molotov summoned Ambassador Schulenburg to the Kremlin to register a protest against the German air violations of the Russian border areas. It was to be the first of two discussions between these two men that night. At 3:30 the morning of the twenty-second, thirteen German armies smashed across the border into Russian-held territory from concentration points in East Prussia, Poland and Galicia.

The surprise was complete. Five days previously General Heinz Guderian, who commanded panzer troops in the attack, had examined the Russian defenses along the River Bug through binoculars and found the strong points unoccupied. It was the same on the twenty-second. Russian tanks carrying practice ammunition were lined up in parks, fuel tanks half filled. Officers were on leave; leave status for the line troops was normal. Bridges over the major rivers were not mined. One Russian unit reported it was being fired on and was told it must be insane. It was reprimanded for sending the message in the clear.

At dawn Ambassador Schulenburg was back in Molotov's office to advise him of the attack, while in Berlin Foreign Minister Joachim von Ribbentrop was telling Russian Ambassador Dekanozov the same news.

Stalin's refusal to heed the warnings or listen to his intelligence services cost him dearly. Russian units were committed piecemeal. Rapidly moving German armored columns encircled hundreds of thousands of Red Army troops at a time, forcing them to surrender. Russia appeared doomed and Hitler's intuition once again appeared vindicated.

Washington expected Germany to defeat the Soviet Union in one or two months at the most. In Japan the inner circle of Prime Minister Fumimaro Konoye thought Russia would collapse, and Japan made the decision to turn its attention in another direction for the time being.

By the end of the summer Leningrad was under siege, all of the Ukraine west of the Dnieper had been overrun and Kiev had been captured. But there had been critical delays. The German Army High Command wanted the major effort directed to Moscow. Hitler wanted to reach the oil of the Caucasus. By the time a decision was reached and the drive toward Moscow resumed, valuable time had been lost and the Russian winter came early.

Already there were indications of Hitler's grave miscalculations. On July 3 in the fighting on the Beresina near Borissov, the new Russian T-34 tank entered the battles for the first time. It was superior to anything the Germans had and their anti-tank guns were ineffective against it. Even more important, the T-34 was built for the worst ground and weather conditions and could move through the mud and snow when the German tanks were bogged down. German intelligence had missed this completely.

German intelligence had missed many other vital elements of information. The maps used by the army were faulty. "The Glinka-Klimiatino road which was shown as 'good' on our maps, did not in fact exist," said tank force commander Guderian.[65] The Germans did not even know with certainty in which villages in Russia the volksdeutsche lived. Hitler told Italian Foreign Minister Galeazzo Ciano with dismay that they were unaware of some industrial plants in the Soviet Union where as many as 65,000 persons were employed.

The lack of intelligence and Hitler's miscalculations led to major errors. He had allotted only 300 tank engines and no new tanks as replacements for the whole of the eastern front, assuming that the quality of his panzer force was so superior that the German armies would soon eliminate any threat from the Russian armor. After the battle of Kiev in October, Panzer Group 2 had only 30 per cent of its tanks operative.

Hitler told Ciano on October 25 that he would have acted differently had he realized the strength of Russian military forces: the armament, the training of the troops, the ability of the staff and the conduct of the soldiers in battle were infinitely superior to that anticipated. The attitude of the population showed much more support for the regime than he believed existed.[66]

Hitler had not just misjudged the Communist government, he had not understood Russia or the Russians. If he had had any thought of the Russian people turning against the regime, he should not have treated them as *Untermenschen* (inferior people). The Sonderkommando (special units) which followed the combat troops into the occupied territories of the Soviet Union were ruthless, cold-blooded murderers who quickly drove the Russians into guerrilla bands which operated in ever-growing numbers behind the German lines.

Hitler was blind to the vastness of Russia and the severity of its climate. The unpaved roads choked the engines of the German tanks and trucks with dust in good weather, became bottomless bogs in wet weather and were impassable to non-winterized vehicles in the snow and ice of winter. The Russians left little rolling-stock intact on the railways, and the German railway engines were not built for the Russian climate. Those that did not freeze or break down were often ambushed by guerrillas.

When Stalin realized that his intelligence service was good, he took seriously reports from Sorge that Japan would not attack Russia in the east. On June 23, Sorge reported to Moscow that General Eugen Ott, the German Ambassador in Tokyo, had instructed all German officials to exert pressure on the Japanese to intervene in the war but that Admiral Wenneker, the Naval Attaché, was convinced they would not attack Russia because the interest of the Japanese Navy was to the south. Four days later Moscow asked Sorge to report on Japanese intentions and troop movements. On July 2, Sorge was able to report that the Imperial Conference had decided on maintaining neutrality in the Russo-German war. His subsequent reports assured Moscow that the Japanese would not attack, certainly not until they were convinced that Russia was defeated.[67] Stalin was able to move reserves from the Far Eastern armies to defend Moscow, and on December 5, 1941, the Russian counteroffensive started.

In most respects, then, Adolf Hitler and Joseph Stalin were captains without eyes. Hitler, riding on the crest of waves of victories, smashed into the Soviet Union impatient with and intolerant of reports of Russian strength and fighting ability; he was so obsessed with his own sense of infallibility that he ignored the warnings and strategic advice of his generals, compounded error with error and led Germany to "unconditional surrender." Stalin, a victim of the system he himself had forged, blind to what was happening because he did not want it to happen, frantically threw Russian forces into the opening clashes, needlessly sacrificing them in battles that need never have been fought, until he regained his composure and used space and manpower to gain the time needed for Soviet victory. From the viewpoint of people killed and property destroyed, *Barbarossa* constitutes one of the most costly of intelligence failures on both sides.

3.
Pearl Harbor:
A Lost Battle v.
A National Disaster

DECEMBER 7, 1941

ON DECEMBER 7, 1941, Japanese carrier-based aircraft attacked the United States Pacific Fleet at Pearl Harbor on the island of Oahu in the territory of Hawaii. The Americans were caught by surprise and the damage to the fleet was extensive.

Simultaneously the Japanese launched assaults against the Philippines and against British forces in Hong Kong and Malaya, and against American bases on Guam and Wake Island.

Two days before the attack on Pearl Harbor, on December 5, German troops desperately attempting to capture Moscow, reported they were within sight of the spires of the Kremlin. The day immediately before Japan opened war on the United States a massive Russian counteroffensive was launched in the Moscow area and drove the Germans back from the capital—never seriously to threaten it again.

Simultaneously Japan had made war on the world's two greatest sea powers: Great Britain, on the assumption that it had been defeated by Germany in Europe and would be unable to defend its empire in Asia; and the United States, on the theory that America was so committed to the war in Europe—even though not yet a belligerent—that it would seek terms after losing its Pacific Fleet.

The Japanese had not advised their German allies of their intention to attack the United States, nor had the Germans advised Japan of when they were going to attack the Soviet Union. The Germans were delighted to give Japan a free hand against the United States and Great Britain in the Pacific and fulfilled their commitment under the Tripartite Alliance by declaring war on America on December 11.

The Japanese decision to attack the United States had been made definite only a week before, although the deterioration of relations between the two nations had been an almost continual process since the First World War, despite the most strenuous efforts of men of good will on both sides to develop friendship and understanding. Japan bitterly resented the racially discriminatory immigration laws of the United States, the American determination to maintain its naval superiority in the Pacific and most particularly the attempts to block Japanese efforts to establish complete control over China. The United States had watched with dismay Japan's activities in China and Manchuria and the rise to complete domination of the Japanese government in Tokyo by the military; but until after the outbreak of the war in Europe in 1939, took no positive action to restrain Japan beyond protests.

Japan had agreed at the Washington Naval Conference in 1922 to a position subordinate to the United States and Great Britain and had accepted the policy of maintaining its fleet at 60 per cent strength of each of those two powers. Despite a smaller navy than Britain and the United States, Japan nevertheless had preponderant military and naval power in the Far East. In exchange Japan pledged not to take advantage of chaotic conditions in China to extract further concessions.

In 1930 the naval powers met again in London. This time Japan demanded that its fleet be at least 70 per cent the strength of either the British or American fleets. The final agreement raised small cruiser and destroyer strength to this level and gave her equality in submarine tonnage while retaining the 60 per cent level in large cruisers. The agreement was to last only four years. On December 29, 1934, Japan gave the required two years' notice that it would no longer adhere to the Washington Naval Treaty of 1932. It did agree, however, to another conference and met in London with the British and Americans on December 9, 1935. When the Anglo-Saxon powers refused to grant it equality, Japan left the conference.

By this time Japan had embarked on a program of expansion on the mainland of Asia. Mukden in Manchuria had been occupied by Japanese troops on September 19, 1931. Both the League of Nations and the United States, a nonmember of the League, condemned the Japanese action and declared it a violation of treaty obligations. In 1932 Manchuria was declared to be "independent," but Japanese officials controlled all important activities. In 1933 Japan withdrew from the League of Nations.

Japanese politics after World War I were characterized by violence and the progressive rise of military influence. In 1921 Prime Minister Takashi Hara was assassinated. In

1923 an attack on the life of the Prince Regent forced the resignation of the cabinet. In 1930 Premier Yuko Hamaguchi was murdered. And in 1932 the assassination of Prime Minister Ki Inukai by military reactionaries marked the end of the influence of the political parties.

By 1936 the army had moved into a predominant position in Japanese politics. On February 26 of that year Viscount Hoboru Saito and the Finance Minister Korekiyo Takahashi were assassinated by army officers. The plotters were brought to trial and sentenced, but the action against the conspirators did not lessen military influence. The army was sufficiently influential to make certain conditions for the formation of the cabinet by Koki Hirota.

On November 25, 1936, Japan signed the so-called Anti-Comintern Pact with Nazi Germany. This agreement was described as directed solely against the Soviet Union. In fact, it was the first step in the German effort to acquire control over Europe and the Japanese attempt to seize Asia.

On January 23, 1937, the Koki Hirota cabinet fell and was replaced by one headed by General Senjuro Hayashi. On July 7 of that year the undeclared war against China resumed in full fury after a shooting incident between Japanese and Chinese troops near Peking. Japanese actions made it quite clear that there would be no respect shown for the interests of other nations in China. Again the League of Nations and the United States condemned the Japanese action and demanded Japan's withdrawal from China. Japan ignored the protests and continued its military action. On December 12, Japanese bombers sank the U.S. gunboat *Panay* and bombed ships of other nationalities near Nanking. Japan explained that it had been a case of mistaken identity.

By early 1938 Japan had moved to what was almost a full war economy. The National Mobilization Bill of March 26 gave the government unlimited powers. The Japanese, after repudiating the London treaty, refused to reveal any details of their shipbuilding program but the Anglo-Saxon powers were well aware that the Navy was being rapidly expanded. The United States and Great Britain decided to stop limiting their capital ships to 35,000 tons.

In May 1939 intensive fighting broke out between Japanese and Russian troops along the Manchurian and Outer Mongolian border. This little war was to last for three months, with heavy casualties on both sides. Relations between Japan and the United States also deteriorated. In July, Washington advised Tokyo that the commercial treaty between the two countries would be allowed to expire. This paved the way for cutting off shipments of war materials to Japan. In August, Japan was shocked by Germany's signing a trade pact and non-aggression treaty with the Soviet Union and promptly denounced its Anti-Comintern Agreement with Germany and Italy. A week later Germany attacked Poland, and Britain and France declared war on Germany.

The war in Europe did little to help Japan for the first nine months. Then, in May 1940, with one blow in western Europe, Hitler made vulnerable the territories held by Great Britain, France and the Netherlands in Asia. With France and Holland occupied by German troops and the British Isles apparently in a perilous position, Japan commenced more aggressive moves for the domination of Asia.

In July 1940 the army again forced a change in the Japanese cabinet, and Prince Fumimaro Konoye, believed to be one who could reconcile the differences between the warlike military and the civilian moderates, became Prime Minister. On September 22, Japanese troops moved into Indochina and forced the Vichy French government to agree to the occupation of its colony. On the twenty-seventh, Japan signed a mutual assistance pact with Germany and Italy. And in December 1940 the army ordered three divisions in South China trained for jungle warfare.

The same month that the Japanese Army was starting to prepare for the conquest of Southeast Asia, Admiral Isoroku Yamamoto began to study the possibility of attacking the American Pacific Fleet when it was at anchor in Pearl Harbor. Yamamoto wanted to prevent the American fleet from interfering with the Japanese offensive to the south. He was convinced that a surprise air attack could do this. He had been impressed by the British naval air action against the Italian fleet at Taranto in the Mediterranean on November 11, 1940, in which twenty-one planes carrying torpedoes sank three battleships, and he called for full details on that battle. The former naval attaché in London was assigned to his staff, to provide him with all available information on the tactics of the British naval air arm.

Yamamoto was also convinced of the feasibility of a limited war against the United States, reasoning that if America lost its Pacific Fleet in one action it would be willing to have the dispute with Japan mediated without further fighting. Had not President Theodore Roosevelt extended his "good offices" to settle the Russo-Japanese War of 1905?

If the United States had believed the Russians should settle with Japan after losing its fleet at Tsushima, would it not wish to do the same if its own Pacific fleet were lost at Pearl Harbor?

In April 1941 Foreign Minister Yosuke Matsuoka visited Germany and Russia. He was in Berlin when the Germans attacked Yugoslavia and Greece; and then, on April 13 he signed a neutrality pact with the Soviet Union in Moscow. That same month in Washington Ambassador Kichisaburo Nomura opened discussions with the American government in an effort to improve relations with the United States.

On June 22 the Japanese were again shocked by their ally Germany when they learned of Hitler's attack on the Soviet Union. The next day the Vichy government of France agreed to Japanese military control of Indochina, and preparations were under way to move into the southern part of that colony despite American warnings against it.

The pace of events quickened during the summer of 1941. On July 2 the Japanese Imperial Conference approved plans for continuing negotiations with the United States, even though some military elements considered this a waste of time. The conference also approved plans for acquiring complete control over Indochina as a base for operations in Southeast Asia. On July 14 the government instituted censorship of all cable and telephone messages. On the sixteenth, in another crisis over military plans, the Konoye cabinet resigned; but two days later, on the eighteenth, Prince Konoye formed a new cabinet, with Admiral Teijiro Toyoda replacing Matsouka as Foreign Minister. The external observer could have drawn several conclusions from this switch. With Toyoda moving to the Foreign Ministry, certainly the role of the navy was enhanced. Matsuoka had concluded the neutrality pact with Russia and one could interpret the change as a possible rejection of that policy.

Japan gave France an ultimatum on Indochina on July 19, and on the twenty-fifth occupied the southern half. The reaction of the United States was swift and unexpected.

President Franklin Roosevelt froze all Japanese assets, a move immediately duplicated by Great Britain and the Netherlands. For Japan this had catastrophic implications: a loss of raw materials, especially petroleum, that spelled a shortage within less than two years which could bring industry to a halt and immoblize the navy.

In August 1941 the Japanese began detailed planning for the conquest of Southeast Asia. Targets for conquest were Malaya, the Netherlands Indies and the Philippines. Meanwhile, Admiral Yamamoto pushed forward plans for the attack on Pearl Harbor. At the Imperial Conference of September 6 the plans for the campaign in the south and the attack on Pearl Harbor were reviewed. With the Emperor's consent preparations for both operations were ordered completed by the end of October. It was made clear to all concerned, however, that negotiations with the United States were to continue which, if successful, would cancel the attack on Pearl Harbor.

Japan had very specific objectives to obtain in negotiations with the United States. It was essential for survival that the flow of raw materials to Japan be resumed, and promptly. This meant that Japanese assets held by the United States, Britain and the Netherlands be released and that the embargo on shipments to Japan be lifted. A minimum of 4,500,000 tons of petroleum was needed. The Allies would not agree to lift the embargo unless Japan agreed to cease its conquest of Southeast Asia and withdraw from China. Japan was unwilling to give up its gains. On these major issues the discussions were stalemated.

On September 13, final training for the Pearl Harbor attack commenced. Twelve days later there were extensive personnel changes in the Japanese combined fleet as the final moves in preparation for war were made.

Prime Minister Konoye resigned on October 16. The military were becoming increasingly impatient with his attempts to negotiate with the United States. That same day the Japanese press carried comments by Captain Hideo Hirade, the Director of Naval Intelligence, on the possibility of war between Japan and the United States. Two days later General Hideki Tojo assumed the post of Prime Minister of Japan.

On the first of November all of the radio call signs for the ships of the Japanese fleet were changed. It was a normal change. The Japanese Navy made it a practice to change call signs every six months to make it more difficult for potential enemies to plot the location of the ships of the fleet by listening to their radio traffic. On November 5 a deadline of November 25 was set as the last possible day for the conclusion of successful negotiations in Washington. That same day Admiral Yamamoto set December 7 Hawaiian time as the day for the attack on Pearl Harbor.

On November 15, orders were issued to requisition and arm additional merchant ships. A week later the ships designated for the task force for the attack on Pearl Harbor sailed to their assembly point—Tankan Bay on the island of Etorofu in the Kuriles, well out of sight of foreign observers. This northern fleet maintained radio silence, while the fleet for the attack on Southeast Asia and the home fleet in the Inland Sea increased radio traffic. Four days later the northern fleet sailed, headed east, well north of any merchant shipping. On November 29 in a speech widely quoted throughout the world, Prime Minister Tojo declared that the influence of the United States and Great Britain must be eliminated from the Orient.

On December 1 all of the radio call signs of the Japanese Navy were changed again. Japanese merchant ships were recalled to home waters. The final decision was made: the American fleet at Pearl Harbor would be attacked. On the third the Japanese attack force refueled and turned south toward the Hawaiian Islands. It had orders to turn back if detected, but it moved through empty seas.

The following day, in Berlin, the Japanese Ambassador asked the Germans if they would declare war if hostilities developed between Japan and the Anglo-Saxon powers. He was told that Germany would honor the commitments of the Tripartite Pact.

On the night of December 6 the Japanese fleet, approaching Hawaii from the north, increased its speed to 26 knots. At 6 A.M. on the morning of December 7, 275 miles north of Oahu, it launched the first attack wave of 183 aircraft.

The Japanese had precise intelligence as to the exact location of each ship in Pearl Harbor when they attacked. For months a Japanese naval officer assigned to the consulate in Honolulu had filed detailed reports on ship movements to and from the naval base. The Japanese knew that the principal units of the fleet would be in Pearl Harbor on December 7. It was an American habit to bring the fleet into port over the weekends. Thus Yamamoto chose Sunday morning for the attack.

UNITED STATES INTELLIGENCE

While Japanese intelligence was precise about the American fleet in the Pacific, American information on the Japanese fleet was inadequate. Even more important, the United States had no hard intelligence, no conclusive evidence as to what Japan might do: move north to attack Russia, already heavily engaged in fighting the Germans in

Europe? or move south to conquer the rest of Southeast Asia? Although waiting for Japan to make the first hostile move—and quite confident it would do so—the Americans had no concept of the immensity of the disaster ahead.

The most important source of the information available to the top officials in Washington was the secret diplomatic traffic of Japan known as "Magic." American cryptographers had succeeded in cracking the Japanese "Purple" code, used for the most sensitive and highly classified messages between the Japanese Foreign Ministry and embassies and consulates abroad. American listening stations in the Philippines and the Hawaiian Islands intercepted and recorded the messages being transmitted. Cryptographers then transcribed the code into Japanese and translators changed the Japanese into English. Occasionally the process was so fast that the message was available to the Americans on the same day it had been transmitted by the Japanese. On one occasion American officials were reading a message from Tokyo to Washington before the Japanese embassy had finished processing it.* More frequently it took twenty-four to forty-eight hours to process the intercept, and sometimes there were lengthy delays in decoding a message because of garbles in the text or because of a shortage of cryptographers or translators.

The messages were intercepted and processed by two different organizations: the Naval Communications Division and the Signal Intelligence Service of the Army. The organizations worked closely together; duplication was thus avoided and there was a mutual exchange of the processed messages.

The Navy Communications Division was responsible

---

* This was the 14-part message delivered by the Japanese Ambassadors to Secretary of State Hull on December 7, 1941.

for disseminating its messages to a very limited number of authorized persons: the Director of Naval Intelligence, the Chief of the Far Eastern Section of the Office of Naval Intelligence (ONI), the Chief of the War Plans Section, the Assistant Chief of Naval Operations, the Chief of Naval Operations, the Secretary of the Navy, and the President. (In the White House, Harry Hopkins and Captain John R. Beardall, the Naval Aide to the President, also saw the messages.)

The Army Signal Intelligence Service delivered the messages to the Chief of the Far Eastern Section of the G-2 Staff (Intelligence), who was responsible for their delivery. The Army was authorized to show copies to the Assistant Chief of the G-2 Staff, to the Chief of War Plans, to the Chief of Staff and to the Secretary of War, and was required to deliver a copy to the Secretary of State. Thus there were thirteen officials in Washington who were authorized to see the messages. Obviously there were a few others who saw them officially or otherwise, but the number was very limited.

The method of handling the messages was equally restricted. For most recipients the high-level couriers, a Navy commander and an Army colonel, usually waited in the outer office while the messages were read and then carried them onward. In some instances, as with the President and the Secretary of State, the locked dispatch case was left with an assistant who had been cleared to hold the case but not to read the messages; he was responsible for the top secret case until his superior was ready to unlock it, read its contents and return it to the original courier. After the authorized recipients had seen the messages, the only copies retained were kept by the chiefs of the Far Eastern sections of Army and Navy Intelligence. The only distribution permitted outside Washington was of paraphrased excerpts which did not reveal the source. The Intelligence Officer of the Pacific Fleet in Honolulu discovered that such messages existed and requested that copies be sent to him, but this request was turned down by Washington.

The reason for the limited distribution was security. If the Japanese had discovered that their "Purple Code" had been broken, they would have changed it immediately and it might have taken months to break a new code. Thus every precaution was taken to prevent the Japanese from learning that their most secret communications were being read in Washington. By limiting the number of recipients to a handful of top officials it was assumed that the possibility of leakage was reduced to an absolute minimum. Presumably top-level officials are absolutely secure and discreet, but a former shipbuilder commenting on this subject in Washington once remarked that "the ship of state is the only vessel I know of that leaks at the top." It was not assumed that a recipient would blurt out in public that he had been reading intercepted Japanese diplomatic messages, but it was feared that someone would use an item of information that could only have been obtained from those messages, thus revealing the source.

It is presumed that prior to being placed on the distribution list for the intercepts, each of those officials was "briefed" by a security officer on the highly sensitive nature of the material and the need for utmost discretion. He was undoubtedly told who the other recipients were and that he could discuss the material only with them, and not with any "uncleared" persons. He was *not* told however what the messages would or would not contain, nor was he warned that some key messages might not be sent by this channel or that Tokyo might mislead even its own ambassadors as to its true intentions.

It is most unlikely that anybody presumed to tell President Roosevelt or Harry Hopkins, or Secretaries Cordell Hull, Frank Knox or Henry L. Stimson, about what information could or could not be obtained from communications intelligence, or that it was only one source and should be evaluated in conjunction with all other available sources. These highly intelligent men probably appreciated some of the subtleties, but whether they were aware of all the pitfalls is most unlikely.

Were they told that even though the "Purple Code" had been broken there would still be some messages—perhaps very important ones—that would not be available? Not all messages would be intercepted in transmission. Wave lengths could be changed and there might be a lapse of time before the new frequencies were discovered by the monitors. Operator errors could cause garbles that would make decrypting difficult, if not impossible. Sometimes the volume of traffic was so great that many days would elapse before a message could be decoded and translated.

The top officials were probably aware that there would be some highly sensitive messages that the Japanese would not transmit by electronic means but would send by courier; but were they aware that if the Japanese suspected the code was broken it would be changed instantly or used for deception—messages to purposely mislead the United States? Or did they believe that the Japanese ambassadors in Washington would receive a message saying, "We are going to attack Pearl Harbor tomorrow at dawn"?

In a society which abhorred secrecy and generally lacked guile, the Americans did not appreciate that the two ambassadors in Washington, both respected admirals, could be used as dupes. If this thought had crossed the mind of American officialdom, then the attack on Pearl Harbor would not have come as such a surprise. Ambassadors

Nomura and Kurusu, ignorant of their government's intentions to attack Pearl Harbor if the United States would not yield to the Japanese demands, conducted themselves in a manner which added to the deception. In fact, they knew little more about their country's war plans than the Americans: both sides in Washington were reading the same cables. And there were only a few of the most senior officials in Tokyo who knew of the plans to attack the United States naval base.

Washington officials did not wholly trust the security arrangements of U.S. field commands, and they worried lest there be errors in transmission; thus the reluctance to send messages to Hawaii or the Philippines. Further, by having the messages always in the custody of one officer and filed in only one location, the possibility of an unauthorized person seeing any message was reduced to an absolute minimum.

That the handling of the "Purple" or "Magic" messages was secure is beyond question. That it was the proper way to use the information is another matter. It was, in effect, making each of the top officials his own intelligence officer because what he was receiving was raw, unevaluated intelligence. It had not been processed in any manner except for the decoding and translating and was still in the usual cable format: to, from, time of transmission, time of receipt (and, of course, the time intercepted and processed by the military communications service). Only one form of evaluation had taken place. The Army and Navy had weeded out those messages which they did not consider important.

In effect the President of the United States, the secretaries of State, War and Navy, the Chief of Staff of the Army, the Chief of Naval Operations and the Intelligence and War Plans chiefs of the Army and the Navy became each, in his own right, an intelligence officer on Japanese military and diplomatic matters. In the crucial six months preceding the attack on Pearl Harbor each received more than 200 cables and dispatches to and from the Japanese Foreign Ministry. Most of the messages related to the crucial discussions between Japan and the United States over China, Indochina and the oil embargo. Some days the recipients would see no messages because there was no traffic. Other days the top officials might see several messages. Much of the material was repetitive. Some of it was very important; a great deal was inconsequential. Yet from this raw material the leaders of the United States were supposed to glean profound and precise knowledge of Japanese intentions and to be able to say that at dawn of December 7, 1941, the Imperial Empire of Japan would start a war with the United States by an air attack on the Pacific Fleet in Pearl Harbor.

Only if each one of the recipients of "Magic" were an expert on Japan, knew the Japanese way of thinking, were familiar with the intricacies of Tokyo politics—the relative power and ambitions of the army and the navy and the royal family—were aware of the vital needs of the economy for oil and raw materials from the United States and Southeast Asia and had accurate knowledge of the strength and quality of the armed forces, would it have been possible for him to convert the Japanese traffic into hard intelligence.

Of all the recipients, Secretary of State Cordell Hull had the greatest capability in this regard. The Secretary had other sources of information. He was in almost daily receipt of cables and dispatches from Ambassador Grew in Tokyo, one of the outstanding diplomats in the service of his country and a shrewd observer and analyst of the situation in Japan. Hull also received cables and dispatches from all other important posts in the world and, of course, he followed closely the development of the war in Europe. Hull met constantly with the President, with the Secretaries of War and Navy, with members of Congress, with the foreign diplomatic corps in Washington and with countless others. He repeatedly met with Japanese Ambassador Nomura to discuss at great length the differences between the two nations. In the intercepted material Hull read Nomura's reports on their discussions and saw how the Ambassador interpreted his statements. He also read what Tokyo was telling Nomura and how the Japanese evaluated developments in the United States. From all of this, Secretary Hull arrived at his own evaluation of the situation—an evaluation which proved to be remarkably accurate.

The intelligence which the Secretary of State examined during the crucial six months before Pearl Harbor included the texts of intercepted cables, principally between Tokyo and the Japanese embassy in Washington, and was preponderantly concerned with the negotiations in which he was participating personally. While these cables enabled the Secretary to check on the accuracy of the Japanese Ambassador's reports on the American views—and on what he had said—there was little in the messages to shed additional light on Tokyo's intentions. But the cables did provide some clues, if such could be believed, of Japan's intentions toward Russia in the north and on the raw materials of Asia to the south, and reinforced the impression given by the negotiators of an obdurate position on China. In October and November of 1941 the cables conveyed an increasing sense of urgency, but also gave an impression of a great Japanese desire to avoid war with the United States.

Of some 294 cables circulated to the cleared officials in Washington between July 1, 1941 and the December 7 attack, 239 were between Tokyo and Washington. But there also were significant messages between the Foreign Ministry and other Japanese missions and between some of the embassies. A dozen messages between Tokyo and Berlin which were intercepted tended to confirm what Japan had been saying, that it would interpret the Tripartite Pact as it saw fit—just as Germany had done. Messages between Japanese missions in Europe and Latin America and "book messages" (the same message to several or all missions) from Tokyo gave the impression that Japan was planning to take an action that would result in hostilities. An exchange of messages between Hanoi and Tokyo and several with Bangkok gave every evidence of Japanese intentions to extend Japan's influence in Southeast Asia. In all, the Washington officials saw messages from Tokyo to sixteen other posts in addition to Washington, and from twelve missions to Tokyo.

Not one of the hundreds of messages carried a clear statement of what the Japanese government intended to do if and when negotiations with the United States failed.* There were plenty of implied possibilities to choose from. These included the following possibilities:

1. *An attack on Russia.* On July 8, Washington read an intercept of July 2, (identified as Circular #1390) to Berlin, which began with the eye-catching sentence, "At the conference held in the presence of the Emperor on July 2nd 'The Principal Points in the Imperial Policy for Coping with the Changing Situation' were decided." The cable went on to say:

Inasmuch as this has to do with national defense secrets, keep the information only to yourself. Please also transmit the content to both the Naval and Military Attachés, together with this precaution.

* In addition, the messages contained errors in spelling and grammar either on the part of the originator or as a result of the decoding or translation. All quotations used here are as printed in the Pearl Harbor Attack Hearings (except that in several instances obvious typographical errors have been corrected).

The Policy

1. Imperial Japan shall adhere to the policy of contributing
to world peace by establishing the Great East Asia Sphere of Co-
prosperity, regardless of how the world situation may change. . . .

The Principal Points

. . . As regards the Russo-German war, although the spirit
of the Three-Power Axis shall be maintained, every preparation
shall be made at the present and the situation shall be dealt
with in our own way. In the meantime, diplomatic negotiations
shall be carried on with extreme care. . . .[1]

Little was said about the Russian problem for three
weeks; then, in a long, four-part cable to Washington and
Berlin on July 3, Foreign Minister Matsuoka said:

From time to time you have been sending us your various
opinions about what we ought to do to help Germany who
desires our assistance now that she is at war with Russia.

After mention of the China problem and Indochina, he
went on to say:

Needless to say, the Russo-German war has given us an
excellent opportunity to settle the northern question, and it is a
fact that we are proceeding with our preparations to take advantage of this occasion. Not only will we have to prepare,
however, but we must choose well our chance. In view of the
real situation facing our Empire, this should be easily understood. If the Russo-German war proceeds too swiftly, our Empire would inevitably not have time to take any effective
symmetrical action.

Here Matsuoka was reflecting the view generally held
that Russia would quickly collapse under the German on-
slaught. In the same message, he soon showed irritation at

not having been informed about the German plans when he had been in Berlin three months earlier:

> For that matter, did not Germany start a war with Russia because of her own military expediency when it was least desirable on our part? Now we have not only to settle the Chinese incident but have to meet a new challenge in the north as well as in the south, and this is quite inconvenient.[2]

Ambassador Nomura, in Washington, in a lengthy two-part cable on August 7 advised that the Americans had reports of troop reinforcements in Manchuria and gave Tokyo his estimate of what the United States would do if Japan attacked Russia:

> With regard to a northward move by us, it must be remembered that the United States has suddenly established very close relations with the Soviet Union. In view of this fact, it is highly doubtful that the United States would merely watch from the sidelines if we should make any moves to the north.[3]

Perhaps the clearest indication of what Japan planned to do about Russia came in two cables of August 15 from Tokyo to Berlin. In #739 Foreign Minister Matsuoka said:

> At the time of my conversation with Ambassador [Constantin] Smetanin the other day, I mentioned our desires in regard to the full realization of our rights and interests in Northern Saghalien and also the removal of danger zones in the waters of the Far East. Since then, we have been asked by the Soviet as to the attitude of Japan toward the German-Russian war; to which we have replied that there has been no change in our intentions of continuing friendly relations between Japan and Russia, that thus far we have maintained an attitude of observing the neutrality pact, and that it is still our desire to continue this in the future, but, that whether or not we can continue thus is a question that depends on the way in which

the Soviet Union responds to this. For instance if (a) any of the Soviet Union's territory in East Asia should be ceded, sold, or leased to a third power, or offered as military bases, (b) the Soviet Union should take any steps that would cause the sphere of any third power's military movements to be extended into East Asia, or should conclude with a third power an alliance that might have the Empire as its object, we certainly could not overlook the threat that this would be to our nation.

To this the Soviet Ambassador replied, that the Soviet government is rigidly observing the Japanese-Soviet neutrality pact, and that as far as the above-mentioned two points are concerned he could give assurance that there has been nothing of the kind and that there will be none in the future.

I furthermore took this opportunity to call the attention of the Soviet to the fact that of late it is persistently rumored that the United Staes will be shipping munitions to the Soviet via Vladivostok, and that if this should be true, Japan would have to take a serious view of it, as it would involve the three power pact relations.

In regard to the Japanese Government's attitude to the German-Russian war, I reiterated that there has been no change in our foreign policy, which has as its keynote the spirit and the objectives of the three power pact, even as Foreign Minister Matsuoka had communicated to the Soviet Government 2 July, and that this point is well understood by the Soviet.[4]

In #740 Matsuoka advised both Berlin and Rome of his conversations with the ambassadors of those countries in Tokyo:

On the 15th I told the German and Italian Ambassadors in Tokyo, confidentially, of my recent conversations with the Soviet Ambassador along the lines of my separate message #739. Ambassador Ott expressing a desire to understand the basic problem, said that according to the notice sent to the German Government on 2 July, he understood that the possibility of Japan's participating in the German-Russian war was not precluded, but asked if, now since the Soviets have given assurances regarding the two points which Japan considers vital, to the effect that there has been nothing of the kind and will not be in the future, the Soviets do not have the impression that

Japan will not take part in the German-Soviet war. To this I replied that, in view of the military expansion the Empire is at present effecting, I think under present existing conditions the above-mentioned arrangement with the Soviet is the very best means of taking the first steps toward carrying out future plans concerning the Soviet, which will be undertaken together with the German Government, that this is entirely in harmony with the spirit and objectives of the Tripartite Treaty, and that I hoped that the German Government would fully understand this point. Ambassador Ott thereupon asked if it is proper to understand that this present arrangement is the first step toward future measures that are to be taken against Russia, that this is merely a temporary arrangement, in other words that it partakes of the nature of a restraint upon the Soviet until preparations can be completed. To this I replied in the affirmative.[5]

How Washington reacted to these two messages is not hard to imagine. It was diplomatic double-talk that could mean anything. There was sufficient ambiguity in the Japanese statements to the Germans, Russians and Italians to leave open any course of action. That the possibility of an attack on Russia was still under consideration came in a cable of August 20 from Tokyo to Washington which, after discussing the possibility of a Russian collapse, said:

The Japanese Government has decided to increase the Japanese forces in Manchuokuo to the minimum number necessary to cope with such a possibility. On the other hand negotiations are being carried on in Tokyo with Soviet officials in order to arrive at a friendly solution to various matters having to do with this area. I understand that the Soviet officials have been instructed by the party leaders to be cautious in their attiude toward the forces stationed in Manchuokuo. This is solely for your information.

—————* the United States Government asks you questions concerning the increase of Japanese troops in the North, will you explain to them suitably as your own view of the matter

* Words missing in cable.

what I have pointed out above. Impress upon their minds that the movement of the troops has for its objective purely preventive precautions against unforseen emergency and that by it we will be able to forestall any possibility of peace in the Far East being disturbed.

Recently when the Soviet Ambassador in Tokyo inquired about this matter, I replied that so long as the Russian Government lives up to the treaty Japan also will be faithful to it. The Ambassador was very much pleased to hear this, saying that my statement had clarified the matter. This is solely for your information.[6]

A month passed before another significant comment about the possibility of an attack on Russia occurred in the intercepted Japanese diplomatic traffic. This was a brief mention in a lengthy analysis of the attitude of the United States by Ambassador Nomura in Washington on September 22: "Japan, in the event of the Russian downfall, might move either to the south or to the north."[7]

Then a week later, on September 27, in commenting on the draft of a proposal that Japan was considering presenting to the United States, Nomura said: "The deletion of the item reading 'no northward advance shall be made without justification' will no doubt be the point which will invite the most suspicion."[8] Two days later Councillor Sadao Iguchi in the embassy in Washington sent Tokyo his views on the negotiations and commented: "The United States is of the opinion that the scene of the negotiations was shifted to Tokyo by us so as to bring about delays. They think that we are watching developments of the German-Soviet war, and that we shall launch a northward move if indications seem to favor it."[9]

Tokyo's reply to these comments came on September 30 and read:

The reason why I left out the expression, "As there is no real objection we will make no northward invasion" in part 2 of your message is that if we were to insert this into the body of the text it might only give them a suspicion that we have direct designs against the Soviet. This whole matter, after all, concerns the China incident and the South Seas question. There is no particular problem in the north. In the preface to the clause concerning the stability of the Pacific area, this matter is fully included so I am willing to leave it up to the leaders on both sides and if necessary to clarify this in the minutes. In my proposal of the 4th I made it plain that there is no objection to this statement.[10]

The Japanese negotiators kept insisting that there was no problem in the north, but simultaneously put pressure on the United States to stop the shipments to the Soviet Union through the port of Vladivostok. On November 16, Tokyo once again explained to Washington why it had used the expressions "without provocation" and "as long as the Soviet Union remains faithful to the Soviet-Japanese Neutrality Treaty" and "without justifiable reasons," and argued that "this qualification by no means either limits nor minimizes our peaceful intentions."[11]

On November 24 there was available to the United States government a cable from Tokyo to Berlin in which Japan indicated a willingness to mediate the Russo-German war so that Germany could transfer her entire fighting force to some other front. It was fairly obvious that the Japanese wanted to see German strength concentrated against the Anglo-Saxon powers as explained in the cable: "In other words, our relationship with Great Britain and the United States has a great bearing on the future of our national greatness."[12]

Then, on December 5, Washington officials read a cable from Tokyo to Hsinking, which did not make matters any clearer; not the fault of the message alone, not all of which could be decoded:

————* In the event that Manchuria participates in the war————* in view of various circumstances it is our policy to cause Manchuria to participate in the war in which event Manchuria will take the same steps toward England and America that this country will take in case war breaks out.

This immediately raised the question of how Manchuria could participate in a war unless it was against the Soviet Union. But the balance of the message made it appear far more likely that the belligerents would be Britain and the United States and not the Soviet Union:

A summary follows:
1. American and British consular officials and offices will not be recognized as having special rights. Their business will be stopped (the sending of code telegrams and the use of short wave radio will be forbidden). However it is desired that the treatment accorded them after the suspension of business be comparable to that which Japan accords to consular officials of enemy countries resident in Japan.
2. The treatment accorded to British and American public property, private property, and to the citizens themselves shall be comparable to that accorded by Japan.
3. British and American requests to third powers to look after their consular offices and interests will not be recognized.

However the legal administrative steps taken by Manchuokuo shall be equitable and shall correspond to the measures taken by Japan.
4. The treatment accorded Russians resident in Manchuokuo shall conform to the provisions of the Japanese-Soviet neutrality pact. Great care shall be exercised not to antagonize Russia.[13]

Some of the Washington recipients of the cable intercepts believed that the Japanese would attack Russia. They were influenced not only by the cables but also by the fact that the fall of Moscow seemed imminent and that the success of the Russian counteroffensive, launched only a few

* Words missing in cable.

hours before, had not become apparent. The messages were so ambiguous that a Japanese attack on Russia certainly remained a good possibility. There had been fighting between the Japanese and the Russians in the Far East. In Washington there was the general belief that Moscow might fall. Finally, in the intercepted cables Washington had read a report of the assurances of the Japanese Foreign Minister to the German Ambassador in Tokyo that ". . . future plans concerning the Soviet, which will be undertaken together with the German Government . . ."

But there were other possibilities for Japanese action.

2. *A conquest of Southeast Asia.* Inasmuch as the freezing of Japanese assets had been triggered by the occupation of Indochina, the possibility of further Japanese advances in Southeast Asia was considerable.

In the cable of July 2 reporting on the conference with the Emperor, the statement was made: ". . . Preparations for southward advance shall be reenforced and the policy already decided upon with reference to French Indo-China and Thailand shall be executed."[14]

A message from Canton to Tokyo on July 14, translated in Washington five days later, began with the ominous statement:

. . . from military officials to the Attaches . . .

1. The recent general mobilization order expressed the irrevocable resolution of Japan to put an end to Anglo-American assistance in thwarting her natural expansion and her indomitable intention to carry this out, if possible, with the backing of the Axis but, if necessary, alone. . . .

2. The immediate object of our occupation of French Indo-China will be to achieve our purposes there. Secondly, its purpose is, when the international situation is suitable, to launch therefrom a rapid attack. This venture we will carry out in spite of any difficulties which may arise. We will endeavor to the last

to occupy French Indo-China peacefully but, if resistance is offered, we will crush it by force, occupy the country and set up martial law. After the occupation of French Indo-China, next on our schedule is the sending of an ultimatum to the Netherlands Indies. In the seizing of Singapore the Navy will play the principal part. As for the Army, in seizing Singapore it will need only one division and in seizing the Netherlands Indies, only two. In the main, through the activities of our air arm (in your city, the Spratley Islands, Parao, Thaiese Singora, Portuguese Timor and French Indo-China) and our submarine fleet (in the South Seas mandate islands, Hainan Island, and French Indo-China) we will once and for all crush Anglo-American military power and their ability to assist in any schemes against us.[15]

After the occupation of Indochina and the freezing of Japanese assets—in effect an embargo on all shipments to Japan—the Foreign Office on July 31 sent the embassy in Washington a policy review in which the following statement was made: "Commercial and economic relations between Japan and third countries, led by England and the United States, are gradually becoming so horribly strained that we cannot endure it much longer. Consequently, our Empire, to save its very life, must take measures to secure the raw materials of the South Seas."[16]

On September 4, Washington officials saw a September 2 cable from Batavia to Tokyo reporting on Japanese activities among the Chinese in the Netherlands Indies and advising that strong police action by the Dutch authorities made the work very difficult.[17] During the next two months not much progress was made toward reaching an agreement in Washington, and on November 18 a six-day-old cable from Tokyo to Vichy, which indicated that the Japanese were accelerating their military buildup in Indochina,[18] was circulated.

On November 26 a message of the previous day from Hanoi to Tokyo asked for immediate guidance, saying, ". . .

no doubt the Cabinet will make a decision between peace and war within the next day or two."[19] Tokyo replied to Hanoi on the twenty-eighth telling the Japanese mission there: "Even though the worst possible situation developed, and it will in all likelihood, the Imperial Government has made no decisions with regard to changing the position of the French Indo-Chinese Government. Therefore, I would like to have you give due consideration to the policy of maintaining the status quo for the time being. If you have no objections, bearing this in mind, I would have you act with prudence."[20]

A message from Bangkok on November 26 opened with: "In the event of the Empire's taking decisive action in a southward advance . . . In the event of an attack upon Burma and Malay . . ."[21]

Tokyo tried to counteract reports reaching Washington of troop movements in Indochina on December 3, with cable #875:

> There seem to be rumors to the effect that our military garrisons in French Indo-China are being strengthened. The fact is that recently there has been an unusual amount of activity by the Chinese forces in the vicinity of the Sino-French Indo-China border. In view of this, we have increased our forces in parts of northern French Indo-China. There would naturally be some movement of troops in the southern part as a result of this. We presume that the source of the rumors is in the exaggerated reports of these movements. In doing so, we have in no way violated the limitations contained in the Japanese-French joint defense agreement.[22]

With this evidence there were many in Washington on December 7 who were convinced that Japan's next move would be to the south, even though the last cable quoted made such reports ambiguous. A number of officials, including some who thought Japan would attack Russia, believed that Japan would try to avoid war with the United States. The intercepted cables were redundant with statements on the desirability of avoiding war with the United States.

3. *Avoidance of war with the United States.* The policy message of July 2 already referred to above contained what was probably the most accurate statement of intention: "Although every means available shall be resorted to in order to prevent the United States from joining the war, if need be, Japan shall act in accordance with the Three Power Pact and shall decide when and how force will be employed."[23]

On August 7 the Foreign Minister cabled the embassy in Washington: "Through my previous messages on the subject, you are perfectly well aware of the fact that the Konoye Cabinets have been sincerely interested in the betterment of Japanese-U.S. relations."[24] The message then went on to propose a meeting between Prime Minister Konoye and President Roosevelt, a proposal that was the subject of dozens of cables over the next several weeks. The United States indicated its willingness to have such a meeting, but only after the discussions in Washington reached a point which indicated that some agreement was possible.

On September 27, Tokyo sent Washington the next of an off-the-record statement by Foreign Minister Toyoda to American Ambassador Joseph C. Grew in which Toyoda said: "Should the United States and Japan come to blows . . . No greater misfortune could befall mankind."[25] Reporting back to Tokyo on October 13 on a discussion with Under Secretary of State Sumner Welles, Ambassador Nomura said that the point had been made that ". . . our proposal of 6 September expressed a willingness to sacrifice a practically unanimous desire of the people for a northward and/or southward military move, for the sake of an adjusted relationship with the United States."[26] Three days later the

Foreign Office told Nomura of German pressure on them to warn the United States that unless it ceased its belligerent activities toward the Axis powers, Japan might ". . . join immediately the war in opposition to the United States." The Foreign Office also said that Japan had not done so because ". . . she is desirous of making a success of the Japanese-American negotiations."[27]

After the replacement of the Konoye cabinet by that of General Hideki Tojo, Tokyo advised Washington on October 21: "The new cabinet differs in no way from the former one in its sincere desire to adjust Japanese-American relations on a fair basis."[28] This was followed on November 2 by: "The Government has for a number of days since the forming of a new Cabinet been holding meetings with the Imperial headquarters. We have carefully considered a fundamental policy for improving relations between Japan and America, but we expect to reach a final decision in a meeting on the morning of the 5th and will let you know the result at once. This will be our Government's last effort to improve diplomatic relations. The situation is very grave. When we resume negotiations, the situation makes it urgent that we reach a decision at once. This is at present only for your information. When we take up these negotiations once more, we trust you will handle everything with the greatest of care."[29]

To Washington, the ominous tone of this message was tempered by a short message to Berlin on November 21, which stated: "Our relations with the United States may have considerable effect on our southward program, depending, of course, on what turns those relations take. In other words, our relationship with Great Britain and the United States has a great bearing on the future of our national greatness.

"For this reason, we would like to avoid the rise of any violence at this time. . . ."[30]

The next day Tokyo advised Washington that on the twenty-fifth the Anti-Comintern Agreement would be renewed for five years but that Japan intended ". . . to handle the matter circumspectly. You know we have Japanese-American relations to think about."[31]

On November 29, Tokyo asked Ambassador Nomura to make one more attempt to reach an understanding with the United States.[32] Inasmuch as the American recipients of these intercepted cables were aware of the impasse that had been reached in the negotiations, they must have been skeptical about further discussions. The indications of desire for an agreement in the cables had to be weighed against repeated requests for speed in reaching the agreement, and the setting of deadlines by Tokyo. From mid-November on, twenty-five messages revealed Japan preparing at least for a break in diplomatic relations with the Anglo-Saxon nations and their friends and—at most—for war.

On October 13 the Foreign Minister advised Washington: "The situation at home is fast approaching a crisis and it is becoming absolutely essential that the two leaders meet if any adjustment of Japanese-U.S. relations is to be accomplished."[33]

On October 21: "We urge, therefore, that choosing an opportune moment, either you or Wakasugi let it be known to the United States that our country is not in a position to spend much more time discussing this matter."[34]*

On November 5: ". . . Time is exceedingly short and the situation very critical. Absolutely no delays can be permitted. Please bear this in mind and do your best. I wish to stress this point over and over.

* Kaname Wakasugi, Minister of the Japanese Embassy in Washington.

". . . We wish to avoid giving them the impression that there is a time limit or that this proposal is to be taken as an ultimatum. In a friendly manner, show them that we are anxious to have them accept our proposal."[35]

A second message from Tokyo on the same day, #736, said: "Because of various circumstances, it is absolutely necessary that all arrangements for the signing of this agreement be completed by the 25th of this month."[36]

On November 11: "Judging from the progress of the conversation, there seem to be indications that the United States is still not fully aware of the exceedingly criticalness of the situation here. The fact remains that the date set forth in my message #736 is absolutely immovable under present conditions. It is a definite deadline and therefore it is essential that a settlement be reached about that time."[37]

On November 19, Ambassador Nomura cabled Tokyo that he assumed the November 25 date was unalterable, but asked that any announcement of the breakdown of negotiations be postponed for four or five days to see if there was any progress in the talks.[38]

During the last two weeks of November the Japanese diplomatic traffic to all parts of the world could best be described as preparing for any eventuality. Interspersed among lengthy reports of the discussions on November 15 was a message from Tokyo to most major missions: "The following is the order and method of destroying the code machines in the event of an emergency."[39] On the same day Ambassador Nomura in Washington asked Tokyo for the government's instructions on how to handle Japanese interests in the United States if diplomatic relations were tionals.[41]

On November 18, Tokyo replied, saying: "It is hard to prophesy the future course of events . . ." The cable then gave priorities for the order of evacuation of Japanese nationals.[41]

On November 19 the Japanese embassy in Washington received Circular #2353 providing for emergency procedures in the event of a breakdown in communications:

Regarding the broadcast of a special message in an emergency.

In case of emergency (danger of cutting off our diplomatic relations), and the cutting off of international communications, the following warning will be added in the middle of the daily Japanese language short wave news broadcast.

(1) In case of a Japan-U.S. relations in danger: HIGASHI NO KAZEAME.*

(2) Japan-U.S.S.R. relations: KITZNOKAZE KUMORI.**

(3) Japan-British relations: NISHI NO KAZE HARE.***

This signal will be given in the middle and at the end as a weather forecast and each sentence will be repeated twice. When this is heard please destroy all code papers, etc. This is as yet to be a completely secret arrangement.

Forward as urgent intelligence.[42]

It was twelve days before this message was decoded and translated, so the Americans did not see it until November 28. Another message on November 19, Circular #2354 (read by the U. S. on the twenty-sixth) gave some code words that could be used in open broadcasts:

When our diplomatic relations are becoming dangerous, we will add the following at the beginning and end of our general intelligence broadcasts:

(1) If it is Japan-U.S. relations, "HIGASHI."

(2) Japan-Russia relations, "KITA."

(3) Japan-British relations (including Thai, Malaya and N.E.I.), "NISHI."

The above will be repeated five times and included at beginning and end.[43]

* East wind rain.
** North wind cloudy.
*** West wind clear.

On November 26 the Foreign Ministry told Washington:

The situation is momentarily becoming more tense and telegrams take too long. Therefore, will you cut down the substance of your reports of negotiations to the minimum and, on occasion, call up Chief Yamamoto* of the American Bureau and make your report to him. At that time we will use the following code:

[These columns would more appropriately be entitled "Code Word" and "True Meaning," respectively.]

English	*Japanese*
Nyuu Yooku (New York)	Sangoku Joyaku Mondai (Three-Power Treaty question)
Shikago (Chicago)	Musabetsu Taiguu Mondai (The question of nondiscriminatory treatment)
Sanfuranshisuko (San Francisco)	Shina Mondai (The China question)
Itoo Kun (Mr. Itoo)	Soori (Premier)
Date Kun (Mr. Date)	Gaimudaijin (Foreign Minister)
Tokugawa Kun (Mr. Tokugawa)	Rikugun (The army)
Maeda Kun (Mr. Maeda)	Kaigun (The navy)
Endan (Marriage proposal)	Nichi-bei kooshoo (Japan-American negotiations)
Kimiko San (Miss Kimiko)	Daitooryoo (President)
Fumeko San (Miss Fumeko)	Haru (Hull)

* Kumaicho Yamamoto, head of the American Division of the Japanese Foreign Office; not to be confused with Admiral Isoroku Yamamoto, who planned the Pearl Harbor attack.

English	Japanese
Shoobai (Trade)	Kokunaijoosei (Internal situation)
Yama Wo Uru (To sell the mountain)	Jooho Suru (To yield)
Yama Wo Urenu (Not to sell the mountain)	Jooho Sezu (Not to yield)
Kodomo Gaumareru (The child is born)	Keisei Kyunten Suru (Situation taking critical turn)

"For your information . . ."[44]

The communications intelligence experts broke this code on the day it was sent and that evening were able to listen to a telephone call to Tokyo by Ambassador Saburo Kurusu; Admiral Kurusu had been sent to Washington to assist Ambassador Nomura in the negotiations.

The telephone conversation that evening did not reveal much to the American listeners; but on the 27th at 11:27 P.M. Ambassador Kurusu had a seven-minute conversation with Kumaicho Yamamoto, the Chief of the American Division in the Foreign Office. The intercepted version that was available to the U. S. officials the next day read like this:

LITERAL TRANSLATION

DECODE OF VOICE CODE

Kurusu: "Hello, hello. This is Kurusu."
Yamamoto: "This is Yamamoto."
Kurusu: "Yes, Hello, hello."
(Unable to get Yamamoto for about six or eight seconds, he said aside, to himself, or to someone near him):
Kurusu: "Oh, I see, they're making a record of this, huh?"
(It is believed he meant that the six-second interruption was made so

LITERAL TRANSLATION

DECODE OF VOICE CODE

that a record could be started in Tokyo. Interceptor's machine had been started several minutes earlier.)

Kurusu: "Hello. Sorry to trouble you so often."

Yamamoto: "How did the matrimonial question get along today?"

"*How did the negotiations go today?*"

Kurusu: "Oh, haven't you got our telegram* yet? It was sent—let me see—at about six—no, seven o'clock. Seven o'clock. About three hours ago.

"There wasn't much that was different from what Miss Fumeko said yesterday."

"*There wasn't much that was different from Hull's talks of yesterday.*"

Yamamoto: "Oh, there wasn't much difference?"

Kurusu: "No, there wasn't. As before, that southward matter—that south, south—southward matter, is having considerable effect. You know, southward matter."

Yamamoto (Obviously trying to indicate the serious effect that Japanese concentrations, etc., in French Indo-China were having on the conversations in Washington. He tries to do this without getting away from the 'Miss Fumeko childbirth, marriage' character of the voice code): "Oh, the south matter? It's effective?"

Kurusu: "Yes, and at one time, the matrimonial question seemed as if it would be settled."

"*Yes, and at one time it looked as though we could reach an agreement.*"

Kurusu: "But—well, of course, there are other matters involved too, but—that was it—that was the monkey wrench. Details are included in

LITERAL TRANSLATION · DECODE OF VOICE CODE

the telegram* which should arrive very shortly. It is not very long and you'll be able to read it quickly."

Yamamoto: "Oh, you've dispatched it?"

Kurusu: "Oh, yes, quite a while ago. At about seven o'clock."

(Pause.)

Kurusu: "How do things look there? Does it seem as if a child might be born?"

"Does it seem as if a crisis is at hand?"

Yamamoto (In a very definite tone): "Yes, the birth of the child seems imminent."

"Yes, a crisis does appear imminent."

Kurusu (In a somewhat surprised tone, repeating Yamamoto's statement): "It *does* seems as if the birth is going to take take place?"

"A crisis does appear imminent?"

(Pause.)

Kurusu: "In which direction
. . ."

(Stopped himself very abruptly at this slip which went outside the character of the voice code. After a slight pause he quickly recovered, then, to cover up the slip, continued.)

Kurusu: "Is it to be a boy or a girl?"

Yamamoto (Hesitated, then, laughing at his hesitation, took up Kurusu's cue to re-establish the voice code character of the talk. The "boy, girl, healthy" byplay has no other significance): "It seems as if it will be a strong healthy boy."

Kurusu: "Oh, it's to be a strong, healthy boy?"

"* JD-1:6915 (S.I.S. #25495). Outline of interview on 27 November with Roosevelt-Hull-Kurusu-Nomura."

LITERAL TRANSLATION   DECODE OF VOICE CODE

(Rather long pause.)
Yamamoto: "Yes. Did you make any statement (to the newspapers) regarding your talk with Miss Kimiko today?"
Kurusu: "No, nothing. Nothing except the mere fact that we met."
Yamamoto: "Regarding the matter contained in the telegram** of the other day, although no definite decision has been made yet, please be advised that effecting it will be difficult."
Kurusu: "Oh, it is difficult, huh?"
Yamamoto: "Yes it is."
Kurusu: "Well, I guess there's nothing more that can be done then."
Yamamoto: "Well yes."
(Pause)
Yamamoto: "Then today ..."
Kurusu: "Today?"
Yamamoto: "The matrimonial question, that is, the matter pertaining to arranging a marriage—don't break them off."
Kurusu: "Not break them? You mean talks." (Helplessly) "Oh, my." (Pause, and then with a resigned laugh) "Well, I'll do what I can." (Continuing after a pause) "Please read carefully what Miss Kimiko had to say as contained in today's telegram."*
Yamamoto: "From what time to what time were your talks today?"
Kurusu: "Oh, today's was from 2:30." (Much repeating of the num-

"Did you make any statement regarding your talks with the President today?"

"Regarding negotiations, don't break them off."

*"Please read carefully what the President had to say as contained in today's telegram."**

"** Probably #1189 (S.I.S. #25441-42). (JD-1: 6896). Washington reports the two proposals presented by the U. S. on 26 November."

LITERAL TRANSLATION

DECODE OF VOICE CODE

eral 2) "Oh, you mean the duration? Oh, that was for about an hour."

Yamamoto: "Regarding the matrimonial question.

"I shall send you another message. However, please bear in mind that the matter of the other day is a very difficult one."

Kurusu: "But without anything —they want to keep carrying on the matrimonial question. They do. In the meantime we're faced with the excitement of having a child born. On top of that Tokugawa is really champing at the bit, isn't he? Tokugawa is, isn't he?"

(Laughter and pause.)

Kurusu: "That's why I doubt if anything can be done."

Yamamoto: "I don't think it's as bad as that."

Yamamoto: "Well—we can't sell a mountain."

Kurusu: "Oh, sure, I know that. That isn't even a debatable question any more."

Yamamoto: "Well, then, although we can't yield, we'll give you some kind of a reply to that telegram."

Kurusu: "In any event, Miss Kimiko is leaving town tomorrow, and will remain in the country until Wednesday."

Yamamoto: "Will you please continue to do your best."

Kurusu: "Oh, yes. I'll do my best. And Nomura's doing everything too."

Yamamoto: "Oh, all right. In

"Regarding the negotiations."

"But without anything—they want to keep on negotiating. In the meantime we have a crisis on hand and the army is champing at the bit. You know the army."

"Well—we can't yield."

"In any event, the President is leaving town tomorrow, and will remain in the country until Wednesday."

LITERAL TRANSLATION   DECODE OF VOICE CODE

today's talks, there wasn't anything of special interest then?"

Kurusu: "No, nothing of particular interest, except that it is quite clear now that that southward—ah—the south, the south matter is having considerable effect."

Yamamoto: "I see. Well, then, goodbye."

Kurusu: "Goodbye."

The Japanese officials obviously were having difficulty using the new voice code. If Ambassador Kurusu's comment at the beginning about "they're making a record of this" is interpreted as referring to the Foreign Office in Tokyo, as it was then by the Americans, it indicated a happy oblivion to the fact that the Americans were recording the conversation. The effort to disguise the meaning was transparent a few sentences later when he discusses "the matrimonial question" and comments that the "southward matter is having considerable effect." Soon thereafter, "the matrimonial question . . . don't break them off," and it was clear that the matrimonial question referred to the negotiations and the southward movement referred to Japanese activities in Indochina. Ambassador Kurusu's "Oh, my" showed that he was aware of the security breach. By this time the gist of the telephone conversation might well have been apparent even if the code had not been supplied in advance.

On the first of December the American officials read the text of a lengthy cable from the Japanese Ambassador in Berlin reporting on a meeting with Foreign Minister Joachim von Ribbentrop:

Ribbentrop opened our meeting by again inquiring whether I had received any reports regarding the Japanese-U.S. negotiations. I replied that I had received no official word.

Ribbentrop: "It is essential that Japan effect the New Order in East Asia without losing this opportunity. There never has been and probably never will be a time when closer cooperation under the Tripartite Pact is so important. If Japan hesitates at this time, and Germany goes ahead and establishes her European New Order, all of the military might of Britain and the United States will be concentrated against Japan.

"As Fuehrer Hitler said today, there are fundamental differences in the very right to exist between Germany and Japan, and the United States. We have received advice to the effect that there is practically no hope of the Japanese-U.S. negotiations being concluded successfully, because of the fact that the United States is putting up a stiff front.

"If this is indeed the fact of the case, and if Japan reaches a decision to fight Britain and the United States, I am confident that that will not only be to the interest of Germany and Japan jointly, but would bring about favorable results for Japan herself."

I: "I can make no definite statement as I am not aware of any concrete intentions of Japan. Is Your Excellency indicating that a state of actual war is to be established between Germany and the United States?"

Ribbentrop: ". . . Should Japan become engaged in a war against the United States, Germany, of course, would join the war immediately. There is absolutely no possibility of Germany's entering into a separate peace with the United States under such circumstances. The Fuehrer is determined on that point.". . .[45]

The same day a message of November 30 from Tokyo to Berlin was available. "The conversations begun between Tokyo and Washington last April during the administration of the former cabinet . . . now stand ruptured—broken. . . . Say very secretly to them [Hitler and Ribbentrop] that there is extreme danger that war may suddenly break out between the Anglo-Saxon nations and Japan through some clash of arms and add that the time of the breaking out of this war may come quicker than anyone dreams."[46]

Also on the first of December, Tokyo advised Washington to use chemicals available in the Naval Attaché's office to destroy codes. London, Hong Kong, Singapore and Manila were told to dispose of their code machines, while the U. S. office was told to retain theirs.[47] It was noted that the machine in Batavia had been returned to Japan.[48] On December 2, the Washington Embassy was told to destroy one of its code machines.[49] On December 5 (in a message read by the United States on December 6) Tokyo ordered some of the personnel in Washington "to leave by plane within the next couple of days."[50] On the same day Iguchi, the Councillor of Embassy, said they were keeping one code machine because negotiations were still going on.[51]

In a short message, on December 6, Tokyo advised the embassy that Japan was replying to the American proposal of November 26 and that the reply would be sent separately in a fourteen-part cable. The cable reported the situation to be extremely delicate; that the Ambassador should keep the reply secret for the time being, and that he would be advised when to present it. The first thirteen parts of the Japanese cable were decoded and available to the senior American officials on Saturday evening, December 6.[52] The fourteenth part and the message specifying the precise time when the reply was to be handed to the Secretary of State were not available until the morning of December 7.[53]

The first thirteen parts of the Japanese reply were a detailed review of the differences between Japan and the United States. The last sentence of Part 14 read: "The Japanese Government regrets to have to notify hereby the American Government that in view of the attitude of the American Government it cannot but consider that it is impossible to reach an agreement through further negotiations."[54]

The time prescribed for delivery was 1 P.M., December 7, Washington time. The reaction of the Washington officials to these two items was that they meant war, and after hurried consultation it was decided to send an additional warning to the forces in the Pacific.*

The diplomatic traffic contained other clues as to possible Japanese action. American officials could assume that the Japanese government might be influenced by what their embassy in Washington was reporting as to the attitude of the United States and the course of action it would take under different circumstances.

JAPANESE VIEWS OF U. S. COURSES OF ACTION

On August 7, Ambassador Nomura described the general outlook in the United States as he saw it: ". . . the United States is under the impression that the ties between the Axis partners are closer than appear on paper. . . . It assumes that the aims of Germany and Italy in the West and Japan in the East are to conquer the world. . . . There is no doubt whatsoever that the United States is prepared to take drastic action depending on the way Japan moves, and thus closing the door on any possibility of settling the situation. . . . the Pacific, of late, has become the center of attention and there is a good possibility that, depending on developments in Europe, this trend will be considerably invigorated in the near future."[55]

---

* For a review of the warnings sent the American forces in the Pacific, see p. 140.

Two days later he reported: "... I am convinced that as long as we proceed along the lines of our present policy, the United States, too, will undoubtedly undeviatingly follow the course whose trend has already been established. The United States assumes that our occupation of South French Indo-China indicates that Japan has already set her course."[56] On August 16, Ambassador Nomura reported that while the United States was divided over participation in the European war, "... the people are unanimous with regard to taking a strong hand in the Far East."[57]

A month later Ambassador Nomura was a bit more optimistic. He reported to Tokyo: "According to information from that usual source, the atmosphere of the Cabinet meeting held here last Friday showed considerable signs of anticipation of a Japanese-U.S. Conference."[58]

On September 22 he reported the attitude of the American people toward a war with Japan:

... a war between Japan and the United States will be one within the scope of the navy alone: Japan's economic strength cannot stand a long war; the United States excels greatly in its ability to replace warships lost in battle; saying these things, they boast of their ability to win out in a short while. There are only a few who are at all conscious of the danger of a war with Japan. . . .

... The people generally here are maintaining an extremely happy-go-lucky frame of mind. There are practically none at all who think that as a result of this war the United States will be destroyed. With regards to their will to enter the war, they feel that naval participation is sufficient. And, aside from the preparations being undertaken by military authorities, there are practically none who anticipate the dispatch of expeditionary forces on a large scale.

However, most recently there has been a sharp decline in the isolationist opinion expressed in the houses of Congress. One group is already going over to the majority group who back up the Government's foreign policy.

. . . Today the greater portion of the American navy is being kept in the Pacific.[59]

On September 29, Councillor Iguchi reported that the embassy did not feel the United States would back down and expressed the view that Tokyo was too optimistic.[60] The next day Ambassador Nomura said that he had called on the Chief of Naval Operations, Admiral Harold R. Stark, and had been told that an agreement was impossible unless the China incident was settled.[61]

On October 3, Ambassador Nomura in a long cable reported on developments in the United States, saying in part: "The general public has been becoming more and more favorable to the President's foreign policy, until today it is being supported overwhelmingly." He then went on to discuss the possibility of Russia's making peace with Germany, and the latter's turning its effort against Britain to the detriment of the United States:

On the other hand, however, the United States has not decreased her economic pressure against Japan one iota. It should be carefully noted that the United States is proceeding along a policy of making this her threatening power. Should the United States continue along her present economic policy, without resorting to the force of arms, she shall gain her objectives of a war against Japan without once resorting to a battle. Moreover, I am of the opinion that unless there is a radical change in the world situation or unless Japan changes her foreign policy, the United States will not alter this policy of hers against Japan.
. . .
Incidentally, in the course of a friendly discussion with a Cabinet official, he advised me that both the President and the Secretary of State are sincere in their desire to bring about an "understanding" between Japan and the United States and that the matter of the removal of the troops [Japanese troops from China] is the only thing that blocks the attainment of this goal.[62]

On October 14, Ambassador Nomura talked to Admiral Richmond Kelly Turner, the Chief of War Plans for the U. S. Navy, whom he had seen in Admiral Stark's office two weeks before. He reported that Admiral Turner told him the U. S. wanted a definite promise, not a pretense:

He said that should the Russo-German war suddenly end and should Germany offer Great Britain peace, it would be after all a German peace and England would not now accept it. Now, this man is a responsible fellow in an important position and I take it that this is the view of the Navy. On the other hand, Hoover and his following consider that should Moscow make a separate peace with Berlin and should Berlin then turn to London with generous peace terms, this whole fray would end with unimaginable quickness. Castle* told me that Hugh Gibson feels the same way and that Japan, too, should be on the alert for this possibility. This, however, I take to be a minority view entertained by the Isolationists. [Frederick] Moore** reports that Secretary Hull told Senator Thomas that he is proceeding patiently with the Japanese-American negotiations, but he hopes that Japan will not mistake this for a sign of weakness on America's part, and that no answer had arrived to the memo of October 2nd. Kiplinger*** reports that there is a very good basis for rumors of a cessation of hostilities between Russia and Germany and that the chances for war between Japan and the United States are fifty-fifty.[63]

After the new Japanese cabinet was appointed, on October 20, the Ambassador sent Foreign Minister Tojo a cable of congratulations on his appointment. Nomura acknowledged that he had thought the United States would be conciliatory toward Japan because of the European war but that the United States was unyielding on China. He ad-

* Former U. S. Ambassador to Japan.
Author's note: Hoover and Hugh Gibson are not identified in reference 63, but are presumed to be (1) Herbert Hoover, former President of the U. S., and (2) Career Diplomat.
** American legal advisor to Japanese Embassy in Washington.
*** A Washington newspaper correspondent.

mitted he was "in the dark" and asked to be relieved, a request which he repeated in another message two days later.[64]

On October 27 the Ambassador cabled another report on a discussion with an American naval officer:

> On the 25th, I met and talked with Admiral [William V.] Pratt. The Admiral is one who recognizes the fact that in the final analysis, the aims of economic warfare and actual armed conflict are one and the same. He is of the opinion that as long as Japan stays within the scope of the China Incident, there will be no shooting war between Japan and the United States. He said, however, that if Japan moved either northward or southward, he feared the consequences. He added that the final decision rested in the Emperor and the President.[65]

On October 29 the Minister of Embassy in Washington, Kaname Wakasugi, sent his analysis of the situation. He expressed the view that the United States had established Great Britain and China as the first line of defense and was strengthening its wartime structure. He went on to say that the United States considered China as part of the over-all Pacific problem, which included equal opportunities for all nations to have access to the raw materials of Indochina and Thailand. Wakasugi said: "Her preparations in the event of the worst have been completed. Therefore, I cannot believe that she is stalling for time. On the other hand, I am of the opinion that she is not so anxious to enter into the agreement that she will sacrifice any of her terms."[66]

That same day the Ambassador also reported on U. S. public opinion:

> I report the following points to you merely as reference material in connection with the adjusting of national relations.
> 1. Admiral [William H.] Standley, Retired, told Member of Parliament Kasai that the more influential Congressmen from the Middle West (where there are many Americans of German

descent) state that the majority of the Middle Westerners are opposed to a war against Germany, but that at the same time, a great number of them favor a U. S.-Japanese war. This is due, in part, he said, to Germany's superior propaganda work. I have heard O'Laughlin, who is familiar with that area, express similar opinions.

2. Secretary Hull has told Congress that the U. S. Government looks upon the Tripartite Pact as an instrument to be used to intimidate the United States. Its aim is to make impossible the aiding of Great Britain by the United States and thus gradually to force the United States to give up the control of the seas and bring back the first line of U. S. defense to the U. S. shore line. The United States desires peace; however, it is a well established fact that there is a better chance to have peace if strength can be shown. If I (Hull) were to make too many concessions to the Axis powers, there is danger that they would be interpreted as weaknesses on my part and no doubt their demands would be increased. (This is particularly true in Tokyo.) There are indications, Hull continued, that the degree of enthusiasm in Tokyo to proceed on selfish courses, is determined to a considerable extent on how the German-Soviet war is going.

It is said that he went on to say that the situation was "very delicate and very changeable." (Reported in *The New York Times*, 28th.)[67]

On November 10, Ambassador Nomura reported again the opinion of a prominent member of the Senate:

1. I sent Moore to contact Senator Thomas of the Senate Foreign Relations Committee and Hull. His report reads as follows:

"The United States is not bluffing. If Japan invades again, the United States will fight with Japan. Psychologically the American people are ready. The Navy is prepared and ready for action."

2. Yesterday evening, Sunday, a certain Cabinet member, discarding all quibbling, began by saying to me: "You are indeed a dear friend of mine and I tell this to you alone." Then he continued: "The American Government is receiving a number of reliable reports that Japan will be on the move soon. The American Government does not believe that your visit on Monday to

the President or the coming of Mr. Kurusu will have any effect on the general situation."

I took pains to explain in detail how impatient the Japanese have grown since the freezing; how they are eager for a quick understanding; how both the Government and the people do not desire a Japanese-American war; and how we will hope for peace until the end.

He replied, however: "Well, our boss, the President, believes those reports and so does the Secretary of State."

In the newspapers and magazines, with the exception of the *Daily News* and the Hearst Papers, it is reported that the Americans are much more eager for a war with Japan than they are for one with Germany. It is said that some of the British are using this inclination for their own advantage and that already parleys have been started for joint Anglo-American action. Suggestions have already been made to the effect that it is necessary for some of the British fleet to be located in the Pacific. Now even if the President and the other statesmen do not follow this trend, who can say how it will be? The friend I just spoke of told me that the United States cannot stop now because if Japan moves something will have to be done since it is a question of the United States saving its face.

3. Well, in any case, I am going to see the President today and talk with him on the bases of your instructions. You may be sure that I will do my very best.[68]

Four days later Nomura sent another personal analysis. After expressing confidence that he could win out in the negotiations, he said:

I am telling Your Excellency this for your own information only.

I believe that I will win out in the long run in these negotiations, and I will fight to the end. I will do my very best with infinite patience and then leave the outcome up to God Almighty. However, I must tell you the following:

1. As I told you in a number of messages, the policy of the American Government in the Pacific is to stop any further moves on our part either southward or northward. With every economic weapon at their command, they have attempted to

achieve this objective, and now they are contriving by every possible means to prepare for actual warfare.

2. In short, they are making every military and every other kind of preparation to prevent us from a thrust northward or a thrust southward; they are conspiring most actively with the nations concerned and rather than yield on this fundamental political policy of theirs in which they believe so firmly, they would not hesitate, I am sure, to fight us. It is not their intention, I know, to repeat such a thing as the Munich conference which took place several years ago and which turned out to be such a failure. Already I think the apex of. German victories has been passed. Soviet resistance persists, and the possibility of a separate peace has receded, and hereafter this trend will be more and more in evidence.

3. The United States is sealing ever-friendlier relations with China, and insofar as possible she is assisting Chiang. For the sake of peace in the Pacific, the United States would not favor us at the sacrifice of China. Therefore, the China problem might become the stumbling block to the pacification of the Pacific and as a result the possibility of the United States and Japan ever making up might vanish.

4. There is also the question of whether the officials of the Japanese Government are tying up very intimately with the Axis or not. We are regarded as having a very flexible policy, ready, nevertheless, in any case, to stab the United States right in the back. Lately the newspapers are writing in a manner to show how gradually we are tying up closer and closer with the Axis.

5. If we carry out a venture southward for the sake of our existence and our lives, it naturally follows that we will have to fight England and the United States, and chances are also great that the Soviet will participate. Furthermore, among the neutral nations, those of Central America are already the puppets of the United States, and as for those of South America, whether they like it or not, they are dependent for their economic existence on the United States and must maintain a neutrality partial thereto.

6. It is inevitable that this war will be long, and this little victory or that little victory, or this little defeat or that little defeat do not amount to much, and it is not hard to see that whoever can hold out till the end will be the victor.

7. It is true that the United States is gradually getting in

deeper and deeper in the Atlantic, but this is merely a sort of convoy warfare, and as things now stand she might at any moment transfer her main strength to the Pacific.

Great Britain, too, in the light of the present condition of the German and Italian navies, has, without a doubt, moved considerable strength into the area of the Indian Ocean. I had expected in the past that should the United States start warlike activities in the Atlantic, there would be considerable feeling for a compromise in the Pacific, but there has been no evidence of such an inclination as yet. There are even now many arguments against war with Germany as opposed to internal questions, but there is not the slightest opposition to war in the Pacific. It is being thought more than ever that participation will be carried out through the Pacific area.

8. Though I cannot be a hundred per cent sure of the present situation in Japan, having read your successive wires I realize that the conditions must be very critical. In spite of the fact that it is my understanding that the people and the officials, too, are tightening their belts, I am going to pass on to you my opinion, even though I know that I will be harshly criticized for it. I feel that should the situation in Japan permit, I would like to caution patience for one or two months in order to get a clear view of the world situation. This, I believe, would be the best plan.[69]

After many lengthy cables reporting the details of discussions with the State Department, on November 18 Ambassador Nomura sent this message:

On the evening of the 17th, both of us went to call on a certain cabinet member and this is what he told us: "The President is very desirous of an understanding between Japan and the United States. In his latest speech he showed that he entertained no ill will towards Japan. I would call that to your attention. Now the great majority of the cabinet members, with two exceptions, in principle approve of a Japanese-American understanding. If Japan would now do something real, such as evacuating French Indo-China, showing her peaceful intentions, the way would be open for us to furnish you with oil and it would probably lead to the reestablishment of normal trade relations. The Secretary of State cannot bring public opinion in line so long as you do not take some real and definite steps to reassure the Americans."[70]

By the latter part of November 1941 the cable traffic between Washington and Tokyo was loaded with discussion of the emergency measures described above as well as the constant reporting on the discussions with the State Department. On November 27, Washington reported on U. S. discussions with the Netherlands and on the fact that the Dutch Foreign Minister* stopped in Washington en route to Asia. The cable said that there had been a considerable increase in the shipment of military supplies from the United States to the Netherlands East Indies and speculated, ". . . at the time the Japanese-U. S. negotiations break off, Britain and the United States may occupy the Netherlands East Indies."[71]

The next day Nomura sent a brief but more ominous message:

So far silence has been maintained here concerning our talks with the United States; however, now the results of our conference of the 26th are out and headlines like this are appearing in the paper: "Hull Hands Peace Plan to Japanese," and "America Scorns a Second Munich." The papers say that it is up to Japan either to accept the American proposal with its four principles,** or face war, in which latter case the responsibility would be upon Japan.
This we must carefully note.[72]

On the first of December the Ambassador reported in detail on the public reaction to speeches in Tokyo by the Prime Minister and other leaders to the effect that the Anglo-

---

* From the government-in-exile based in London—Holland at that time being occupied by the Germans.
** Author's note: The four American principles were:
  1. Removal of Japanese forces from China;
  2. Recognition of the Chiang Kai-shek government;
  3. Withdrawal of Japanese forces from Indochina;
  4. A multilateral treaty for peace in the Pacific.

Saxon powers were blocking Japan's realization of her natural rights in the Pacific:

The immediate reasons for the President's sudden return to Washington are as I reported in message #1222.* Basically speaking, however, the United States has been aroused against us by the reports of Premier Tojo's speech to Parliament, and by the speech of Cabinet official Kaya and Suzuki to the Convention of the Imperial Rules Assistance Association. The dispatches concerning these speeches gave one the impression that anti-foreignism, crushing of Britain and the United States, were the points most emphasized.

Japan's true motives are being further doubted here because of the reports of increased troop movements in French Indo-China.

Thus, in the midst of this atmosphere, fraught with suspicion as it was, the report of Premier Tojo's speech arrived, in which it was alleged that the Premier advocated the purging of all Britons and Americans out of the Far East.

Since the alleged speech was made at a time when the United States was expectantly awaiting our reply to their official note of the 26th to Japan, particular importance was attached to it. (It is possible that the U. S. Government assumes that the speech was made by way of expressing our complete disapproval of the U. S. proposal and that it foreshadowed our launching a military campaign. Some of the newspapers go to the extreme of commenting that if the speech is given a literal interpretation it can mean nothing except a declaration of war.)

The President's speeches concerning foreign affairs are consistently very cautiously worded, for they are usually taken as a description of U. S. national policy. It is almost natural that people who are accustomed to interpret speeches in that manner, reacted the way they did to the Premier's speech.

I assume that you have already taken measures to do so, but may I suggest that when the Prime Minister or any Cabinet

---

* Author's note: The President suddenly returned to Washington from a rest at Warm Springs, Georgia, as the result of a call from Secretary of State Hull, who considered a speech by Prime Minister Tojo especially alarming. The Premier was quoted as saying, "The exploitation of the Asiatics by the Americans must be purged with vengeance."

officer is to touch upon Foreign Affairs, careful consideration be given to those factors. I make this suggestion only because our country is at a very critical point in her history. Even if the worst eventuality materializes, we should be in a position to show all neutrals and outsiders the complete innocence on our part.[73]

On December 3, Washington reported to Tokyo: "Judging from all indications, we feel that some joint military action between Great Britain and the United States, with or without a declaration of war, is a certainty in the event of an occupation of Thailand."[74] This was to be the last assessment by the Washington Embassy of the probable American course of action in the event of a further move in South Asia by Japan.

For Tokyo the reflections of its embassy's views on the probable courses of action of the United States constituted the most accurate intelligence available. The Japanese at that time were reputed to have a vast espionage network, but its size was exaggerated and the information it produced was low-level. Japan had not been able to crack the United States diplomatic code, and there were no Japanese agents at a high level in the United States government. Consequently, what was available to Japan was a considerable amount of low-level intelligence on ship movements as seen by observers at various American ports and the Panama Canal, and the assessments made by the embassy.

Japan made extensive use of its embassies and consulates for intelligence collection purposes. The consuls used Japanese citizens as unpaid agents to assist them in gathering information, a task which undoubtedly was put to them in the bluntest possible terms. There were hundreds of these agents in Hawaii alone. In June 1944, R. L. Shivers, the Special Agent in charge of the office of the Federal Bureau of Investigation in Honolulu, advised the U. S. Attorney for the District of Hawaii that he believed he could provide the evidence to prosecute successfully several Japanese subconsular agents for violation of the Espionage Act of June 15, 1917; this act had been applicable to such acitivities since August 1939 but had not been enforced in the territory. Shivers also advised that a total of 40 cases had been investigated and were ready for prosecution and that another 200 cases could be brought up to date fairly quickly. The U. S. Attorney, Angus M. Taylor, Jr., advised Assistant Attorney General Wendell Berge in Washington; Berge had the matter reviewed by the Criminal Division and then asked the State Department whether to prosecute. A decision not to prosecute was based on recommendations from the Hawaiian Department of the Army which was trying to win the loyalty of the Japanese on the islands; the Army urged warnings rather than prosecution, on the assumption that not over 10 per cent of the unregistered consular agents were aware they were violating an American law which required the registration of all foreign agents.[75]

The material turned over to the Japanese consulates by those agents to send to Tokyo ranged all the way from regular reports on ships entering and leaving harbors to the precise anchorage of ships in Pearl Harbor and plans of the Panama Canal. In the months preceding the attack there were some twenty-four messages on naval movements in Hawaii, twenty on the shipping in the Panama Canal and fifty-six on activities in the Philippines.[76]

Actually, the Japanese agents started work before the attack plans were made. On December 2, 1940, an agent reported on the ships at Pearl Harbor, advising that one battleship of the *Texas* type had been observed and that other ships in the harbor included three heavy cruisers, eight cruisers, twenty-seven destroyers, six submarines and three special service ships.[77] Additional reports were filed on the twentieth and twenty-fourth of that month, and in January 1941 on the sixth, seventh, ninth, sixteenth and twenty-eighth. Reporting continued with this frequency. On September 24, 1941, Tokyo advised that henceforth the consul should divide Pearl Harbor into five sub-areas and report the precise location of the warships and aircraft carriers and whether they were at anchor, tied up at wharves, buoys or in docks.[78]

On November 15, Tokyo advised: "As relations between Japan and the United States are most critical, make your 'ships in harbor report' irregular but at a rate of twice a week. Although you already are no doubt aware, please take extra care to maintain secrecy." Washington could not read this until December 3rd.[79]

On November 29, Tokyo asked to be advised when there were no ship movements in addition to the regular reports on activity.[80] This message was decoded by December 5. Washington could take alarm over these messages about Pearl Harbor, but there were other indications as well.

Reports from other areas covered vital defense matters. On August 2, 1941, Tokyo asked the consulate in Panama to report when English and American merchant ships transited the Canal.[81] Panama reported on August 18 that one hundred planes, mainly bombers, had "completely disappeared" from Albrook Field.[82] A message from Buenos Aires to Panama on September 23 mentioned maps and charts of the Canal Zone in transit to Tokyo.[83] A report on October 18 gave details of ship movements and military construction work and identified units in the Canal Zone.[84] The Philippines were reported on in equally great detail. On

August 1, Tokyo asked Manila to report on "the camouflage and distinguishing marks of the American naval and military aeroplanes in Manila."[85] Manila reporting was frequent on all items of military interest. On October 4, Tokyo asked for a reconnaissance of the new defense works on Luzon.[86] On November 15, Manila was told to "ascertain by what route bombers went to the Philippines."[87] Tokyo was also receiving reports from Batavia, Singapore, San Francisco and Seattle. From all of these ports, and many others, a flood of details on military activities flowed into Japan.

The intelligence personnel in Washington reading the intercepted messages of the Japanese agents reporting on military matters did not view the messages by themselves as out of the ordinary—considering the world situation of late 1941—or as conclusive evidence of Japanese intention to attack any one place. It is true that Tokyo requested very specific details about the location of ships in Pearl Harbor, information that would be very useful, if not essential for any attack on that base. But it is also true that many specific details were requested from agents in other parts of the Pacific: from Panama to the Philippines, and from Seattle to the Netherlands East Indies.

What was most important was that the messages did not deviate from a familiar pattern. The Japanese were known to be insatiable collectors of information. One of the most frequent caricatures of the time was that of the ubiquitous Japanese tourist with a camera snapping pictures of everything in sight. Viewed together with the worsening situation in Asia, the possibility that Japan would engage in further military conquests and that there would be clashes with the British or Dutch or Americans, this collection effort did not seem unusual.

U. S. REPORTING FROM TOKYO

In addition to intelligence from intercepted messages, the State Department in Washington received reports from Ambassador Grew in Tokyo which reflected his astute views on the situation in Japan. Grew was an exceptionally able diplomat, thoroughly familiar with developments in Asia and a perceptive reporter. He exerted his every effort to prevent the deterioration in Japanese-American relations and did his best to keep each side accurately aware of the views of the other.

In a memorandum to his staff in the Tokyo embassy on October 19, 1939, less than two months after the outbreak of the war in Europe, Grew said: "During my stay in the United States, American public opinion was steadily hardening against Japan. The denunciation of the Treaty of 1911 was almost universally approved and there is an almost universal demand for an embargo against Japan. . . . The present attitude of the administration is that we will not allow American interests to be crowded out of China. . . . I believe that more is now to be gained by discreetly conveying this present attitude (of the U. S.) to the Japanese Government and people in order to offset the prevailing feeling in Japan . . . that in the last analysis the United States will back down."[88]

In December 1939 Grew recorded that he and his staff were convinced that Japan had irrevocably committed itself to the "continental adventure" and was determined to see it through and that even a complete American embargo would not stop Japan.[89] In April 1940 Grew noted that many Americans discounted the possibility of Japan's declaring war on the United States and that they did not understand the potential intensity of Japanese nationalistic fanaticism.[90] In August of that year he wrote in his diary that the Japanese who favored expansion were now in the majority and that the successes of Germany had gone to their heads like strong wine. He said that these people were convinced the United States would not dare embroil itself with Japan because of Germany.[91] He had conveyed this view to Washington in his dispatches.

On October 2, 1940, Grew said, "Our reliable and important Japanese channels of information are in general no longer available,"[92] a statement which was not only a true indication of the worsening of relations, but a dangerous omen for intelligence as well. On November 18 the Ambassador recorded that he was now convinced Foreign Minister Matsuoka had persuaded his government to sign the Tripartite Pact on the grounds that war with the United States was inevitable whether or not Japan was aligned with the Axis.[93]

On December 14, 1940, Ambassador Grew wrote a letter to President Roosevelt giving his views on the situation in Asia. Among other things he said: "Unless we are prepared with General Hugh Johnson to withdraw bag and baggage from the entire sphere of 'Great East Asia including the South Seas' (which God forbid) we are bound eventually to come to a head-on clash with Japan."

He went on to say: ". . . The principal point at issue, as I see it, is not whether we must call a halt to the Japanese program, but when. . . . Only if they become certain that we mean to fight if called upon to do so will our preliminary measures stand some chance of proving effective and of removing the necessity for war."[94]

Grew recorded in his diary on January 7, 1941, that an editorial in *Kokumin* of that date said war between Japan and the United States would start within the year.[95] He noted the consternation and fury of the Japanese when the

United States, Great Britain and the Netherlands froze all Japanese assets after its forces moved into Southern Indochina in July 1941.[96] On September 29 he advised the Secretary of State that if the talks between the United States and Japan were unproductive, the cabinet of Prince Konoye would fall.[97] The Konoye government fell on October 16.

On October 25, Grew said that the new cabinet of General Tojo had made a commitment to the Emperor to continue to seek an agreement with the United States.[98]

On November 3, Grew told Washington: "What has happened to date . . . does not support the view that a continuation of trade embargoes and imposition of a blockade (proposed by some) can best avert war in the Far East." He went on to note that the Japanese were more likely to risk national hara-kiri than to yield to foreign pressure and warned: "The Ambassador's purpose is only to ensure against the United States becoming involved in war with Japan because of any possible misconception of Japan's capacity to rush headlong into a suicidal struggle with the United States. While national sanity dictates against such action, Japanese sanity cannot be measured by American standards of logic."[99]

THE AMERICAN ESTIMATE OF THE SITUATION

All through 1941 the United States had been engaged in a determined effort to reinforce and fortify its military outposts. America concentrated on building the "arsenal for democracy" and sending aid to Great Britain and to the Soviet Union in an effort to halt the conquests of Hitler. Failure to reach an agreement with Japan for a modus vivendi in Asia was recognized by Washington to have created an increasingly ominous situation in the Pacific.

On July 2, 1941, the American Director of Naval Intelligence was informed by his staff that sources close to Japanese industrialists expected Japan to make an aggressive move against Russia on July 20. The staff in Washington said that they did not place too much credence in this report and considered the Japanese more likely to move south.[100]

On July 25, 1941, in a memorandum for the Chief of Staff on the subject of "Sanctions Against Japan," the G-2 of the Army said: "Effective economic sanctions against Japan imposed by us, today, would not, in the opinion of this Division, force Japan to take any steps in the way of aggressive action which she does not plan to take anyway, when a favorable opportunity arises, nor would they precipitate a declaration of war on us by Japan."[101] The same unit on September 15, in a Brief Periodic Estimate of the World Situation, said: ". . . Japan, beset with uncertainties, may do nothing, may attack the Maritime Provinces, may seek to expand to the Southwest; it is even possible that she may withdraw from the Axis."[102] The Navy at that time also saw a variety of possibilities for Japanese action. In a memorandum of September 25 to the Chief of War Plans, the Office of Naval Intelligence said: "The undersigned believes that Japan will: 1. Continue the negotiations with the U. S., but not yield on any points which she considers would endanger the 'East Asia co-prosperity sphere.' 2. Watch closely the Russo-German fighting and the naval warfare in the Atlantic. 3. If Russia collapses, attack Siberia. 4. If the bulk of the U. S. fleet is withdrawn to the Atlantic, strike south. She does not expect this development but could quickly exploit it.* 5. If Russia is still resisting strongly by December, wait, at least until late next spring, before taking any decisive action."[103] Here was a strong expression that Japan would regard the U. S. Pacific Fleet as a major obstacle to any further move south.

* Underlining in the original text.

On October 2 the Army G-2, in a memorandum that was addressed to the President and the Secretary of State as well as to the Army, repeated the conviction that strong diplomacy and increasing economic and military pressure by the United States offered the best possibility for preventing the spread of hostilities in the Pacific area.[104]

On October 21, ONI said, "The Naval forces of Japan may now be considered to be fully mobilized for imminent action."[105] In a memorandum on "Recent Developments in the Far East" on November 27, the G-2 of the Army concluded that the Japanese had completed plans for further aggressive moves in Southeast Asia to be put into effect when the negotiations with the United States broke down and that the initial move would be against Thailand.[106] The Navy in its estimate of December 1 also saw the same move in the offing: "An eventual control or occupation of Thailand followed almost immediately by an attack against British possessions, possibly Burma and Singapore."[107] In its Fortnightly Summary of the same day, ONI noted that the Japanese-American negotiations had virtually broken down and that the deployment of Japanese forces southward clearly indicated that extensive preparations for hostilities were under way.[108]

In the final Military Intelligence Estimate issued in December before the attack and discussing possible developments in the period December 1, 1941, to March 31, 1942, the G-2 of the Army said: ". . . Japan already extended militarily has a multiplicity of strategic objectives; but for a variety of reasons, she cannot concentrate the required forces to attack any of them on a large scale and with assurance of success. A possible exception to the latter statement lies in the contingency of a serious depletion of Russian forces in eastern Siberia. But even in this case, a large-scale

Japanese strategic offensive against Siberia during the period in question is somewhat doubtful. . . ."

After noting that there had been a decline in Axis morale and that Japan was weary of an unsuccessful war (in China) and economically distressed, the estimate conceded that Japan possessed the initiative in Asia despite being over-extended and could attack the Philippines or Hong Kong, seek a settlement with the United States or withdraw from the Axis, but that the most probable line of action would be the occupation of Thailand. In a supporting annex on Japan, the G-2 reported: "The whole political machinery is geared to preparation for expansion into the maritime provinces of Siberia, for further expansion in Southeast Asia, and the southwestern Pacific, and to the solution of the China 'Incident.' . . . in order to secure a better position for herself, she might disregard her obligations, and even withdraw from the Axis. Japan has boundless ambitions in the Far East, but in view of the increasing American and British strength in the Far East, and the continued stalemate in China, she finds herself in a more and more unfavorable strategic position to realize these ambitions. Japanese government leaders are aware of the perils of further military adventures; they want to avoid a general war in the Pacific. . . . Thus her economic situation contributes largely to the indecision of her leaders. This is a problem which she must solve within the next few months."[109]

Within forty-eight hours of the issuance of this report in Washington, Japan set about solving this problem by attacking Pearl Harbor, the Philippines, Malaya and the Netherlands Indies.

At a higher level in the United States government the danger of an attack was more keenly appreciated. Secretary of War Henry L. Stimson, Secretary of Navy Frank Knox and Secretary of State Cordell Hull met frequently to exchange views on the deteriorating relations with Japan. The President held regular meetings with these three plus the Chief of Staff of the Army and the Chief of Naval Operations. These senior officials had the benefit of the military estimates and summaries, the details of the discussions in Washington with the Japanese and the information provided in the intercepted cables.

Secretary Stimson kept a record of what was said at these top-level policy meetings. On November 25 he recorded: "At the meeting were Hull, Knox, Marshall,* Stark and myself. There the President brought up the relations with the Japanese. He brought up the event that we were likely to be attacked perhaps as soon as—perhaps next Monday, for the Japs are notorious for making an attack without warning. . . ."[110]

Two days later the Secretary recorded: "November 27, 1941: News is coming in of a concentration and movement south by the Japanese of a large expeditionary force moving south from Shanghai and evidently headed towards Indo-China, with the possibility of going to the Philippines or to Burma or to the Burma Road or to the Dutch East Indies, but probably a concentration to move over into Thailand and to hold a position from which they can attack Singapore when the moment arrives.

"The first thing in the morning I called up Hull to find out what his final decision had been with the Japanese— whether he had handed them the new proposal which we had passed on two or three days ago or whether, as he had suggested yesterday, he had broken the whole matter off. He told me now he had broken the whole matter off. As he put it, 'I have washed my hands of it, and it is now in the hands of you and Knox, the Army and Navy.' "[111]

* General George C. Marshall, U. S. Army Chief of Staff.

It is not surprising that Secretary Hull had broken off the discussions. He had met with the Japanese for months and there had been no progress in reaching an agreement between the two governments. Hundreds of messages had passed back and forth between Washington and Tokyo, both on the Japanese and the American diplomatic circuits. Formal notes had been exchanged between the two governments. There had been endless debate of the conditions demanded by the two nations. Japan would not agree to give up its conquest of China or expansion in Southeast Asia, and the United States would not lift the embargo on the shipment of raw materials without these concessions.

On November 28, Stimson recorded that G-2 had sent him a statement of Japanese movements in the Far East and that it amounted to such a formidable statement of dangerous possibilities that he decided to take it to the President even though Mr. Roosevelt had not yet awakened. The statement was discussed later in the day at a meeting of the so-called war council. "It was the opinion of everyone that if this expedition was allowed to get around the southern point of Indo-China and to go off and land in the Gulf of Siam, either at Bangkok or further west, it would be a terrific blow at all of the three powers: Britain at Singapore, the Netherlands, and ourself in the Philippines."[112]

Secretary Stimson's notes reflect the thinking at the top level of the government. Further Japanese expansion was expected. The conquest of the rest of Southeast Asia seemed likely. The United States would become involved if the Japanese attacked the Philippines, and this was considered to be a good possibility. What the United States would have done if the Japanese had not attacked American interests— left Pearl Harbor alone and bypassed the Philippines, and confined their expansion to occupation of Thailand and conquest of Malaya and the Netherlands Indies—poses an interesting question. The President's War Council did not have to face that dilemma.

When the news of the attack on Pearl Harbor was received in Washington on the afternoon of December 7, 1941, some of these officials may have been surprised that Hawaii was the target—Knox, when he heard the news, said that the report must have meant the Philippines—but the outbreak of the war was expected.

WARNINGS SENT TO THE FORCES

The forces in the field had been kept apprised of Washington's estimates of the situation and of the grave concern over the course of developments.

On January 13, 1941, Admiral Harold R. Stark, the Chief of Naval Operations, wrote Admiral H. E. Kimmel in Hawaii to congratulate him on being named Commander in Chief of the Pacific Fleet. In the course of a long letter Stark said: "In my humble opinion, we may wake up any day with mines deposited on our front door step or with some of our ships bombed, or whatnot, and find ourselves in another undeclared war. . . . I have told the Gang here for months past that in my opinion we were heading straight for this war, that we would not assume anything else and personally I do not see how we can avoid, either having it thrust upon us or of our deliberately going in, many months longer. And of course it may be a matter of weeks or of days."[113]

On January 24, 1941, the Secretary of the Navy wrote a letter to the Secretary of War dealing with the defenses of Pearl Harbor:

Op-12B-9-McC (SC)A7-2(2)/FFI
Serial 09112 *Secret*
My Dear Mr. Secretary: The security of the U. S. Pacific Fleet while in Pearl Harbor, and of the Pearl Harbor Naval

Base itself, has been under renewed study by the Navy Department and forces afloat for the past several weeks. This re-
examination has been, in part, prompted by the increased gravity of the situation with respect to Japan, and by reports from
abroad of successful bombing and torpedo plane attacks on
ships while in bases. If war eventuates with Japan, it is believed
easily possible that hostilities would be initiated by a surprise
attack upon the Fleet or the Naval Base at Pearl Harbor.

In my opinion, the inherent possibilities of a major disaster
to the fleet or naval base warrant taking every step, as rapidly as
can be done, that will increase the joint readiness of the Army
and Navy to withstand a raid of the character mentioned
above.

The dangers envisaged in their order of importance and
probability are considered to be:

(1) Air bombing attack.

(2) Air torpedo plane attack.

(3) Sabotage.

(4) Submarine attack.

(5) Mining.

(6) Bombardment by gun fire.

Defense against all but the first two of these dangers appears to have been provided for satisfactorily. The following
paragraphs are devoted principally to a discussion of the problems encompassed in (1) and (2) above, the solution of which I
consider to be of primary importance.

Both types of air attack are possible. They may be carried
out successively, simultaneously, or in combination with any
of the other operations enumerated. The maximum probable
enemy effort may be put at twelve aircraft squadrons, and the
minimum at two. Attacks would be launched from a striking
force of carriers and their supporting vessels. . . .

The balance of the letter was devoted to a review of the
Army aircraft, antiaircraft and other defenses available at
Pearl Harbor. It urged that the Army assign "the highest
priority to the increase of pursuit aircraft and anti-aircraft
artillery, and the establishment of an air warning net in
Hawaii," and suggested that "the Army and Navy forces in
Oahu agree on appropriate degrees of joint readiness for

immediate action in defense against surprise aircraft raids against Pearl Harbor."[114]

On February 1 the Chief of Naval Operations relayed to the Commander in Chief of the Pacific Fleet a message from Ambassador Grew in Tokyo: "The Peruvian Minister has informed a member of my staff that he has heard from many sources, including a Japanese source, that in the event of troubles breaking out between the United States and Japan, the Japanese intend to make a surprise attack against Pearl Harbor with all of their strength and employing all of their equipment. . . . The Division of Naval Intelligence places no credence in these rumors."[115] ONI was absolutely correct in its assessment at this time. Admiral Yamamoto was only beginning to think about such an attack and such intelligence could only have come from him or one or two others.

That same day Admiral Kimmel in Hawaii wrote a lengthy letter to the Chief of Naval Operations on the preparations by the Pacific Fleet, in which he said: "I feel a surprise attack (submarine, air, or combined) on Pearl Harbor is a possibility."[116]

Another warning was contained in Pacific Fleet Confidential Letter No. 2 CL-41 from the Commander in Chief to all units—Subject: Security of Fleet At Base and in Operating Areas. Issued in February (and re-issued October 14, 1941), it said: ". . . The security of the Fleet, operating and based in the Hawaiian Area, is predicated, at present, on two assumptions. . . ." The second of these assumptions was "that a declaration of war may be preceded by (1) a surprise attack on ships in Pearl Harbor. . . ."[117]

On February 25, Stark wrote Kimmel: "The difficulty is that the entire country is in a dozen minds about the war— to stay out altogether, to go in against Germany in the Atlantic, to concentrate against Japan in the Pacific and the

Far East—I simply can not predict the outcome. Gallup polls, editorial talk on the Hill (and I might add, all of which is irresponsible) constitute a rising tide for action in the Far East if the Japanese go into Singapore or the Netherlands East Indies. . . ."[118]

On April 1, 1941, OPNAV sent a Top Secret dispatch to all Naval Districts warning them to take special precautions on Saturdays, Sundays and holidays because past experience had indicated that the Axis powers often started something on those days.[119]

On April 4, Stark told Kimmel: "I realize that you all, just as much as I, are vitally interested in the matter of 'timing.' Something may be forced on us at any moment which would precipitate action, though I don't look for it as I can see no advantage to Mr. Hitler in forcing us into the war unless, of course, Matsuoka agrees to fight at the same time. On the surface, at least, the Japanese situation looks a trifle easier, but just what the Oriental really plans, none of us can be sure. I have had several long talks with Admiral Nomura and unless I am completely fooled, he earnestly desires to avert a Japanese crisis with us."[120]

On May 14, Admiral Stark sent a memorandum to the Commandants of the Naval Districts stressing the seriousness of the situation and saying, "Though the danger of mines, raiding and diversions, and even of sporadic or stunt air attack, may be remote in the Eastern Pacific, we cannot discount it, and hence should be bending every ounce of effort of which we are capable not to be caught napping in that area."[121] Copies went to the Fleet Commanders.

On June 20, following a visit to Washington, Admiral Kimmel in Hawaii received a note saying that Admiral Stark had meant to suggest to him the use of a smoke screen around Pearl Harbor in the event of an air attack.[122]

A postscript on a letter of July 3 from Stark to Kimmel

said: "It looks to us at the moment as you will judge by a dispatch you will receive ere this as though the Germans had persuaded the Japs to attack Russia within the next month. It is anybody's guess and only time will tell."[123]

In a long letter dated July 31, Stark told Admiral Charles M. Cooke in Hawaii that opinion in Washington was that Japan would not go into the Netherlands East Indies but that an attack on the Russian Maritime Provinces was possible. He suggested Cooke show the letter to Kimmel.[124] A dispatch to Kimmel of August 19 replying in great detail to one from the Pacific Fleet Commander again discussed the possibility of a Japanese attack on Russia.[125]

In a postscript on September 23, Stark advised Kimmel that conversations with the Japanese in Washington had practically reached an impasse.[126]

On October 16 the Chief of Operations sent a dispatch to the Fleet Commanders, which said in part: "The resignation of the Japanese Cabinet has created a grave situation. . . . Since the U.S. and Britain are held responsible for her present desperate situation there is also a possibility that Japan may attack these two powers. In view of these possibilities you will take due precautions. . . ."[127] On November 24 the fleets were advised: "Chances of favorable outcome of negotiations with Japan very doubtful. . . . A surprise aggressive movement in any direction including attack on Philippines or Guam is a possibility. . . ."[128]

The next day Stark wrote Kimmel: "Personally I do not believe the Japs are going to sail into us and the message I sent you merely stated the 'possibility'; in fact I tempered the message handed me considerably. Perhaps I am wrong, but I hope not. In any case after long pow-wows in the White House it was felt we should be on guard, at least until something indicates the trend."[129]

THE EMPTY SEAS

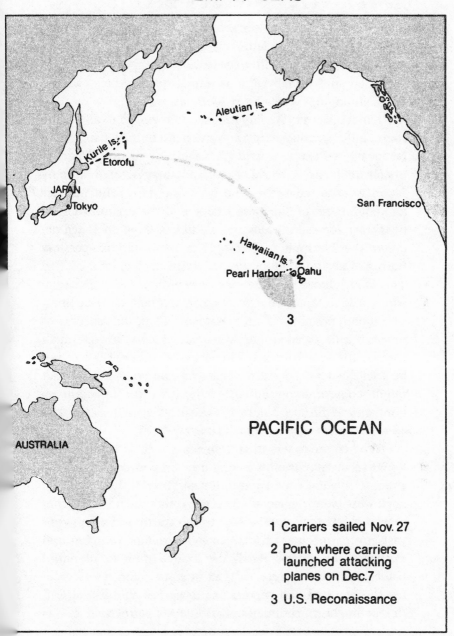

Aleutian Is.

Kurile Is. 1
Etorofu

JAPAN
Tokyo

San Francisco

Hawaiian Is. 2
Pearl Harbor Oahu

3

AUSTRALIA

PACIFIC OCEAN

1 Carriers sailed Nov. 27

2 Point where carriers
launched attacking
planes on Dec. 7

3 U.S. Reconaissance

In late November, Stark warned Kimmel of the gravity of the situation. In a letter on the twenty-fifth Stark said that neither President Roosevelt nor Secretary of State Hull would be surprised by a Japanese surprise attack, adding that he thought it would be in Southeast Asia.[130]

November 27, Washington sent a message to all Pacific commands, starting with the sentence "This dispatch is to be considered a war warning." It went on to say, "Negotiations with Japan . . . have ceased and an aggressive move by Japan is expected within the next few days. The number and equipment of Japanese troops and the organization of naval task forces indicates an amphibious expedition against either the Philippine Thai or Kra peninsula or possibly Borneo. Execute appropriate defensive deployment. . . ."[131] This was followed up the next day with another dispatch, which said: "Japanese future action unpredictable but hostile action possible at any moment. If hostilities cannot repeat not be avoided the United States desires that Japan commit the first overt act. This policy should not repeat not be construed as restricting you to a course of action that might jeopardize your defense. Prior to hostile Japanese action you are directed to undertake such reconnaissance and other measures as you deem necessary. . . ."[132]

The commanders in Hawaii did not consider any additional security measures necessary. Air and sea reconnaissance was being conducted to the southwest; the north and northwest were neglected. The air commanders were concerned about the "empty seas" to the north and northwest, vast stretches seldom transitted by merchant shipping and uncovered by patrols. With the limited number of patrol planes available a sector of 128 degrees could be covered, not the required 360 degrees. As it was, Rear Admiral Patrick Bellinger, in command of the Navy's patrol planes, was not shown the "war warning" message probably on the assumption that his forces were already sufficiently alerted. The Commander in Chief of the Pacific Fleet had direct sources of warning, as well as the messages from Washington. The Federal Bureau of Investigation put telephone taps on suspected Japanese agents in Hawaii. On December 6 the FBI delivered to Army and Navy Intelligence the transcript of a telephone conversation between a Japanese named Mori in Honolulu and Tokyo. It was a far-ranging conversation, discussing how many airplanes were flying around, the number of sailors, if the Japanese in Hawaii were alarmed, the building boom, searchlights, comments in the Honolulu newspapers, the impression Mr. Kurusu made when he passed through, the climate, flowers in bloom, liquor and so on. Unless one assumed there was a hidden code in the message, the principal question that would be raised was why somebody would pay for such an expensive telephone call to discuss such trivia.[133]

There was also the Navy's Radio Intelligence units, which provided an analysis of the call signs of the Japanese navy. The call signs were used for locating the major units of the Japanese fleet and were considered to be a principal source for warning of potential hostilities. When the Japanese fleet changed its call signs on December 1, fleet intelligence in Hawaii was concerned. Captain Edwin Layton, chief of intelligence for the Pacific fleet, had asked Washington to include his staff in the distribution of intercepts of Japanese diplomatic traffic but had been refused on the grounds that the facilities at Pearl Harbor were not as secure as those in Washington.

On December 2, Captain Layton advised Admiral Kimmel that he did not have sufficient information on the location of Japanese Carrier Divisions 1 and 2, to which the

Admiral replied, "Do you mean to say that they could be rounding Diamond Head and you wouldn't know it?" Layton replied, "I hope they would be sighted before now."[134] By the next day the Radio Intelligence Unit had identified two hundred of the new Japanese call signs but drew an almost complete blank on carriers and submarines. The same ominous lack of information continued for the next four days.

At 3:42 A.M., Sunday morning December 7, the minesweeper U.S.S. *Condor* reported a periscope in a restricted area outside of Pearl Harbor to the destroyer U.S.S. *Ward,* which searched for the unidentified submarine for an hour and a half without results. At 6:30 the U.S.S. *Antares,* with a barge in tow, advised the *Ward* she had sighted a suspicious object. Ten minutes later the *Ward* saw a submarine following the *Antares* and opened fire. At 6:51 the *Ward* advised the Fourteenth Naval District of the action. This news reached headquarters at 7:40.

At 7:55 the first wave of Japanese planes from the six carriers hit the fleet at anchor. The attack lasted one half hour. At 8:40 horizontal bombers attacked for thirty-five minutes, and at 9:15 there was another attack by dive bombers. By 9:45—less than two hours after the first shot was fired—the battle was over.

Despite the lack of advance warning, the Americans fought back. The Navy had been on an "augmented No. 3" stage of readiness. On each battleship two five-inch guns and two 50-caliber machine guns were manned at all times. Within ten minutes most of the antiaircraft guns were firing. But antiaircraft fire from ships at anchor was not enough. Japanese planning and training had been effective, and surprise had been achieved.

The United States Pacific Fleet had been seriously

damaged. Of the battleships, the *Arizona* blew up and the *Utah* capsized, neither to fight again. The *Oklahoma* had capsized, but later was raised. The *West Virginia* and the *California* had been sunk or beached. The *Tennessee*, the *Maryland* and the *Pennsylvania* were damaged, as were the cruisers *Helena, Honolulu* and *Raleigh*. A total of 188 American planes had been destroyed and another 128 damaged. American dead numbered 2,400.

The Japanese attacking force had consisted of six aircraft carriers, two battleships, nine destroyers and three submarines. Of the 324 planes in the attacking force, 29 were lost. The Japanese also lost five midget submarines and one large submarine. About one hundred Japanese were killed.

Immediately after the third wave of planes had returned to the carriers, Admiral Chuichi Noguma turned his fleet and headed for home waters. He was undoubtedly concerned about the location of the three American aircraft carriers, at least two of which the Japanese hoped to catch in Pearl Harbor. With the carriers at sea, Noguma did not want to risk a counterstrike.

No Japanese planes had concentrated on the vast petroleum storage areas at Pearl Harbor nor the dry docks or ship repair facilities. This was a major mistake. The United States Pacific Fleet had been dealt a staggering blow, but with unexpected speed it returned to battle.

WHY IT HAPPENED

In the brilliance of hindsight it would be improper to say that the surprise of the attack at Pearl Harbor was the result of negligence of any one individual or any single unit of the U.S. government. Intelligence was not the sole factor that failed—command and leadership failed too. The attack can be viewed correctly only as a national error for both countries, the fault of the people, the organizations of the government and the leaders.

The attack was a disaster for both sides. For the United States it was a humiliating defeat, the worst naval losses in battle in its history. For Japan it was a miscalculation that led to national surrender. In both instances it was clear that there was inadequate information available about the potential adversary and insufficient attention paid to the information that was available.

As the details of the course of events have revealed, the United States had a great deal of information indicating what Japan might do. The information came from a variety of sources: specific Japanese action in moving troops and ships and supplies; extensive exchanges of diplomatic messages between Tokyo and Washington indicating Japanese goals; discussions between Japanese and American officials in both capitals; the astute observations of Ambassador Grew in Tokyo; the revelations in the Japanese official cables decoded by the cryptographers; the reports of Japanese agents in Hawaii tapped by counterintelligence efforts; the location of Japanese naval ships given by their radio call signs.

In no one place in Washington were all of the reports on Japan assembled, analyzed and assessed as a totality, but were scattered through several departments and bureaus. Each department and agency processed the information it collected, provided its own interpretation and occasionally shared it with others. If the department considered the information important, it tried to push it to the highest possible level of government that was possible—the Chief of Staff, the Cabinet Member, or the President himself. Only rarely was material from one source weighed against material from another. Sources were not weighed and evaluated and judged by their comparative accuracy over a period of time. There was no single objective view produced by the best-qualified analysts. Given some of the other weaknesses of the system and prejudices of the time, there is no guarantee that such a centralized system would have served to place the military commands on a more guarded alert, but it might have.

The method of handling intelligence in the United States government in 1941 made each of the top policy makers his own intelligence officer. Had there been a sophisticated centralized system of handling intelligence, all information on Japanese intentions would have been analyzed in depth by experts and sent to the policy level in the form of an estimate of probable developments. "Raw intelligence," such as the texts of the intercepted cables, would have reached the President and the Cabinet-level officials only on rare occasions and then probably as documentary evidence to support an estimate.

President Roosevelt and Harry Hopkins, when shown the intercepted fourteen-part message to be delivered by the Japanese ambassadors on December 7, said; "This means war." Army Chief of Staff General George C. Marshall said the same thing when he saw Part 14 of the message. Even more serious than the fact that these top officials received and evaluated their own raw intelligence information was the method of distributing and controlling "Magic" messages—intercepts or communications intelligence.

The intercepted material was so closely held that only a few of the top intelligence officials, the most senior of the military officers and the top policy officials were allowed to see the text of the material. This very tight control was based on the presumption that the information was very valuable—which it was; that broader distribution would create a security hazard because of the increased possibility of leaks or careless talk—which is not necessarily true; and that if the Japanese ever discovered that their diplomatic code had been broken they would change the code and even send the most important messages by courier—which was certainly true. As a result, the material was too closely held, preventing centralized intelligence. Some analysts—a mere handful—processed the intercepts; other analysts processed the normal U.S. diplomatic reports from Tokyo; still others processed the naval material; and a fourth group processed the Army's material. The analysts handling "Magic" were too hard-pressed with the volume of material they had, and the rest were ignorant of the existence of the highly classified information.

A by-product of this tight control over the communications intelligence material was even more serious. This was a tendency to create too great reliance on the intercepts as the best source of information—infallible and all-revealing. Perhaps even subconsciously the intelligence chiefs and policy makers were confident that they would learn *all* of the Japanese intentions through this source.

It would be erroneous to fault the U.S. leaders in this regard. In a country as unsophisticated on intelligence matters as was the United States of 1941, who would believe that a source as lucrative as "Magic" would not keep them informed of what they needed to know about Japan's next move? It had revealed the fact that Tokyo was planning to move south, that there was no intention of getting out of China, that an attack on Russia would wait until the Soviet Union was mortally wounded and that there was desperate anxiety to make a deal with the United States.

Nevertheless, one of the dangers in intelligence work is the tendency to place too great reliance on one source; this was an even greater danger in 1941, when information from the one source was handled separately and apart from all other intelligence sources. Had the communications intelligence been pooled with all other material, it is possible that a different estimate might have been reached. The simple truth is that the Japanese diplomatic and military traffic never once hinted at or mentioned the possibility of an attack on Pearl Harbor.

It has been claimed that a careful study of the intercepted diplomatic traffic alone should have placed the United States on an all-out war alert and that the fleet at Pearl Harbor should not have been caught by surprise. And yet—more startling—the U.S. forces in the Philippines were also caught by surprise. Nine hours after the attack on Pearl Harbor, twenty-seven Japanese bombers attacked Clark Field near Manila and destroyed seventeen of the eighteen B-17 bombers on the field and fifty-six American fighters, with the loss of only seven Japanese planes.

Pearl Harbor clearly did not look for an attack. As evidence: Joseph L. Lockhard and George E. Elliot, Jr., of the 515 Signal Aircraft Warning Service were practicing with a radar at Opana on a bluff on the north side of Oahu at 7:02 on the morning of December 7 and got the blips of the Japanese attacking force on the screen; when they reported to their headquarters, they were told to forget it because it was either a mistake or some planes arriving from the mainland! Even when the "war warning" message of November 27 had been received in Hawaii, no increase in air or sea patrolling was ordered. Nor was any extra precaution taken when the "call signs" of the Japanese carriers were no longer heard by the radio monitoring service.

U.S. forces were on an alert, but it was the alert of military forces who had not been in combat and who greatly underestimated the potential enemy in every respect.

The estimates and memoranda of the intelligence staffs

cited above show the depth of the miscalculation. It was inconceivable to them that economic pressure would drive Japan to war. They ignored Japan's truly desperate position as a result of the stoppage of shipments of oil and raw materials from the United States and from the British and Dutch possessions in Southeast Asia. As one Japanese admiral stated shortly before the attack on Pearl Harbor, if the U.S. embargo continued Japan might have to surrender without firing a shot.

It was also believed that Japan was so exhausted both militarily and economically by the war in China and consequently that she could not possibly embark on another major campaign.

The extended discussions in Washington also tended to confuse some of the American officials as to what Japan might do. The talks gave the impression that Japan was most anxious to reach an agreement with the United States. Indeed Japan was, but on its own terms. The discussions also seemed to indicate indecision in Tokyo. The Japanese preparations were regarded as a form of political pressure and a technique to exact more concessions from the United States.

There was a conviction that Japan wanted to avoid war with the United States. This was correct. Japan did wish to avoid war with the United States, provided it could be guaranteed at least 4,500,000 tons of petroleum a year, access to the raw materials of Southeast Asia and a free hand to deal with China. If the United States had agreed to these terms, the attack on Pearl Harbor would have been canceled.

Japanese diplomatic reports about war with the Anglo-Saxon nations was regarded in Washington as a belief by Japan that the United States would go to war only if the

British and Dutch possessions in Southeast Asia and the
Philippines were attacked. President Roosevelt shared the
conviction of Winston Churchill that the Japanese would
not enter the war until they were convinced the British Empire was defeated, as they did not wish to fight both America and Britain simultaneously.[135] This belief was strengthened by Japanese messages to Berlin offering to mediate the
Russo-German war, in order to permit Hitler to turn the full
fury of his war machine against the British Isles.

A Japan heavily engaged in China, in severe economic
difficulties, ambitious to move north or south in Asia, anxious to reach an agreement with the United States and hesi-
tant to fight Britain and America simultaneously was not
likely to attack Pearl Harbor and challenge the entire
United States Pacific Fleet. If it did take offensive action, it
was much more likely to occupy Thailand and then move on
Malaya and the Netherlands Indies, perhaps seizing the
Philippines to protect the flank of its southward drive. This
was the reasoning in Washington.

The rationale that Japan would avoid a head-on clash
with the United States was supported by a lack of appreciation of the power or ability of the Japanese military forces.
The American Navy had had rather friendly relations with
the Japanese Navy. It was not inclined to suspect them of
evil intentions—at least as far as the United States was concerned. If there was concern at Pearl Harbor it centered on
sabotage, not on carrier-borne attack with bombers and torpedo planes. Moreover, the Pacific Fleet did not believe a
torpedo plane attack was possible in Pearl Harbor because
of the shallow water. They obviously had not made the
same intensive study of the attack by British torpedo planes
on the Italian fleet at Taranto as had Admiral Yamamoto's
staff.

The Japanese also had serious gaps in their understanding of the United States. They were convinced that the United States would not fight a war against Japan because of the determination to crush Hitler, despite Admiral Nomura's reports. Nor did Japan believe that America could fight simultaneously in both Europe and Asia. This reasoning suited the conviction of some Japanese who believed they could fight a limited war with the United States—that destruction of the American Pacific Fleet at Pearl Harbor would lead Washington to seek mediation of the dispute in order to concentrate its full force on assisting in the defeat of Hitler. President Theodore Roosevelt had mediated in the war between Japan and Russia in 1905. President Franklin Roosevelt had indicated his willingness to arrange talks between Japan and China in 1941. Americans traditionally favored mediation—or so the Japanese reasoned.

The German victories in Europe led the Japanese to underestimate both the fighting ability and the determination of the Americans. The democracies seemed to them soft and weak. The United States Pacific Fleet with its three carriers was no match for Japan's ten carriers. Even though the American carriers were not at Pearl Harbor on December 7 and thus escaped damage or destruction, Admiral Noguma, who commanded the attacking task force, apparently felt that the damage to the battleships had rendered the fleet impotent. His second wave neglected the oil tank farms, the submarine flotillas and the dockyards at Pearl Harbor—all vital factors in the fast resurgence of American naval power in the Pacific.

It would be unwise to predict that a Pearl Harbor could not happen again. It would be equally foolish to say that such a surprise attack could never be duplicated, or that no nation would ever again be so foolish and/or deceit-

PEARL HARBOR | 157

ful to attempt it, or even that no other nation will be so ill-prepared or lax as to invite surprise.

Those are vain presumptions. As long as nations have territorial, or political, or economic, objectives which they cannot achieve through peaceful means, they will resort to war. As long as nations resort to war to achieve national objectives, there will be surprise attacks if the target is sufficiently tempting and there is a good possibility of success.

The only guarantee against surprise attack is advance information, and the potential enemy must know that the intelligence is so good that he cannot achieve surprise. Of course if a nation allows its defenses to deteriorate, then even good intelligence cannot guarantee it against attack from a predatory nation.

If defenses deteriorate, and intelligence on the increasing strength of a potential enemy is good, one could assume that the warning would be clear and the military power would be restored to meet the danger. This is not necessarily so. In most instances the intelligence is not clear concerning the threat. In some cases the intelligence will be ignored.

It might be assumed that after the disaster at Pearl Harbor the United States would never again let its defenses down. Yet less than nine years later America was involved in another war, this time in Korea. On this occasion U.S. intelligence had many reports on the possibility that North Korea might attack South Korea, but once again intelligence did not say when the attack was going to take place nor under what conditions. Nor had the United States government made it clear to the world that it would defend South Korea, if indeed it knew this itself.

Intelligence can help avert surprise. Powerful and alert defenses may deter attack. Together they may prevent war. At Pearl Harbor neither was available in the proper amount.

4.

Dieppe: Prelude
to D-Day

AUGUST 19, 1942

WITH THE AMERICAN battleships out of action
in Pearl Harbor, Japanese forces swept southward in east
Asia in a seemingly irresistible avalanche. Two days after
Pearl Harbor the British battleships *Prince of Wales* and
Repulse were sunk by Japanese aircraft off the coast of
Malaya.

By December 25 the British forces at Hong Kong were
forced to surrender. On January 2 the capital of the Philippines, Manila, was captured. On January 11 the Japanese
landed in the Netherlands East Indies. For three days, January 24 to January 27, a running battle between Japanese
and Allied naval forces took place in the Macassar Straits.
Four Japanese transports, one cargo ship and a patrol boat

were sunk by a Dutch submarine and four American destroyers, but the drive southward was only momentarily slowed. On February 15, Singapore fell and the great British naval base was lost to Japanese forces sweeping down the Malay Peninsula. The principal Allied naval forces defending the Netherlands Indies were defeated by the Japanese in the battle of the Java Sea at the end of February, and by early March the Dutch islands were occupied. In the meantime a Japanese army was moving west to occupy Bruma, close to the vital supply road to China, posing a threat to India.

The Japanese had quickly overwhelmed the United States defenses on Guam, which fell on December 13, and Wake Island, which was captured on the twentieth. In the Philippines the American and Filipino forces which had retreated to the Bataan Peninsula were forced to surrender on April 9, and the fortified island of Corregidor at the entrance to Manila Bay yielded on May 6.

Toward the end of April a powerful Japanese invasion force sailed for New Guinea with the objective of capturing Port Moresby. It was intercepted in the Coral Sea by Allied forces. In the ensuing battle the Japanese lost the light carrier *Shoho*, and the heavy carrier *Shokaku* was severely damaged. The Americans lost the aircraft carrier *Lexington*, but the Japanese force withdrew and the threat to Australia was momentarily averted.

By the middle of May 1942 the Radio Intelligence Unit at Pearl Harbor had clear evidence that the Japanese were planning an attack in great strength on the Aleutians and Midway. A Japanese force of four fleet carriers and seven battleships with numerous escort vessels headed for Midway. Three American carriers constituted the principal defensive forces supported by aircraft based on Midway. In the furious air battle that ensued the four Japanese fleet carriers were sunk as against the loss of the U.S. carrier *Yorktown*. On June 5, Admiral Yamamoto's fleet retired and the tide of Japanese victory in the Pacific turned.

British forces in North Africa had counterattacked against the Italian forces which had invaded Egypt from Libya, driving them back, but the German Afrika Korps under General Erwin Rommel, sent to bolster the Italians, had in turn driven the British forces back to the Egyptian border. A second British offensive in December 1941 was countered by Rommel's return attack, which drove them to within seventy miles of the key British naval base in Alexandria. There the front became static in the summer of 1942. All of Italian East Africa had been occupied by the British by the end of 1941.

In Russia, the Germans, having failed to capture Moscow, were forced back by the Red Army's winter counteroffensive, which liberated such major cities as Mozhaisk, Kalinin and Rzhev. On July 2, 1942, the Germans opened a new offensive in the south, capturing Sevastopol in the Crimea and moved toward the oil fields of the Caucasus, seizing Voronezh, Millerovo and Rostov. The Soviet Union was hard-pressed. Stalin urged Britain and the United States to open a second front in western Europe.

On August 19, 1942, an Allied force of 252 ships under the protection of strong air cover landed more than 6,000 men on the French channel coast in the area of Dieppe, strongly engaged the German defenders and, after eight and a half hours, withdrew.

The British Broadcasting Company told the French people at the time of the landing that it was a "raid," not the Allied invasion hoped for, and warned them not to engage in any activities which could be used as a pretext for reprisals by the Germans.

Churchill called it a "reconnaissance in force" and described it as "an indispensable preliminary to full-scale operations."

German propaganda described it as a desperate attempt to open a second front and the last-minute result of political necessity and pressure.

The Russians denied it was an invasion, saying: "It was simply a more precise testing of calculations connected with great and serious military operations to be undertaken in the near future."

The Canadians looked on it as a disaster. Of the 4,384 Allied casualties, 3,367 were theirs.

From a purely military viewpoint at that moment, little that was done on August 19 could be called of great value. The contribution of the attack on Dieppe toward winning the war would have to be measured at a later date.

WHAT WAS THE ATTACK ON DIEPPE?

The attack on Dieppe was not a "raid" in the sense of the word as it was known in 1942. Raids were popularly identified at this time with commando attacks on Spitzbergen, St. Nazaire, and so on, when the objective was the destruction of an important installation of military value. Field Marshal von Rundstedt, German Commander in Chief in the west, commented: "The operation at Dieppe cannot be considered a local raid. For this the expenditure in men and materials is too great. One does not sacrifice twenty to thirty of the most modern tanks for a raid."[1]

Was it a "reconnaissance in force"? This term comes closer to describing the events of August 19. Taken in the broadest sense, the attack on Dieppe was certainly an effort to discover what would be required to dislodge the Germans from France.

But the losses at Dieppe were so appalling that historians are bound to be disturbed by the relatively simple appellation: reconnaissance in force.

Was it a political necessity? The British were under great pressure in the spring and summer of 1942, primarily by the Russians but also by the Americans, for the opening of a second front in Europe. General George C. Marshall had urged the seizure of Brest and Cherbourg during the autumn of 1942. Molotov's visits to London and Washington had resulted, in addition to the Anglo-Soviet Alliance of May 26, in considerable discussion and comment on a second front. The degree of Russian pressure was proportionate to their desperate military situation at that time. So the element of political necessity cannot be totally discarded in searching for an explanation for Dieppe.

One area that deserves careful examination before leaving the question of what was the attack on Dieppe is that of intelligence. This area provides some clues to the heavy losses in men and material. Was the information on which the operation was based inadequate? Or was it adequate, but the force assembled to do the job insufficient? Was the operation betrayed? Or was there insecurity? If intelligence was adequate, why was it necessary to have a reconnaissance in force, which by definition is to gather information on the enemy?

Examination of the intelligence available to the British in planning for the attack on Dieppe may help to answer these questions and place this greatly misunderstood operation in proper focus.

PLANNING

The plans for the Dieppe attack were developed during one of the darkest periods of the war for the Allies. The military situation was grave in all theaters of war. The British garrison at Tobruk in North Africa surrendered on June 21. The Russians, though they still held Leningrad and Moscow, were hard-pressed along the entire front, with the Germans at the Volga in Stalingrad and driving toward the Caucasus. Molotov had visited London and Washington in April and May of 1942, desperately seeking help. He told President Roosevelt that the Russians might not withstand the German summer offensive unless Hitler were forced to withdraw forty divisions from the east. Roosevelt, after consulting General Marshall, authorized Molotov to tell Stalin that there would be a second front in 1942.

In England, meanwhile, the draft outline of a plan for an attack on Dieppe was first presented to the military chiefs by the Combined Operations Staff on April 25. It called for assault by commandos on the heavy batteries at Berneval and Varangeville flanking Dieppe to the east and west. The main assault would be on Dieppe itself, preceded by a heavy air bombardment. Glider-borne troops would land behind Dieppe at Arques, then suspected to be the main German headquarters for that coastal area, and would assist the sea-borne troops and tanks in capturing the airport at St. Aubin.

Dieppe had been selected by the planners because it met several conditions considered essential for such an operation. Its defenses were typical of those erected by the Germans around average-sized ports along the French coast. It could be reached by sea in a few hours. It was within the range of airfields in England so effective fighter cover could be provided and the Luftwaffe would be forced to battle. It would provide experience in direct assault on a port as well as landing on open beaches with modern technical equipment. There were ample targets of military value to be destroyed.

The objectives were basic. German reactions to a potential invasion would be clearly revealed. It was important to learn when the enemy would commit its reserves. The real strength of Hitler's vaunted Festung Europa (Fortress Europe) would be tested. And perhaps as important as any of these objectives, the weapons used would be subjected to the test of practicality, and ideas would emerge for new techniques and equipment.

On April 30, 1942, Lieutenant General Bernard Montgomery, then commanding the ground forces in the south of England, asked Lieutenant General A. G. L. McNaughton, who commanded the Canadian forces, whether he would like to participate. McNaughton accepted and picked the Second Canadian Infantry Division to provide the ground forces. These Canadians had been training in England since 1939, but as yet had seen no combat action.

On May 11, Lord Louis Mountbatten, adviser on Combined Operations, presented the plan to the Committee of the British Chiefs, indicating that in addition to the military objective of the attack it would be of great training value for the cross-channel invasion or any other major operation. The plan stated that intelligence reports revealed Dieppe was not heavily defended and that the beaches were suitable for landing infantry. It was indicated that some of the assault areas could accommodate armored vehicles. Forty German landing craft were in the port. The removal of these was a major objective. The other objectives of the raid were listed as destruction of enemy defenses around the port, including the airfield at St. Aubin, the radio station, the power plant and dock and rail facilities. Secret documents were to be removed from the division headquarters, reported to be at Arques-la-Bataille, and prisoners were to be taken. The Chiefs of Staff Committee approved the plan.

On May 15, General McNaughton cabled Canada giving a general description of the plan for an assault on a nameless French port. McNaughton stated that he was satisfied the objective was worthwhile and that the land, sea and air forces detailed were sufficient for the task.

The plan was substantially modified by June 5, when it was decided to attempt tactical surprise and to eliminate the heavy aerial bombardment. The Admiralty had already refused to allow heavy ships to enter the dangerous waters off the French coast, fearful that they would be sunk by land-based aircraft. The heaviest fire support from the sea would come from the guns of the destroyers.

On June 30, Churchill had a small conference at 10 Downing Street to review the plans for the operation. The Prime Minister expressed anxiety over the project and asked Lord Mountbatten whether he could guarantee success. The reply was negative. However, General Sir Alan Brooke, the Chief of the Imperial General Staff, indicated that Dieppe or some operation on a divisional scale was indispensable as a preliminary to the invasion of France. Approval was given to continued planning.

Cover stories were devised to deceive German agents suspected of operating in Britain. One spread the tale that the commandos were training for an assault on one of the Channel isles. A second implied that a force being assembled in the south coast ports was the Tenth Anti-Submarine Striking Force, trained for special operations in the Mediterranean.

Early in July the Dieppe assault force was assembled. Two preliminary training exercises were held. The first was very bad; the second a considerable improvement; and approval to proceed with the operation was given. On July 4 all forces embarked and the troops were told they were going to land at Dieppe. A chance German air raid put two of the large infantry landing ships out of action, and on July 7 the raid was canceled.

On August 17 it was reactivated. The same force was reassembled and sailed the next night. Thereby was created one of the controversial questions about the operation that has never been answered satisfactorily. Was the success of the raid jeopardized by the fact that it had been canceled after a large force—probably 10,000 in all—had been told the objective, and then reactivated less than six weeks later with the same force and the same objective? From a purely security viewpoint it was a horrendous performance, almost certain to give advance warning to German intelligence.

But was it that bad? Assuming the Germans had received reports on the July 7 attempt and its cancellation, would they really expect the August effort to be aimed at Dieppe or some other objective? German intelligence was watching for deception and bluff as well as the real thing.

A review of the security breaches between July 7 and August 19 reveals plenty of indiscretions for German intelligence to feed on, provided German agents were at the right place at the right time to hear the careless words.

There had been ample concern for the security of the operation. Surprise was one of the key ingredients to success. Precautions had been taken to prevent leaks. Plainclothes counterespionage agents mingled with the Canadian troops and the naval personnel in pubs and hotels and at dances and checked billets, and particularly, the female companions to be found in the area. Daily reports were made to Combined Operations headquarters and were reviewed by MI-5, the British counterespionage service.

On August 12—just a week before the raid actually took place—MI-5 agents carefully checked the Shoreham-New Haven area, where there was a large concentration of the participating personnel. They reported much indiscreet talk: Canadians of the Calgary Tank Regiment were talking about their waterproofed tanks and an operation in which commandos would participate.[2] Some of the loose-talkers were taken into custody and held incommunicado until after it was all over. A senior Royal Navy Lieutenant Commander left a copy of the naval operational orders in a bar and was arrested.[3] There were other equally horrifying examples of security breaches, but British counterintelligence was very much present and German agents apparently were not, and there is no evidence of any reports reaching the Germans as a result of these lapses.

General Montgomery, having been redirected to new duties in North Africa and therefore in no way connected with the operation, notes that after July he had considered the operation canceled and was very upset when he heard it had been revived. He says he wrote to General Sir Bernard Paget, the Commander in Chief of the home forces in Great Britain, "telling him of my anxiety and recommending that the raid on Dieppe should be considered cancelled 'for all time.' If it was considered desirable to raid the Continent, then the objective should not be Dieppe. The advice was disregarded."[4]

Despite Montgomery's concern, there is no evidence that German intelligence had pinpointed Dieppe as the target of this particular operation.

ALLIED INTELLIGENCE

The sources of Allied intelligence on which to base the plans for the attack were varied. There was considerable basic intelligence on the topography of the area available in the archives and supplemented by tourists' postcards and snapshots collected earlier in the war from all over England on all parts of the world where British forces might be required to fight. There was also extensive aerial photography of the area. Allied aerial reconnaissance planes flew over the occupied areas of Europe every day of good weather, so flights over the Dieppe area caused no unusual interest on the part of the German defenders. Some of the aerial photographs were taken only thirty-six hours before the raid.

The maps and photographs prepared at the Photographic Interpretation Unit at Medmenham were remarkably accurate—to a degree. These pinpointed artillery, antiaircraft and antitank guns, roadblocks, some of the barbed wire and some of the machine gun positions. But the planners obviously gave the caves in the headlands, which flanked Dieppe harbor on each side, inadequate attention. No provisions were made to neutralize these caves, which hid heavy machine guns and sniper nests.

In addition to the photographic intelligence there was extensive reporting from the French underground and from British agents. London was aware that German counterintelligence had penetrated some French networks and agent reports were not accepted as accurate unless confirmed by collateral sources such as photographs, prisoner-of-war interrogations or intercepted German communications.

All of the intelligence received from the Admiralty, the Photographic Interpretation Unit and the Secret Intelligence Service (which processed the reports of the French Resistance) was assembled by Combined Operations Intelligence into a confidential forty-eight-page book, which was not available to the attacking force until long after the plan of attack had been adopted. Even though it was late, the intelligence summary contained nothing sufficiently startling to change the plan.

Most of the historians who have touched on the action at Dieppe have given the amount of intelligence available to the planners good marks. But in calculating what could be accomplished against the German defenses, the Combined Operations Staff may well have been overly influenced by the success of the raid against St. Nazaire which took place on March 28, 1942, and succeeded in knocking out the largest drydock in Europe for the duration of the war.

Remember that Dieppe was selected as the objective because it was a port of average importance, lying on the actual coast which could be reached by sea from England in a few hours and covered by land-based aircraft. Its defenses were apparently considered about standard for ports in the area, and the defending forces were also viewed as not unusually strong.

How thoroughly the planners compared the topography in the area of Dieppe with that of other channel coast ports is difficult to determine. The Germans, recognizing that the topographical features of the area would force any attackers to follow certain courses, prepared their defenses accordingly.

This part of the French seaboard, running from Cape Griz Nez in the east to the Saane River west of Dieppe, is called the Iron Coast. Most of the entire coast consists of vertical chalk cliffs thirty to a hundred feet high, broken only here and there by the mouths of rivers and narrow steep-sided gulleys. At the foot of the cliffs, rocky ledges extend seaward from the face of the cliffs. These ledges are covered with flint stones from three to six inches in diameter and with sand at low tide.

The port of Dieppe is at the mouth of the Arques River, which reaches the channel by cutting through the limestone cliffs. It has a small sheltered harbor with a pebbled beach 1,500 yards long, framed on either side by two practically inaccessible cliffs.

Two miles west of Dieppe the Scie River creates another beach 600 yards wide at the village of Pourville. Another three miles west at Varangeville the Germans had located one of the main shore batteries to guard the port.

To the east of Dieppe, just short of a mile, lies the narrow valley of Puits. At Berneval, just beyond Puits, a second battery of German guns was located.

One of the targets of the attack was the headquarters of the German 302nd Infantry Division, the principal unit defending the Dieppe area, believed to be at Arques-la-Bataille. Allied intelligence had missed the move of this headquarters on April 27 to Envermeu. The 302nd Division was subordinate to the 81st Corps, which had its headquarters at Rouen, and this in turn was a unit of the German Fifteenth Army with headquarters at Tourçoing. The Fifteenth Army defended the coast of western Europe from the Scheldt in Holland to Dives-sur-Mer near Caen in Normandy.

Churchill said that "from available intelligence" it appeared that Dieppe was held by low-category troops amounting to one battalion, which with supporting troops amounted to no more than 1,400 men in all.[5] This was in accordance with the original estimate in April 1942 of Combined Operations Headquarters Staff, which placed the garrison at two companies of infantry, and obviously was on the low side, even for that date.

On July 20 the German 302nd Division received replacements totaling 1,353 men, and on August 12 a second group of 1,150 had reported. Thus by the time of the attack on August 19, the garrison was at full strength if not at full proficiency.

There was some surprise to find the 302nd Division still at Dieppe, because reports had been received that it had been relieved by the 110th Infantry Division, a better combat unit. It is possible that German deception had contributed to this confusion. Agent reports had been received in England from the Dieppe area describing a shoulder patch which resembled the divisional flash of the 110th. At that time, however, the 110th was on the eastern front.[6]

The British were rightfully concerned about the proximity of German armor to Dieppe and noted the move of the 10th Panzer Division from Soissons to Amiens in June, bringing it within eight hours of the target. Thus, if the Allied evacuation were delayed beyond one tide, the attackers might have to face German tanks.[7]

During July the Germans moved the headquarters of the S. S. Panzer Corps to Nogent-le-Rotrou, the 1st S. S. Adolf Hitler Panzer Division to near Paris, and the 2nd S. S. Das Reich Panzer Division to Laval. While none of these moves directly affected Dieppe, they indicated German concern over an invasion attempt.

Intelligence on the German capability to defend the main beaches at Dieppe was obviously deficient in many respects. There was inadequate knowledge of the armament in the pillboxes. There was almost complete ignorance of the observation and fire-control positions hidden along the beach, and equal blindness concerning the many beach-defense and antitank guns and the volume of cross fire that could be expected from the defenses hidden in the highlands on either side of the harbor.

While intelligence appreciated the difficulties the Allied tanks would encounter in getting across the sea wall, inadequate consideration was given to heavy concrete roadblocks set up on all exits from the Promenade into the town.

The after-action report of the German 81st Corps put it quite succinctly: "The Englishman had underestimated the strength of the defenses, and therefore at most of his landing places—especially at Puits and Dieppe—found himself in a hopeless position as soon as he came ashore."

Colonel C. P. Stacey, who wrote the Canadian official history of the war, comments:

Tactically, it was an almost complete failure, for we suffered extremely heavy losses and attained few of our objectives.

The enemy was astonished that, in spite of our generally accurate knowledge of his defenses, we attempted an assault on an area strong both by nature and by art, with weapons which he considered inadequate to the task.

. . . from the beginning the planners underrated the influence of topography and of the enemy's strong defenses in the Dieppe area.[8]

Field Marshal Gerd von Rundstedt, commanding the German forces in the west, personally looked over the documents captured on the beaches at Dieppe and commented on the high quality of the maps. He also noted the necessity for greater use of camouflage and of dummy positions for deception purposes, and issued orders to this effect.

The 81st Corps report noted that Allied intelligence generally lacked knowledge as to the location of regimental and battalion command posts.

Major Reginald Unwin, a professional officer on General McNaughton's staff, warned that the absence of confirmed defenses did not preclude Dieppe from being heavily defended. When the final intelligence estimate on the defenses was produced for inclusion in the operations plan, Unwin refused to sign it as unjustifiably optimistic and he inserted warnings. Unfortunately most of Major Unwin's warnings were either ignored or deleted.[9]

GERMAN INTELLIGENCE

German intelligence, in the spring and summer of 1942, was alert to the possibilities of attacks on the French coast. The raid on St. Nazaire on March 28 made German intelligence particularly sensitive to reports of commando attacks. Admiral Erich Raeder, the German Naval Chief, noted on April 11 that this raid showed British determination and ability "to attack our extensive coastline more frequently and on larger scale," although he thought that for a time these would be raids and not second front attempts.[10]

Many raid rumors are recorded in the German war diaries of this period. One such report said a raid on Dieppe was planned for April 6. A report of May 5 said sufficient Allied forces were available for opening a new front in Norway.[11] The communiqués issued by the Allies following Molotov's visit to London and to Washington in May 1942, with their stress on a second front in the west, served to intensify German anxiety. On June 11 a statement was issued in Washington: "In the course of conversations full understanding was reached with regard to the urgent task of creating a Second Front in Europe in 1942."

General Franz Halder's diary on July 6 noted that Hitler's fear of a landing in the west made him refuse to release the 1st S. S. Liebstandarte Adolf Hitler Panzer Division to join the attack of the 1st Panzer Army at Rostov.

On July 9, Hitler personally signed a directive concerning a possible attack in the west. "Our rapid and great advances may place before Great Britain the alternatives of either staging a large-scale invasion with the object of opening a Second Front, or seeing Russia eliminated as a political and military factor. It is therefore highly probable that enemy landings will shortly take place in the area of the Commanding General Armed Forces, West."[12]

He noted the heavy concentration of shipping along the southern coast of England, commented on the increase in reports from agents on possible landings and then said that he thought the likely target area would be the channel coast between Dieppe and Le Havre and Normandy. There was an immediate reinforcement of the Dieppe area with the addition of mortars and antitank guns.

On August 2 at a Fuehrer Conference, Hitler gave detailed instructions for coastal defense indicating that he wanted a solid line of unbroken fire.

On August 10 the German Fifteenth Army, charged with defending the French coast along the Pas-de-Calais, echoed Hitler's comments: "Various reports permit the assumption that, because of the miserable position of the Russians, the Anglo-Americans will be forced to undertake something in the measurable future." On August 13, Hitler's anxiety was even more apparent when he warned his followers to the effect that a second front must be prevented at all costs.

Oberkommando der Wehrmacht West, the German High Command for western Europe, was no less alert than Hitler to the possibilities of a landing. From mid-June on, the 3rd Luftflotte intensified both photographic and visual reconnaissance of the assembly of landing craft on the south coast of England. OKW assumed that an enemy landing could take place at any time and on any point on the extensive coastline.

By this time in the war the German military intelligence service was in poor shape and many of its key officers were anti-Nazi, even to the point of betraying their country. Consequently, Admiral Canaris' Abwehr was not held in the highest esteem either by the German High Command or by the army, and in 1942 there was a tendency to ignore its reports.

German intelligence was also in receipt of the usual variety of reports from clandestine sources and third-country nationals. A Portuguese sailor who had left Portsmouth on June 13 reported invasion preparations along the south coast of England, with supplies being built up at Dover, Romney, Dungeness, Hastings, Bexhill, Eastbourne, Seaford and Portsmouth.[13] (Surely the Germans must have taken this report with a considerable grain of salt, knowing that British authorities did not allow neutral sailors to wander around the coastal areas.) Further, the report was so general as to be worthless. It was the type of information a sailor could use to pick up pleasure money by peddling it to one of the many Axis intelligence agents in neutral Lisbon—that is, if German intelligence was so stupid or desperate to buy it. There were only two names in the report that had any connection with the Dieppe operation. Some Canadians were billeted at Seaford and left there by truck convoy to go to the port of embarkation, as they also did from Lewes, Horsham, Little Hampton, and Billingshurst. The other name was Portsmouth, a major British port and center of shipping from which the command ship sailed to Dieppe. Not mentioned at all by the Portuguese were: Newhaven, from which the Calgary Tanks, Camerons and No. 3 Commando embarked; Shoreham, from which the Fusiliers Mont-Royal sailed; nor Southampton, the major port of embarkation, from which sailed the No. 4 Commando, Royal Highland Light Infantry, Royal Regiment, Black Watch, Royal Marine Commando, Essex Scottish and South Saskatchewan Regiment.

On April 6 a British agent in the Marseilles area instructed a French Resistance network to report all movement of German armor in the area of Rouen-Amiens-Dieppe.[14] A German counterintelligence agent in the network reported this to the regional Gestapo headquarters in Dieppe, and the Germans prepared to feed false information into the network. The same occurred in Grenoble when an Allied agent sought information on German units in the Pas-de-Calais.[15]

On May 24 the German Foreign Office, also aspiring to be an intelligence organization, warned of an imminent British landing on the west coast of Jutland. In mid-June German agents suggested that large-scale landings could be expected around June 20 near The Hague or La Rochelle or Le Treport.

On July 7, von Rundstedt, while ordering a general alert along the entire channel coast from July 10 to July 24 because the tides and the moon were considered favorable for enemy landings, downgraded Dieppe from "a defended area" to "a group of strong-points," noting that "due to the small capacity of its port, it is not the type of harbor the Allies are likely to choose as an invasion base."[16]

On July 22 another British agent in Angers placed his requirements for a continuous flow of intelligence on German defenses along the channel coast with a man reputed to be the Resistance leader in the area. The Frenchman was also German counterintelligence and is claimed to have personally advised von Rundstedt of the Allied interest in coastal defenses.[17]

Clandestine intelligence operations being what they

are, the Germans concluded that the agents' inquiries did not necessarily indicate Dieppe as the target. Agents were asking about almost the entire coastal area of Europe.

On August 15 the Germans noted a change in British communications procedures which made interceptions much more difficult, although the operational and training traffic showed no deviation from normal.[18] German study of Allied air operations gave no clue, and did not point especially to an impending landing.

THE ACTION

Dieppe was not one battle, but eight separate actions which had only limited effect on each other.

The battle plan was complex. The two heavy batteries covering the port on each flank were to be destroyed or neutralized by commando attacks. The highlands which ominously overlooked Dieppe harbor on both sides were to be seized from the rear by attacks on Puits and Pourville. The force attacking at Pourville was to drive inland to capture the German divisional headquarters believed to be at Arques-la-Bataille, with assistance from tanks coming in through Dieppe. The main force of infantry and tanks would land on the beaches of Dieppe harbor. Overhead the R.A.F. would maintain air superiority and challenge the Luftwaffe to all-out battle.

On August 18, 1942, 252 ships sailed from Portsmouth, Southampton, Shoreham and Newham on the south coast of England. The 9th and 13th mine-sweeping flotillas sailed from Portsmouth, headed toward Newhaven to disguise their true objective and then swung east to open two channels through the minefields for the flotilla. Twenty-four tank-landing craft and nine infantry-landing craft carried a total of 6,086 officers and men of the landing force. Eight destroyers plus steam and motor gun boats and motor launches provided an escort.

The first action joined was the chance encounter of Flotilla Group 5 (carrying No. 3 Commando) with a German coastal convoy bound from Le Havre to Dieppe. This occurred at 0347. Two messages from British naval headquarters at Portsmouth, warning that the German convoy was in the path of the Flotilla, failed to reach Group 5. The first one, sent at 0127 hours, was not received by anybody. A second message, at 0144, was received by the alternate command ship, *Fernie*, which did not realize that the main command ship, *Calpe*, had not received the message, and did not send it on to Group 5.

The German convoy escort struck first, scattering the British. Only seven of twenty-three landing craft carrying the commandos were able to proceed, with only twenty men landing to attack the battery at Berneval. The commandos in the other six landing craft that reached the French coast were unable to reach their target.

The remarkable aspect of the convoy action was that literally nobody but those directly engaged paid any attention to it. The escorting Allied destroyers, which could have intervened perhaps decisively, ignored it, even though they surely saw the gunfire at night. The communications equipment on Steam Gun Boat 5, which was involved in the action, was destroyed, so it was not able to alert the Force Commander that surprise may have been lost. The order to keep radio silence was scrupulously followed by all others concerned. Major General John Hamilton Roberts on the command ship did not hear about the action until 0645. He was thus not aware that one of the commando attacks on a flank battery was seriously weakened. And even though the Germans along the coast both saw and heard the action, it did not increase their state of alert in any way. It was simply dismissed as a routine convoy action. Three German patrol craft off Dieppe watched the battle but were so unconcerned they returned to port.

Perhaps even more remarkable was the little effect the convoy skirmish had on the action at Berneval. One of the landing craft able to proceed after the convoy battle landed Major Peter Young, two officers and seventeen men at Yellow Beach II below Berneval at 0515. Here the target was 2/770 Hurenkusten Artillerie Abteilung which had four 105 mm. and three 170 mm. coastal defense guns as well as two 20 mm. Oerlikons for antiaircraft defense. The battery had 127 men, and there were 114 Luftwaffe personnel manning the radar in the vicinity.

Major Young's small force landed undetected and made their way inland to the Dieppe-Berneval road. A young French boy described the best approach to the battery and led them into Berneval. There Young cut the telephone lines to Dieppe.

The 20 British commandos then moved to within 200 yards of the battery, neutralized it with sniping for more than two hours and re-embarked at 0810. The second landing by six craft carrying the remnants of No. 3 Commando at Berneval on Yellow Beach I was less successful. They were twenty-five minutes late and landed in broad daylight, encountering heavy opposition immediately upon landing. The Germans, who outnumbered the small British force, were soon reinforced by three more companies of the Antitank Battalion of the 302nd Division. Of the 120 commandos who got ashore at Berneval, 82 were captured.

Meanwhile, on the other extreme flank five miles to the west of Dieppe, No. 4 Commando under Lord Lovat* was attacking the heavy German battery, the 813th Abteilung,

* Brigadier S. C. J. P. Lovat.

THE BATTLE OF DIEPPE

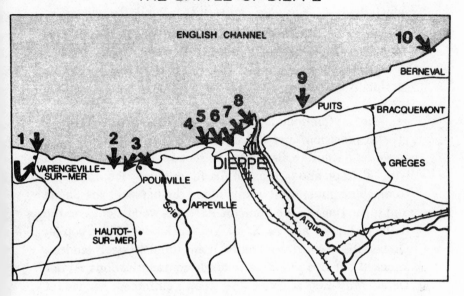

1. NO. 3 COMMANDO

2. CAMERONS
3. SOUTH SASKATCHEWANS

4. FUSILIERS MONT-ROYAL
5. ROYAL HAMILTON LIGHT INFANTRY
6. ROYAL MARINES
7. CALGARY TANKS
8. ESSEX SCOTTISH

9. ROYAL REGIMENT

10. NO. 4 COMMANDO

which had six 150 mm. guns just behind the village of Varangeville. While everything else about the Dieppe operation may have tragically failed, this attack was a classic in its success, despite the fact that the battery had opened fire on the invasion fleet at 0447, three minutes before the landing.

No. 4 Commando's attack was made with training-ground precision, and the timing of each individual unit's move was accurate almost to the second. Lord Lovat landed with "B" troop at 0450 east of the River Saane, lost four men to machine guns, went a mile along the banks of the Saane and turned east to the Blancmenil le Bas wood alongside the battery. Lieutenant A. S. S. Veasey landed "A" troop at Quiberville, scaled the cliffs with tubular steel ladders, knocked out two pillboxes and cut communications. Major Derek Mills-Robert, with "F" troop reinforced, landed at Vasterival opposed by only one machine gun. The noise of his Bangolore torpedoes blowing gaps in the wire along the beach was covered by the roar of the Spitfires attacking the Ailly Lighthouse.

Precisely at 0550 the British mortars opened fire. "B" troop attacked from the right flank, and Major Mills-Roberts and "F" troop from the left flank. An air attack by Spitfires was made simultaneously. It was over in a matter of minutes, aided appreciably by a direct mortar shell hit on piled cordite which blew up, killing or stunning many Germans. But it was the hard-driving infantry attack by Major Mills-Roberts' "B" troop which administered the *coup de grâce* and overran the battery. Four Germans were taken prisoner. The rest were shot or bayoneted. By 0650 the guns were blown up and the commando withdrew toward the beach at Vasterival. By 0900 the unit was on its way back to England. Its casualties totaled forty-six.

On the German side, it was not until 1000 hours that

the 302nd Division learned that the Varangeville battery had been wiped out.

At Pourville, two miles to the west of Dieppe port, the South Saskatchewan Regiment commanded by Lieutenant Colonel Charles C. I. Merritt landed as one wave on Green Beach at 0450 hours without a shot being fired at it. The plan was to land astride the River Scie, which flows into the sea near the middle of the Pourville beach. Unfortunately, almost all of the landing force was put ashore on the west bank. This meant that "A" Company, which was charged with seizing the radar station and the high ground a mile to the east, had to penetrate the village and cross the bridge carrying the main road to Dieppe. Before it could cross the bridge, however, the German defenders were in action. This was a critical development. The seizure of Le Pollet cliff on the west headlands of Dieppe and the silencing of the four 105 mm. guns of "B" battery of the 302nd Division artillery were essential to a successful landing on the Dieppe beach. These steps were not accomplished.

But even though the South Saskatchewan Regiment was not able to drive eastward and clear the cliff, it was able to hold Pourville while the Camerons landed and drove inland along the Scie. These two units fared the best of all the Canadian troops in the Dieppe operation. Of the 523 South Saskatchewans landed, 357 were re-embarked and 268 of the 503 Camerons were taken off. The losses between them still amounted to a staggering 65 per cent or 686 out of 1,026, with 151 killed, 266 taken prisoner and 269 wounded.

The situation at Pourville caused the German High Command the greatest concern. General von Haase, commanding the 302nd Division, ordered the reserve regiment to move up from four miles south to drive out the attackers. Shortly after 0900, von Rundstedt ordered the 10th Panzer Division committed under the 81st Corps and moved from

Amiens to Pourville. Its advance units reached Longueville-sur-Scie at 1355 hours, by which time the battle was over.

Admiral Kanalkuests (the naval command, channel coast) also added to German alarm by reporting at 0640 that he was out of contact with Dieppe and that the outposts at the Ailly Lighthouse reported tank landing craft. This information caused the high command to wonder whether the British intention was to create a beachhead.

At Puits, 1,500 yards to the east of Dieppe, the Royal Regiment of Canada under the command of Lieutenant Colonel Douglas Catto made its approach, under murderous fire from fully alert defenders in unexpected defensive positions. While still well offshore, the landing craft were hit repeatedly and when those who survived reached the beach they had no place to go to escape the German guns. A ten-foot high sea wall, covered with heavy barbed wire (not reported by intelligence) blocked the head of the beach. On the east cliff a concrete pillbox was hidden in the front garden of a brick house. The main slit of this pillbox covered the beach and sea wall at very short range. A few hundred yards south of Puits four German howitzers fired 550 rounds at the landing craft.

The landing was a complete disaster. Being unable to move inland off the beaches, the Royal Regiment had no chance to accomplish its vital objective of seizing the headlands to the east of Dieppe. Of 554 officers and men who had embarked from England, only 67 returned; 227 were dead on the beaches and the rest were prisoners. Only 20 men were able to move inland off the beach. The German defenders lost two killed and nine wounded. At 0835 the 571st Regiment informed its division headquarters that Puits was firmly in German hands and that the enemy had lost 500 prisoners and dead.

In Dieppe itself the German 571st Infantry Regiment, with two battalions defending the port, did not order action stations until 0500, after it had already heard of the landings at Pourville. The 302nd Division went on the alert a minute later.

The frontal attack on the Dieppe beach was made by the Royal Hamilton Light Infantry under the command of Lieutenant Colonel Robert R. Labatt on the right (west) landing on White Beach and the Essex Scottish commanded by Lieutenant Colonel Jasperson on the left (east) landing on Red Beach. Nine tanks of the 14th Tank Regiment were to land with the first wave. The tanks arrived late and the infantry was pinned down before it could get through the wire obstacles.

German riflemen showed exceptional skill in picking off the officers, communications men and engineers, thus effectively hampering command and destroying the attackers' ability to communicate their plight to the command ship or to coordinate an attack, and eliminating any chance of the attackers being able to clear the beach obstacles. German mortar fire was devastating and inflicted severe casualties on the attackers.

The landing of the tanks, nevertheless, was remarkably successful. All ten of the LCT's succeeded in getting tanks ashore, and eight of them landed three apiece. Two tanks were drowned driving off the LCT's into deep water. Twenty-seven tanks reached the beach. Of these, fifteen crossed the sea wall and reached the promenade. Here the tanks were stopped. With all of the engineers either pinned down or killed by the withering German fire, there was no way to remove the heavy concrete roadblocks barring all streets into the town.

The infantry on the main beaches of Dieppe had little

chance. Resistance was much stiffer than had been expected. The tanks that were able to get into action were unable to neutralize or destroy the German gun positions along the beaches or in the flanking cliffs. There was no artillery support and the guns of the supporting ships were too small to be effective. The infantry paid. "D" Company of the Hamiltons was almost wiped out on landing. Between 30 to 45 per cent of the Essex Scottish were dead or wounded by 0545 hours.

There was some limited penetration of the town by the infantry. The Casino was captured and there was street fighting in the area around it. But this slight success only led to a compounding of the catastrophe. At 0610 the command ship received a message, "Essex Scots across the beaches and in the houses." At 0640 General Roberts decided to land the main body of his floating reserve, and at 0700 a battalion of Les Fusiliers Mont-Royal under the command of Lieutenant Colonel Menard headed for Dieppe harbor in twenty-six unarmored landing craft. German artillery had this small fleet under direct fire for ten minutes as it approached the beaches. It suffered heavy casualties before landing, and on reaching the beaches suffered the same fate as the first assault wave.

Major General John Hamilton Roberts, the commander of the Canadian ground forces at Dieppe, was unaware throughout the action of the extent of the disaster, especially on the main beaches at Dieppe where he committed his reserve. At 0817 an entry in the command ship *Calpe's* log reads, "Have control of White Beach." Roberts thereupon instructed the Royal Marine Commandos under Lieutenant Colonel Phillips—the last of the floating reserve—to transfer to armored landing craft and land on White Beach to support the Essex Scottish. When Phillips in the lead landing craft emerged from the smoke screen and saw the disaster on the beaches, he stood up to signal to the landing craft to turn back. Lieutenant Colonel J. C. Phillips was killed almost instantly, but he had saved most of his command.

The air battle was slow in getting under way, but British hopes of engaging all of the Luftwaffe in the west were ultimately realized. The results were not exactly what had been anticipated, even though at the time the British claimed a great air victory. Sixty-nine Allied squadrons were committed to the battle. These planes flew 2,617 sorties during the day, giving the fleet and the troops constant fighter cover, bombing the heavy batteries at Berneval and Varangeville and laying smoke screens.

The Luftwaffe was slow to react. At 0600 it was placed on the alert. It was not until 0711 that 81st Corps advised 302nd Division that bombers were being committed, and not until 1000 that German fighters challenged the R.A.F. over the battlefield. By the end of the battle—at approximately 1400 hours—all Luftwaffe resources in the west had been committed and 945 sorties had been flown.

It was no British air victory as claimed, although the first priority was achieved—that of controlling the air over the battlefield. The R.A.F. lost 106 planes, including 88 fighters, 8 bombers and 10 reconnaissance aircraft—its heaviest one-day loss of the war. It had 113 killed and 40 wounded. The Luftwaffe had 48 planes destroyed and 24 damaged.

The Allied naval losses were comparatively light. One destroyer, the *Berkeley*, was lost during the evacuation, hit by German bombs being jettisoned so the aircraft could escape British fighters. Five of the tank-landing craft and 28 lesser craft were sunk. There were 550 casualties among naval personnel with 75 killed and 269 missing. Naval gunners brought down 29 bombers and fighters—including 5 friendlies!

German ground losses totalled 591 casualties, with the principal defense unit, the 302nd Infantry Division, having 5 officers and 116 men killed, 6 officers and 195 men wounded, and eleven missing. The Kriegsmarine lost 78 killed or missing and had 27 wounded, while the Luftwaffe had 105 killed or missing and 58 wounded.

Field Marshal von Rundstedt said that the first real warning came when part of the landing force blundered into a German coastal convoy at 0350 hours. The Field Marshal's opinion is open to question. He had also gone on record as believing that landings at dawn would not be attempted.

The German 81st Corps claims that the entire coastal area was alerted as a result of the convoy battle, but all units apparently did not go on full alert. The battery at Berneval which could see the convoy battle and while alert, thought it was solely a naval action. No shot was fired on the assault wave at Pourville. When the *Prince Albert* dropped anchor off Dieppe at 0350 hours and began to disembark troops into landing craft, the Ailly Lighthouse and the lights on the jetties of the harbor were still on.

Commander of Naval Group West told von Rundstedt's headquarters at 0445 hours that the firing in the channel near Dieppe was just a "customary attack on a convoy" and made no mention of possible landings. It was not until 0458, or more than an hour after the convoy encounter, that 81st Corps at Canteleu was advised fighting was in progress at Berneval and at 0510 that there were landings at Pourville and Quiberville.

Perhaps the most revealing comment on German confusion was the action taken on the radar sighting. At 0232 hours Flugmeldezentrale (air warning center) advised that

Freya radar 28 had numerous targets in its scope about twenty-one miles off Dieppe. Flugmeldezentrale was told by Kriegsmarine (naval headquarters) West that it was only the Boulogne Convoy, which was expected at Dieppe at 0500.[19] It is possible that the radar report was given such cursory attention because it was a new installation and the commands were assumed to be inexperienced in distinguishing friend from foe. At 0410 the German radio station at Le Havre reported that British surface vessels were attacking the convoy. The naval authorities told Heeresgruppe (Army Group) D and the 3rd Luftflotte that it was probably a routine attack.[20]

The Germans had studied the moon and the tide cycles to determine the most favorable times for landing. On July 20 the Fifteenth Army said there were three periods when the moon and the tide along the French channel coast were best for attacks: July 27 to August 3; August 10 to 19; and August 25 to September 1.[21]

The 302nd Division was charged with defense of the channel coast from the Somme to Veules-les-Roses. It had nearly a year and a half to prepare defenses before it was challenged by an enemy. One of its early orders, issued on April 25, 1941, indicated a slight miscalculation of enemy intentions, for it assumed that the ports of Le Treport and Dieppe would not be assaulted directly but would be subject to flanking attacks. In the area of Dieppe itself, the month of August had been unusually calm with no alert at land or sea for the first two weeks. But Major General Conrad von Haase, who commanded the 302nd division, had the defenses fully manned from high tide every night to sunrise the next morning. On August 8 the 302nd Division ordered *drohende Gefahr* (threatening danger) alert for ten nights, August 10 to August 20.[22]

On August 18 the weather report provided to the German headquarters in France predicted that the next day would have a fine morning but an overcast afternoon. The Luftwaffe gave a third of the pilots twenty-four-hour leave. The staff of OKW West concluded that the night of August 18–19 would be suitable for enemy raiding operations and directed coastal troops to be put on "threatening danger" alert. There did not appear to be any coordination in their actions.

It seems that though some Germans expected a raid or even an invasion attempt anywhere along the coast, this view was not unanimous. Dieppe was not necessarily the target. It was only a possibility along with many other areas.

The raid did achieve tactical surprise, as the planners had hoped, despite blundering into the convoy. The Germans were no more nor less alert than they would have been at any time. The greatest surprise to the Germans was the size of the attack. It confused their thinking and their planning for the future to an important, if not decisive, degree.

The Germans captured documents with which they could better evaluate the raid. A copy of the Detailed Military Plan of the Dieppe landing was found on the body of a dead officer.[23] Concern at possible deception may have prevented full weight being given to the contents of these papers. Despite this information there were those who believed that the landings had actually been intended as the opening phase in the invasion of France. Some of the German confusion was caused by their difficulty in believing that the British would use a regiment of their most modern tanks for a mere raid.

But perhaps an even more grievous error on the part of the Germans arose from a conviction—shared by Hitler and some of his followers on the General Staff—that Dieppe proved that an invasion could be repelled on the beaches. On August 25, just a week after the raid, Hitler ordered Commander in Chief West to build 15,000 fortifications of a permanent nature, thus fatally neglecting the development of a mobile reserve. This was to have a decisive effect on the Normandy battle in June 1944.[24]

The erroneous report which resulted in the most drastic German action, and may have had the most far-reaching effect on German strategy, was the air reconnaissance report of a twenty-six–ship convoy off the south coast of England with the decks of the ships covered with troops. As a result of this report, Field Marshal von Rundstedt at 1030 ordered Alert Two for the whole of the Seventh Army, which covered the coasts of Normandy and Brittany, and for the greater part of the Army Reserve under his command. This alert was cancelled at 0800 the next day (the twentieth). It was also this report which may have convinced some in the German High Command that the raid on Dieppe was actually an invasion attempt which failed. This conviction led Hitler to concentrate on a strategy of coastal defenses as the principal means for repelling invasion and to neglect of mobile reserves as counter to invading forces. It led to the falsely optimistic belief that an all-out assault could be easily repelled.

While the attack on Dieppe was undoubtedly an unsatisfactory substitute for a second front as far as the Russians were concerned, there seems little question that it did nevertheless force the Germans to commit a greater portion of their resources to the west. In January 1942 the Germans had 33 divisions in the west, including 2 panzer divisions, compared to 163 in the east, of which 19 were panzer. By September, just after the raid, there were 35 divisions in the west with the equivalent of 3½ panzer and 1½ motorized. Strength in the east had also gone up—to 182, with 20 panzers. But by November 1942 strength in the west had been increased to 52 divisions.

THE LESSONS: D-DAY

In any military action each side gains important experience and, if wise, is better prepared for the next battle. Dieppe was no exception. There is no question but that the Allies secured valuable information which could not have been obtained without fighting.

Most of the payoff for Dieppe was not collected until June 6, 1944, D-Day in Normandy. How many lives may have been saved in Normandy will become more apparent as we see what was learned. Lord Louis Mountbatten said that for every soldier who died at Dieppe, ten were saved on D-Day.

Two lessons, however, immediately became painfully apparent.

The operation did not succeed in giving any instant and direct relief to the Russians. The threat of an invasion had already led Hitler to reinforce the west with a steady buildup of forces, including such elite units as the 1st. S. S. Liebstandarte Adolf Hitler and 2nd S. S. Das Reich Panzer divisions. Alarmed by the landing at Dieppe, Hitler pulled another crack unit out of the line in Russia—a Panzer Grenadier Division—but the General Staff persuaded him to leave it in the east after the landing was crushed.

The air battle over the French coast caused Luftwaffe units all the way from Denmark to Spain to be placed on the alert. None was moved from the eastern front, understandable since the R.A.F. losses were much higher than those of the German Air Force.

If the British expected gratitude from the Soviets for this attempt, they were wrong. While Moscow's anti-British campaign abated somewhat, the Russians were bitterly disappointed by the size of the attack at Dieppe. Their own situation was desperate. A week before the raid, on his visit to Moscow, Churchill had carefully explained to Stalin that a second front on the Continent was not possible in 1942.

The Allies benefited, however, perhaps indirectly, when Colonel-General Kurt Zeitzler, Chief of Staff to Field Marshal von Rundstedt in the west, loudly and repeatedly trumpeted that an invasion attack had been crushed (which was exactly what Hitler wanted to hear), and he was elevated to replace General Halder as Chief of Staff of the Army. Zeitzler had none of Halder's abilities.

In addition to Zeitzler, who kept telling Hitler that an invasion attempt had been repulsed at Dieppe, many in the German High Command were convinced by the action that attacking forces could be destroyed on the beaches. This led the Germans to concentrate on correcting the defects in the coastal defenses. It also led to a conviction that the Allies would try to capture a major port. During the next two years the Germans expended considerable effort preparing major ports in western Europe for defense against assault from the sea. An assault patterned on Dieppe was not to be repeated, but the Germans did not know it.

The Germans did gain some valuable information from Dieppe. They were impressed by the British ability to land tanks on the beaches and they took additional steps to meet this type of attack. British documents which fell into their hands showed them how clearly their defenses were revealed in aerial photography, and they immediately increased their efforts to camouflage and erected dummy emplacements. Finally, they saw the need for more reliable communications in combat. But all in all, Dieppe gave the Germans more cause for complacency than concern.

No longer was Washington optimistic about the possibilities of an early invasion of Europe. The President and most of the Plans Division in the War Department were profoundly shaken by the Dieppe casualties.

General Haase, the German division commander, commented: "One of the important lessons of the war was learned at Dieppe—how not to go about an invasion." Everyone on the Allied side felt the same way.

The list of lessons learned at Dieppe is a formidable one.

1. It was unwise to launch a direct assault on a port. The resistance was too difficult to overcome without destroying all the port facilities which were needed intact. Further, the direct attack on a port made the plan of battle too rigid and prevented that flexibility essential to overcoming unexpected obstacles, such as clearing the headlands at Dieppe. The Dieppe experience indicated the necessity of achieving a deep penetration quickly with the objective of seizing a port from inland. This was well executed in Normandy nearly two years later when the Allies landed on open beaches, much to the surprise of the Germans, cut the peninsula and took the port of Cherbourg from the rear.

2. Surprise had been substituted for firepower and bombardment at Dieppe. The disaster on the beaches made it apparent that overwhelming fire support was an absolute necessity, with close fire support in the initial stages of the landing. Before Dieppe the British Navy was averse to sending its big ships too close to enemy-held shorelines. The experience on August 19, 1942, demonstrated conclusively that under an air umbrella naval losses could be minimized.

On D-Day, in addition to a formidable air bombardment, battleships and cruisers moved in to give direct fire support against pillboxes, gun emplacements and even tanks. Rockets fired from landing craft blanketed areas of the landing. The firepower of the attacking forces was strong enough to keep the defenders down and cut their communications.

3. At Dieppe the force commander was literally a spectator with the battle beyond his control. Compounding the difficulties already created by faulty intelligence, General Roberts was inadequately informed about the situation on the beaches as communications failed or he received false information. As a result he sent his reserves into action when they could do nothing to affect the course of the battle. Roberts did not have exclusive control over all forces employed, and perhaps even more serious, he was given a plan to implement over which he had no influence. He should have been asked to participate in the advance planning. All of these errors were corrected before General Dwight D. Eisenhower sent his forces ashore on June 6, 1944.

4. A great number of tactical lessons emerged from the ordeal at Dieppe. The failure of communications was one of the most damaging. The leaders on the command ship *Calpe* could not successfully direct a battle when they had no information on its progress. The need for armored landing craft emerged even more clearly after the appalling losses suffered by Les Fusiliers in their unprotected vessels. The value of smoke cover was emphasized. The engineers' casualties prevented them from destroying obstacles that blocked the landing craft and the tanks and exposed them to destruction, and showed the need to protect these specialists in the assault wave. It was also obvious that the infantry must have tank protection from the moment of landing and that the antitank guns defending the beaches must be de-

stroyed in the preliminary bombardment. All these lessons were invaluable in planning D-Day.

5. Dieppe brought major new organizational concepts for amphibious assaults. The handling of assault landings became a specialized aspect of naval training. The two "dry runs" for Dieppe had obviously been inadequate to iron out all of the difficulties that would arise in coordinating such a sizeable force. The need for closer coordination of plans and intelligence was more than apparent.

6. Major General John Hamilton Roberts, the military commander of the Canadian ground forces at Dieppe, was truly without the essential information he needed. The intelligence on which the operation was based had serious gaps which led to catastrophic results. The number of guns the Germans could use to fire on the landing craft and the main beaches at Dieppe was badly underestimated. The emplacements in the east and west headlands were suspected, but their strength and the difficulty in destroying them were completely misjudged. Observation posts for forward artillery observers along the esplanade in Dieppe were apparently a complete surprise to the attackers and provided the Germans with devastating accuracy of fire against the landing craft and the troops on the beaches. This alone might have been a decisive factor in the results.

It could be argued that even if the intelligence on Dieppe had been perfect, which it obviously was not, the planners might still have underestimated what was required for victory. There was lack of knowledge of the German order of battle below the regimental level—important to the assault forces. There appeared to be overreliance on aerial photography as being capable of revealing all that should be known about the German defenses. This, of course, is one of the classic recurrent failures in intelligence: overreliance on one source or collection system.

Finally, the most serious error of all was the apparent complacency of the intelligence personnel that they had all the answers.

Of great importance was the effect German snipers would have on the operation in their ability to kill officers and signal detachments. This factor left Roberts blind as to the condition of his own forces, with the result that three times he sent reinforcements to units that already had been decimated on the beach only to have his reserve forces cut to pieces in the landing craft or die on the beaches.

Communications from the ground units to Roberts on the command ship *Calpe* ranged from inadequate to non-existent, compounded by enemy deception.

R.A.F. communications for the air battle were good between the aircraft, the command ship and the control point at Group II in England. But not knowing how his ground forces were faring, Roberts could not use air support to greatest effect.

Naval communications were less good and could have seriously affected the outcome. The failure of the destroyers to intervene in the convoy battle was one example. The lateness with which Roberts was advised of the convoy battle and that No. 3 Commando was in effect out of action was important. Had it not been for the incredible bravery and achievements of Major Young and those few men who did get to Berneval, that battery could well have disrupted the entire landing operation in front of Dieppe.

General Roberts took all the blame for the failure at Dieppe—a failure undoubtedly compounded by the gaps in information and intelligence. He never again held an important command and at the end of the war went into a self-imposed exile in the channel islands, one of the belated casualties of an intelligence failure.

5.

Arnhem: A Viper
in the Market

SEPTEMBER 17, 1944

F R O M D I E P P E on the coast of France to the Dutch
city of Arnhem on the lower Rhine is about 242 miles as the
crow flies, but in World War II it took two years and thirty-
two days for the western Allies to travel that distance.

The raid on Dieppe had demonstrated beyond doubt
that a major landing on the coast of France was a long time
off. Churchill had told Stalin in Moscow just a few days
before the Dieppe operation that the opening of the Second
Front could not possibly be accomplished in 1942 but that
the landings in North Africa that fall would divert German
resources from the Russian front and ease the pressure
somewhat. Stalin had not been happy with Churchill's refusal to promise a second front—conveniently forgetting

that the Soviet Union had done nothing while the Germans conquered western Europe in 1940. The Russians had pressed for the establishment at least of a six-division beachhead in Normandy. Churchill said this might be possible with the sea-lift and air cover available.

The disaster at Dieppe dramatically indicated the degree of preparation necessary before the Allies would be ready to open the Second Front in Europe. Any consideration of interim measures to placate the Russians was abandoned.

During the summer offensive of 1942 German advances in the east had swept to the Caucasus, and the granaries of that area and the Ukraine were lost to the Russians. Krasnoder and Maikop in the Caucasus were captured and Grosny was threatened. The Nazis crossed the Kerch Straits and seized Novorossisk. Hitler's forces reached the Volga at Stalingrad. Stalin had every reason to plead for a second front in western Europe.

On November 8, 1942, United States forces landed in North Africa and opened a drive from the west that within six months was to link up with the British forces attacking from the east across Egypt and Libya. By 1943 the Germans were cleared from Africa after a massive surrender in Tunisia.

The fortunes of war swung to the Allies in 1943. In Russia the siege of Leningrad was lifted after seventeen months. The remnants of twenty-two German divisions trapped at Stalingrad were captured. Major cities such as Kursk, Kharkov, Rostov, Belgorod, Rzhev and Vyasma were liberated. By October the Russians had reached the Dnieper River.

Elsewhere the Fascist powers were steadily being driven back. Sicily was cleared by August 18, 1943. A landing was made in Italy on September 2. Italy surrendered

September 9, and the Germans had to take over most of the fighting south of the Alps. In October Marshal Tito's Yugoslav guerrillas launched an offensive in the Trieste area, and the German forces throughout the country were harassed and put on the defensive. In the South Pacific the Japanese were destroyed on island after island. The Gilbert Islands were captured by the Americans in July 1943.

The year 1944 also saw considerable political maneuvering. The Casablanca conference of the western Allies in January produced some agreements on strategy and the unfortunate term "unconditional surrender," which was to prolong the war. In May Stalin dissolved the Comintern, which he had never liked or trusted and had already replaced by the apparatus of the Communist Party of the Soviet Union, which was more efficient and effective and under absolute control. In August 1944 a conference in Quebec reached further decisions on the strategy of the war as far as the British and Americans were concerned. In November at Teheran the Anglo-Saxon powers joined the Russians in "complete agreement on the scope and timing of operations." On December 1 a declaration issued from Cairo by the Americans, British and Chinese indicated that only the surrender of Japan would end the war in Asia.

The year 1944 was the year many people expected the war in Europe to end. Perhaps if a German General Staff using a rational approach to the military situation had been making the decisions, it would have. But an irrational dictator, governing by terror, made the policy. He would neither admit defeat nor allow retreat.

From the south the Allies drove northward up the Italian peninsula. Rome was liberated on June 4, Florence in August, and the country south of a line from Livorno to Ancona was freed.

From the west one of the greatest armadas ever assembled landed a force on the beaches of Normandy on June 6 and the Second Front in Europe became a reality. Within six weeks the Allied troops in Normandy under the command of General Dwight D. Eisenhower had grown to four armies and smashed out of the beachhead to liberate quickly most of France.

The lessons of Dieppe had been learned well, and applied to the landing in Normandy. Heavy naval gunfire supported the landing craft. Airborne troops landed in the interior behind the beach defenses. The battle area was isolated by intensive bombing of all transportation facilities. And this time there was no question about air superiority. The Luftwaffe barely made an appearance.

Less than two weeks after the Allied landings in Normandy, Hitler's first secret weapon was ready for use. The "buzz bomb," or V-1, a warhead with stubby wings propelled by a "ram"—jet engine—was launched on June 17 against England from bases along the channel coast of France.

On July 20, Count Claus S. von Stauffenberg, carrying reports from Berlin, placed a bomb under the conference table at Adolf Hitler's headquarters in East Prussia. The blast injured the German leader, but failed to change the course of history. Hitler's security forces quickly apprehended and executed most of the plotters. Such revered military leaders as Field Marshals Erwin Rommel and Erwin von Witzleben were implicated in the plot. Rommel was permitted to take his own life with poison and was given a state funeral. Witzleben was garroted. Any hope of a successful revolt against the Nazis was gone forever. Hitler's injuries may well have destroyed what reason he had left. If he was not a madman before July 20, 1944, he was most certainly highly irrational thereafter.

In Russia in 1944 the German armies were gradually being driven from the country. By March the Russians had reached the Rumanian border. The Crimea was cleared by May. By July 24 Pskov, the last important Russian city held by the Germans, was freed. In August Rumania surrendered, to be followed by Bulgaria in September.

In the Pacific in 1944 the Japanese were being pushed back toward their home islands by the overwhelming force of American arms. Japanese convoys carrying reinforcements and supplies to island garrisons were annihilated by the U. S. Navy. The Japanese merchant marine was being sunk at an irreplaceable rate by American submarines, and the ring of American bases moved closer and closer to Tokyo. In February 1944 the Marshall Islands were seized; in May the Admiralties; in September the Carolinas. The U. S. base at Guam was recovered in August.

By the late summer of 1944 it appeared that a decisive victory in western Europe might bring an end to Hitler's war. Paris had been liberated by the French Forces of the Interior on August 25. Brussels was liberated by the British on September 4. The German armies streamed east from France, badly beaten and in disarray. It seemed inconceivable that the Nazis would be able to mount more than token resistance in the Siegfried Line on the western borders of Germany. It was most likely that they would ask for an armistice. Did it make sense to destroy what was still standing of the German cities after more than four years of Allied air raids by resisting the overwhelming power of advancing armies from west and east?

In the battle for France the four German armies stationed there had lost great numbers of men and vast quantities of equipment. The Seventh Army had taken the brunt of the assault in Normandy. It had been supported by the S. S.

panzer divisions and finally by some elements of the Fifteenth Army which had been located along the French coast between the Seine and Belgium. The Fifteenth Army had not been committed to battle in Normandy because the Germans expected a second Allied landing across the English Channel at its narrowest part—so well had the deception plan worked which was designed to make them believe this. These two armies—the Seventh and Fifteenth—were badly mauled in the Falaise Gap when the Allies broke out of Normandy and drove eastward. The German First Army in the Bordeaux area of France sent some of its units to Normandy, while others tried to retreat eastward across France. The German Nineteenth Army guarding the south coast of France was driven northward and around Switzerland by the U. S. Seventh Army and French First Army, which had landed on August 15.

By early September 1944 the collapse of Germany seemed imminent to the armies in the west. The German losses of both men and equipment seemed irreplaceable. Hitler was known to be scraping the bottom of the manpower barrel. Conscripts appearing in battle were both much younger and much older than the ages normally considered ideal for soldiers. Units were even being formed of men with a common ailment—one such being a stomach battalion. Could such men bolstering the ever-thinning line of army veterans and hardened Nazis continue to defend the Reich much longer?

It appeared that all the staggering German military forces needed was a *coup de grâce*. The G-2 summary of SHAEF* on August 26 expressed it in this fashion: "The August battles have done it and the enemy in the west has had it. Two and a half months of bitter fighting have

* SHAEF—Supreme Headquarters Allied Expeditionary Forces.

brought the end of the war in Europe within sight, almost within reach." The same intelligence unit was even more optimistic on September 2. It said: "Organized resistance under control of the German High Command is unlikely to continue beyond 1 December 1944."

Perhaps the most optimistic of all intelligence reports of this period was published by the First United States Army, which predicted the possibility of political upheaval in Germany in thirty to sixty days.[1]

Allied optimism was further bolstered by the conviction that German materiel losses could not be replaced. It seemed certain that tank and artillery production had been seriously reduced, if not stopped, by Allied bombing and that the railroads were in deep trouble through loss of engines and rolling stock and difficulty in keeping the lines repaired.

The Allied advance in the west appeared irresistible. The success was not one which had been anticipated. The staging lines calculated by the planners for *Operation Overlord* (the landing in Europe) had been overrun. By D-Day plus 90 (September 6) the troops were advancing beyond the position scheduled for D-Day plus 300. In early September Allied positions were already at the line planned for April 1945.

There was one obstacle which many discounted in the euphoria of victory. The armies had outrun the lines of supply. Despite superhuman feats in high-speed bulk transportation—a gasoline pipeline built at the rate of thirty miles each day; highways used exclusively by the "Red Ball" express trucks rushing shells, food and other essentials forward to the troops at fifty miles an hour; an airlift carrying thousands of tons of cargo each day—the effort was insufficient to support the continued advance of seven armies.

The port of Antwerp in Belgium had been liberated,

but the Germans still controlled the Scheldt Estuary and no Allied ships could enter until the waterborne approaches were cleared. The French port of Brest in Brittany had been freed after a violent battle which would limit its usefulness for some time to come, but it was now more than 500 miles from the front. Consequently the bulk of supplies for forces on the border of Germany still came across the beaches in Normandy, through Cherbourg and other distant ports.

Apparently neither General Eisenhower nor General Bernard Montgomery put top priority on the supply problem. The Supreme Commander was anxious to continue the push forward on all fronts. The newly formed 6th Army Group, with the French First and U. S. Seventh armies, was pressing forward through the Vosges toward the Upper Rhine. General George S. Patton's Third U. S. Army was attacking across the Moselle into the Saar. Montgomery had the most daring plan of all—a drive northward to cross seven waterways at one blow, with the Neder Rijn (Lower Rhine) at Arnhem most important of all. Montgomery may have considered the clearing of Antwerp as a secondary accomplishment of his drive, which if successful could reach the Zuider Zee and cut off the Germans still to the west.

Montgomery's real goal was to flank the Siegfried Line to the north and open the way across the German plains north of the Ruhr. For this he wished Eisenhower to stop all attacks and to give his forces top priority for all required supplies.

General Montgomery already had two armies under his command, the First Canadian and the Second British. To these he proposed to add the First Allied Airborne Army to secure the essential bridges over the major waterways and to act as a carpet for the armor to rush across Holland. He also wanted the Ninth U. S. Army transferred to his command from General Omar Bradley's 12th U. S. Army Group. This army he would use to protect the right flank of the attack.

The proposed use of the airborne troops evoked an enthusiastic response in the First Allied Airborne Army. Two of the units concerned, the U. S. 82nd and 101st Airborne Divisions, had not been in battle since Normandy. The British 1st Airborne, while composed of seasoned troops, had not yet been in battle as a division. The airborne units had planned no less than eighteen operations to be used in the battle for France, but none had been mounted for one reason or another—the advance of the ground troops was too rapid or higher headquarters disapproved.

On September 10, after an exchange of letters on the subject of future strategy, General Eisenhower flew to Brussels at Montgomery's urgent request. The unusual case of a Supreme Commander flying to see one of his subordinates at his call occurred because Montgomery felt he should not leave his headquarters at that stage of the battle. In the brief meeting Montgomery urged that he be given full priority for his operation. This was refused. He was given the airborne troops. The general plan for the operation was approved and he was promised 1,000 tons of supplies a day. His request for one of Bradley's armies to cover his flank was also turned down.

With these provisos, detailed planning for an operation to be known as *Market Garden* began on a high priority basis, with the target date set for just one week later, Sunday, September 17. Speed in mounting the operation was considered essential to destroy the German forces before their retreating troops could be regrouped to form any cohesive line of defense. There was some concern with regard to the adequacy of the information available on the location and strength of the Germans, but not much. No commander is greatly concerned with intelligence when he is pursuing an apparently defeated and disorganized enemy. Certainly the intelligence summaries did nothing to cause concern about severe or prolonged German resistance. German generals and other officers captured in France had reported to their interrogators that very little in the way of combat forces remained between the Allies and Berlin. The captured senior officers said that there were no troops in the Siegfried Line and that they knew of no plans for resistance. (Of course they were unaware of the plans for defending the Reich. Adolf Hitler never imagined it would be necessary to fight on German soil.)

The plan for *Market Garden* was bold and daring. Its audacity surprised friend and foe alike, especially since General Montgomery's reputation was that of a cautious tactician. He proposed with one blow to cross all the water barriers standing between the western Allies and the key German industrial area of the Ruhr, to turn the end of the Siegfried Line in the north and to open the way across the North German plains.

There would thus be not one massive assault but a series of four simultaneous attacks that would ultimately merge into a continuous front and provide a massive dagger thrust across Holland from south to north. With the Rhine River barrier crossed, the heart of Germany would be exposed.

General Montgomery's advance forces had reached the Meuse-Escaut Canal close to the Belgian-Dutch border. There was a small bridgehead across the canal at Neerpelt. He proposed to launch the ground assault from this point, using the XXX Corps of the Second British Army to drive up the main road leading to Eindhoven. The principal objec-

THE SIX BRIDGES TO ARNHEM

tives were the great bridges that spanned the broad reaches of the Maas, Waal and Rhine rivers where they flowed through the flat lands of Holland toward the North Sea. Anticipating that ground forces alone could not move fast enough to capture the bridges before German demolition crews could destroy them, Montgomery proposed to drop airborne troops on these targets and to provide a carpet over which the ground forces could advance. This was the *Market* portion of operation *Market Garden*.

The audacity of this plan, the greatest airborne assault in history, lay in the length of the carpet to be spread by the men landing from the sky. The XXX Corps was seventeen miles from Eindhoven, where the nearest airborne forces were to land. Here the U. S. 101st Airborne Division was charged with securing the road from Eindhoven to Grave. The U. S. 82nd Airborne Division was responsible for capturing the bridges at Grave, forty-two miles away, and at Nijmegen, fifty-four miles from the nearest ground forces. At the end of the carpet, sixty-four miles away, the British 1st Airborne Division was to land on the far side of the Lower Rhine at Arnhem and capture that vital bridge.

To keep the plan in proper perspective it should be noted that advances of many miles a day had not been uncommon for the British and American armored divisions during the battle for France. The British Guards Armored Division, given the assignment of the principal assault force to link together the airborne units, had made similar advances against German forces presumably better organized and in greater strength than those expected to be in the area between the Belgian border and Arnhem. The British Second Army had advanced between twenty to twenty-five miles each day from the Seine River to the Dutch border.

Yet one very important intelligence factor seems not to

have been given adequate attention, and it was information available to the planners. This was the condition of the terrain to be crossed. An earlier airborne operation planned for the Flanders area had been turned down because of the many water barriers.[2] The area in Holland chosen for *Market Garden* had exactly the same obstacles: rivers, canals and low-lying polder-ground mostly impassable for tanks and heavy equipment.

In such country the vehicles are forced to stay on the roads. The roads are built above the countryside, making vehicles prominent targets. The limited number of roads tended to channelize the forward movement and to make defense easier against the attack.

On September 10 the decision was made to proceed with operation *Market Garden*, and the operation was launched on the scheduled date, Sunday, September 17. The week was spent perfecting plans for the operation. Intelligence was a rather subordinate aspect of the considerations —not unreasonable in consideration of the generally held view of the western Allies that the Germans were beaten. The sources of intelligence were not unlimited, nor was the information reported always precise, accurate or timely. In battle there is almost a direct relationship between the proximity of the enemy and the information available. When lines are tightly held and there is daily contact between the opposing forces, prisoners of war, captured documents, patrols and reconnaissance produce a considerable amount of information on the identity of enemy units, the strength of defenses, and even on occasion what the enemy plans to do. When the situation is fluid, contact with hostile forces sporadic and no fixed front established, accurate intelligence is difficult to produce.

It was the latter situation which prevailed in September 1944. The Germans had been retreating for nearly two months, standing to fight where possible, but unable to hold out against Allied air power, armor and abundant infantry. The tenacious and bloody resistance in Normandy, and the bitter effort to dam up the Allied breakout at Mortain, had turned a disaster in the Falaise Gap into a desperate effort to get back to Germany. For the Allies it was a case of pursuit, cautious only to the degree of not wanting to lose men unnecessarily, against a retiring but still dangerous enemy who might decide to try to hold this town or that river. Allied intelligence became primarily a matter of counting the numbers of prisoners from the various German units.

This was how the situation appeared to intelligence personnel providing information to the planners for *Market Garden*. It was really a question of what remnants of what German units would be found in Holland and what the defeated enemy could do when found and with what.

There were no prisoners of war to be interrogated who could provide useful information, because the Germans were going in the wrong direction—falling back into Holland and Germany. Thus there were none who had passed through Arnhem on the way to the front and who could report having seen the shoulder patches of the Hohenstaufen and Frundsberg divisions.

Aerial reconnaissance could spot vehicles and tanks which in turn might reveal bivouac areas or collection points if the commanders were careless enough to allow them to make tracks or paths across open fields or through wooded areas. But this provided only approximate locations (perhaps temporary at that), not identity or capability.

Clandestine sources in the target area were limited as to what they could produce. The Dutch Resistance was active and bold and kept up a steady flow of reports to London. It did indeed provide valuable information; but one is apt to ascribe to the underground greater capability than actually existed. London had to be very circumspect in its queries to agents in German-held territory prior to an attack. If a message said, "We are planning to stage an airdrop at Arnhem" and the agent was captured and forced to talk, or if the message was intercepted by the Germans, then the enemy would be waiting. Indeed, if queries were consistently pointed at one target, this could be dangerous. London knew that German counterintelligence was dangerous and ubiquitous and that Resistance personnel were constantly falling into their hands.

The net result was a jigsaw puzzle with too few pieces. There were not enough solid facts, and there were different interpretations of what information was available.

There was no *hard* intelligence in the strict sense of the word on German dispositions in the area. Dutch Resistance reported that battered panzer units were resting and refitting in the Eindhoven and Nijmegen areas. This was repeated in the intelligence reports of both XXX Corps and Second Army on September 7. On September 12, Second Army speculated that the 9th and 10th S. S. Panzer divisions might be in Holland, and four days later further speculated that those units might be in the area of Arnhem. SHAEF's report on September 16, located the units in the Arnhem area, but General Montgomery's 21st Army Group intelligence staff did not agree.

A Dutch intelligence report dated September 15 had said the "S. S. Hohenstrufl was along Issjel."[3] While the name of the 9th S. S. Panzer Division was actually Hohenstaufen, there was a garble in the radio report and the name was sufficiently close for any order of battle officer to give it credence. The report was too late to affect the operation being launched (having come from Holland less than two days before the attack). If indeed it was called to the attention of the top commanders, one would expect that it would have had little impact—they would have assumed it to refer to remnants of a badly mauled division.

One can only conclude that the information was sketchy and given different interpretations. The man most directly concerned, Major General R. E. Urquhart, commanding the 1st British Airborne Division, could use his own judgment. Certainly he was not warned that his lightly armed airborne troops would land almost on top of two panzer divisions especially trained to contest airborne landings and possessing enough armor and guns to constitute a major threat to his achieving his objective.

We have dealt thus far with the intelligence available on the 9th and 10th S. S. Panzer divisions. These were well-known and respected adversaries, which had fought well and effectively in Normandy and France. Had it been accepted that significant portions of these units were in the Arnhem area, it would seem almost a certainty that the 1st Airborne would not have been dropped there—or at least not in the area where it did land.

The general assessments of German strength would have added little information:

On September 13 the 1st Airborne Corps intelligence summary said that the Germans had few infantry reserves and not more than fifty to one hundred tanks in the area.[4]

On September 16 Second Army Intelligence reported that no tanks had been seen by aerial reconnaissance over the area and that their presence near Arnhem was highly unlikely.

Also on September 16, the SHAEF intelligence summary said that the Germans had the equivalent of only eleven infantry divisions and four armored divisions to defend the entire Siegfried Line from the Swiss border to Holland. This is an interesting analysis, but rather meaningless to lower echelons interested not so much in the over-all picture as in how many enemy there might be in their assigned path of attack. If one makes the SHAEF estimate more meaningful by changing it into a net evaluation—how many Germans versus how many Allies—it produces even greater euphoria: 15 German divisions to stop seven armies with a total of 50 divisions.[5]

The intelligence officer of the 2nd Battalion of the Parachute Regiment in the 1st Airborne Division told that unit's staff that they could expect to meet about 2,000 S. S. recruits in the Arnhem area, supported by Luftwaffe ground troops from the Deelen airfield less than seven miles away.[6]

Lieutenant General Sir Frederick Browning, who commanded the 1st Airborne Corps, told General Urquhart that the 1st Airborne Division was not likely to meet more than a brigade group supported by a few tanks.[7] General G. I. Thomas briefed his 43rd Infantry Division staff to the effect that the Germans were unlikely to offer prolonged resistance and that they were not likely to be supported by more than a squadron of armor.[8]

It was with this background, and obviously with supreme confidence, that operation *Market Garden* was launched on Sunday, September 17, 1944. The weather seemed auspicious for the occasion. It was clear and sunny at the bases of the airborne troops in England and in Holland where they were to land.

The sky was filled with an air armada: 2,800 airplanes carrying paratroopers and towing 1,600 gliders loaded with more men and equipment. A considerable portion of three airborne divisions was in the sky at one time: 30,000 men were to descend on their target from above. The early hours of the operation boded well.

The 101st Airborne Division landed 6,769 men between 1:00 and 1:30 that afternoon with less than 2 per cent casualties—not much more than would be expected on a normal training exercise, let alone a landing in enemy-held territory. The 82nd Airborne was nearly as successful. And the two brigades of the 1st Airborne Division landing north of Arnhem encountered seemingly light resistance.

The 101st put the greatest number of troops on the ground most quickly. It went in on one lift—on the theory that landing closest to the actual front at that time, it would encounter the greatest enemy resistance. The 82nd went in with two lifts, while the 1st Airborne—the farthest away at Arnhem—was scheduled to go in on three lifts on three successive days: two brigades the first day and one each on the next two days.

Had the planners for *Market Garden* been more concerned about the weather or about the enemy at Arnhem, they would perhaps have reversed the priority of lifts and put all of the 1st Airborne in at once. More likely, they would have decided not to go as far as Arnhem and been content to take the bridge at Nijmegen as the farthest objective. General Browning had said that they might be going one bridge too far—and he was right.

Simultaneously with the airdrop, XXX Corps attacked out of its bridgehead at Neerpelt on the road to Valkenswaard. The Guards Armored Division used the main highway for its advance. It was flanked on the left by the 43rd British Infantry Division and on the right by the 50th British Infantry Division, which had the unenviable task of crossing low-lying, reclaimed land without many roads or paths. For XXX Corps it was a case of trying to move 20,000 vehicles down one highway.

General Montgomery had assumed the paratroopers at Arnhem would have to hold the bridge for only twenty-four hours before they received assistance from the ground troops, especially from the tanks of the Guards Armored Division. General Urquhart said his men could hold the bridge for forty-eight or even seventy-two hours.

The task of capturing the bridge at Arnhem was assigned to the 1st Parachute Brigade. It parachuted in on its drop-zone on schedule and immediately set out on the six-mile march to the bridge. The paratroopers' first choice had been to land on the polder land immediately south of the bridge but had been told that the ground was too soft. The Royal Air Force had also vetoed the nearer drop-zone as too close to the antiaircraft guns protecting the bridge. Both contentions were in error. The ground was not too soft for the landings, and the limited antiaircraft around the bridge could have been quickly put out of action by fighter bombers at the time of the drop.

It was the six miles from the drop-zone at Wolfhezen through the city of Arnhem to the bridge that may have been the most important factor in the battle, but it was the speedy reaction of the Germans that made that distance decisive.

Under normal conditions troops sixty miles from the nearest enemy—which was what the Germans at Arnhem were before the British dropped in on them—would not be expected to react quickly. Furthermore they were resting and refitting in an area presumably safe from enemy attack. It was not that the Germans did not anticipate the possibility of an airborne assault, but rather that they expected it to come to the southeast on the far bank of the Rhine at

Wesel (where in fact it did come in February 1945) and not in Holland.

The German reaction was very fast because Field Marshal Walther Model, the commander of Army Group "B" defending the area, was lunching at the Tafelberg Hotel in Oosterbeck and the British paratroopers landed almost on top of him. He barely escaped in his staff car, drove immediately to the headquarters of 2nd S. S. Panzer Corps at Doetinchem, ordered the 9th S. S. Panzer Division to get to the bridge at Arnhem and hold it. He also sent the 10th S. S. Panzer Division with utmost speed to the bridge at Nijmegen. Model was confident he could cope with the lightly-armed airborne troops if he could block off the drive north by the armor of the British Second Army.

The 1st Parachute Brigade ran into immediate trouble in trying to reach the bridge at Arnhem. Unknown to Allied intelligence, an S. S. battalion under Major Krafts had been transferred from the coastal area to the vicinity of the landing zone on the night of September 3. It went into immediate action against the British and was quickly reinforced by infantry and armor from the 9th S. S. Panzer Division.

Only one of the three battalions of the British Brigade made it to the bridge—the 2nd, commanded by Lieutenant Colonel J. D. Frost. These men were able to reach and secure the houses at the north end of the bridge by eight o'clock that Sunday evening, September 17. The 2nd Battalion missed possibly greater success by just half an hour. At 7:30, units of the 9th S. S. Panzer Division had gained control of the bridge itself and the British could not dislodge them.

The epic of Colonel Frost's battalion at Arnhem must be one of the great ones in military history. While the paratroopers could not actually take the bridge, the Germans were denied its use while the British held the northern terminus. Thus the 10th S. S. Panzer Division could not pass through Arnhem and cross the bridge enroute to Nijmegen; it had to cross the Rhine to the east on a pontoon bridge, which slowed its trip.

Frost and his men held their position not for twenty-four hours but for three and a half days—until dawn on September 21—well beyond the seventy-two hours which Urquhart had thought possible.

The other two battalions of the 1st Parachute Regiment fought desperately to get through Arnhem to their beleaguered companions at the bridge but were nearly annihilated in their efforts. Only the brigade headquarters staff, "C" Company of the 3rd Battalion and several small units got through. The second lift of the division, the 4th Parachute Brigade, which landed on Monday, was five hours late arriving and was immediately caught up in a desperate battle not far from its drop-zone, which the 1st Airlanding Brigade (glider troops) was hard-pressed to hold.

In the early stages of the fight the 2nd Battalion at the bridge took prisoners from both the 9th and 10th S. S. Panzer divisions. News that these units were in the battle made little impression either at division headquarters or elsewhere. Either these divisions were believed to have been so badly chewed up by the battles in France that their presence was not considered significant, or communications were so poor that the intelligence never seeped back.

The paratroopers were not facing 2,000 poorly equipped S. S. recruits just learning the rudiments of soldiering, as the advance briefing had predicted. They were facing 6,000 battle-hardened veterans, mostly from the 9th S. S. Panzer Division, equipped with artillery and tanks. It was more than sheer bravery could overcome; and nature, too, was on the side of the Germans.

The weather in the area, which one pre-operation report had said was "very unreliable and subject to rapid change,"[9] turned bad. On D-Day plus 2, Tuesday, September 19, the major element of the third lift—the Polish Parachute Brigade—was unable to leave the bases in England. On Wednesday, September 20, it was drizzling in Holland and the bases in England were still closed down. On D-Day plus four, Thursday, September 21, when the remnants of Frost's men surrendered at Arnhem bridge, the third lift was able to leave the airfields in England, but less than half found the drop-zone in Holland, on the south side of the Rhine. This time the Germans were waiting for them. The 1st Jagd Division had been moved up to airfields in the Ruhr to intercept the airdrops. It received advance warning by radio from the isolated German garrison at Dunkirk on the channel coast, which had been bypassed during the Allied advance, that Allied troop-transport planes were en route. The German fighters were able to inflict heavy losses on the transport planes and gliders bringing in the Polish troops. Further, since the Americans had insisted that the Allied 2nd Tactical Air Force stay out of the area during reinforcement and resupply missions, the German fighters were virtually unopposed in attacking the transport planes and gliders. Friday, September 22, was another gloomy, rainy day and air operations were grounded. By Saturday the situation at Arnhem was beyond help from the air.

The bad weather also hampered resupply by air, and as the Germans pressed in on the British, the drop-zones became fewer and more difficult to hit. Added to the intense antiaircraft fire and the presence of enemy fighters was the unhappy fact that the Germans had captured ground markers and smoke signals and used them to mislead the R.A.F. Despite heroic efforts by the flyers, who took heavy losses, most of the supply drops fell into enemy hands.

To the south, what was to have been a sprint by the Guards Armored Division up the carpet of airborne troops through Eindhoven and Nijmegen to Arnhem turned into a plodding advance and a colossal traffic jam as thousands of vehicles of XXX Corps tried to move up the one main highway. German resistance was anything but negligible; pressure from both sides of the corridor was intense as the divisions protecting the flank of the armored advance made slow progress across the low country crisscrossed by canals and waterways.

The 43rd Division took three days to advance from the Albert Canal to the Maas. It was able to help the 1st Airborne at Arnhem withdraw its survivors south across the Rhine on the morning of September 25 only by using its artillery to pound the surrounding Germans.

The 82nd Airborne captured the road bridge over the Maas at Grave and over the Maas-Waal Canal at Heuman, but collided with the 10th S. S. Panzer Division 400 yards from the road bridge over the Waal at Nijmegen. It required help from the tanks of the Guards Armored Division to secure this key bridge on September 22.

On September 22 also, the Germans had counterattacked against the narrow Allied-held corridor at Veghel and for a time all movement north was stopped until the enemy was cleared out. By then the remnants of the 1st Airborne Division at Arnhem bridge had surrendered and the plight of the rest of the division was serious.

If poor intelligence alone was not sufficient to cause defeat, there were other problems. The radios of the 1st Airborne Division failed to work on the battlefield. Radio contact between the division and the units to the south was not established until September 21, four days after the start of the battle. Hampered by a lack of information on his units, the division's commander, General Urquhart, set out to see for himself and found himself in the center of the battle, surrounded by Germans. He was out of touch with his headquarters for a considerable period of time.

Within two hours of the air landings on Sunday, September 17, the complete order for the entire airborne operation was on the desk of General Student, commander of the German First Parachute Army, whose headquarters was in Vught just seven miles from a drop-zone of the 101st Airborne Division.[10] An American officer, violating all security and intelligence regulations, had carried the order with him. When his glider was shot down and he was killed, the defenders had a prize of incalculable value.

The operation, however, was not betrayed as some have claimed. Colonel Orestes N. Pinto, a counterintelligence officer assigned to SHAEF during the period of the battle, wrote a series of articles in 1950 alleging that a double agent in the Dutch underground told Giskes, the head of the Abwehr in Holland, that the British would land airborne troops at Eindhoven. This did indeed happen, but there were two things wrong: the agent had no hard information on which to base his guess, and the Germans did not believe him.

The battle of Arnhem lasted from September 17 to September 26. It failed to accomplish its objective of securing a crossing of the Lower Rhine. It failed to open a passageway across the North German plains to Berlin. It was not a decisive mistake, since it did not cost the Allies victory in the west. It did secure important objectives, and it did provide a base for future advances. What happened at Arnhem was the result of a major intelligence error: a gross underestimation of the enemy and serious misjudgment of the terrain.

Winston Churchill commented on the battle, writing after the war: "Heavy risks were taken in the Battle of Arnhem, but they were justified by the great prize so nearly in our grasp. Had we been more fortunate in the weather, which turned against us at critical moments and restricted our mastery in the air, it is probable that we should have succeeded."[11]

The Chief of the Imperial General Staff, General Sir Alan Brooke (later Lord Alanbrooke), did not agree. In his diary he wrote: "I feel that Monty's strategy for once is at fault. Instead of carrying out the advance on Arnhem he ought to have made certain of Antwerp in the first place." (The Germans were not cleared from the banks of the Scheldt Estuary until November 26.)

Montgomery's colleague General Omar Bradley commanding the Army Group to the south, while lavish in his praise of the plan, describing it as one of the most imaginative of the war ("If successful, it would outflank the Siegfried defenses and carry Montgomery across the Lower Rhine on the shortest route to Berlin"), nevertheless objected strenuously. He said he feared that Montgomery underestimated the German capabilities on the Lower Rhine and was too ambitious for the forces at his disposal.[12]

General Sir Brian Horrocks, who commanded the British Corps, seems to substantiate General Bradley's fears. He wrote: "The failure at Arnhem was primarily due to the astonishing recovery made by the German armed forces after their crippling defeat in Normandy."[13]

Field Marshal Montgomery was inclined to place the major blame for the failure at Arnhem on Eisenhower, at

least by implication. In his memoirs he discusses why Arnhem was not a complete success and lists as the first reason
the fact that Arnhem was not regarded as the spearhead of a
major thrust to the north. But the Field Marshal fails to
make a case as to the difference this would have made.
There is no evidence that the operation was at all hampered
by any shortage of men or materiel. In fact, it could be
argued that it would have been impossible to cram more
into the assault corridor. If anything, Eisenhower's decision
to push forward on all fronts should have helped the attack
by preventing the Germans from diverting more troops to
the Arnhem area.

Montgomery is more candid in his appraisal of the
other reasons for the failure at Arnhem. He notes that the
airborne troops were dropped too far from the bridge at
Arnhem, that the weather was bad after the first day, preventing effective resupply and reinforcements, and that
even though the 2nd S. S. Panzer Corps was known to be in
the area, "We were wrong in supposing it could not fight
effectively."

Montgomery made one additional assessment. He notes
that the difficulties in clearing the approaches to Antwerp
had been underestimated.[14] It is true that if Antwerp had
been in use as a port the problem of resupply would have
been considerably eased. Resupply by air from bases near
Antwerp might conceivably have been possible on days
when the airfields in England were closed. If Montgomery
meant that first clearing the approaches to Antwerp would
have made matters easier for a major thrust to the north, he
is undoubtedly correct.

Major General Urquhart, the man on the spot commanding the 1st British Airborne Division at Arnhem,
agreed with Montgomery that the airborne troops were

landed too far from the objective, the bridge; but he points out that intelligence reports had erroneously described the polder country south of the bridge as unsuitable for airborne landings. He also notes the handicap created by committing his division piecemeal in three airlifts. In a very restrained and soldierly manner, he is the most critical of the intelligence of any of the captains involved.[15]

Urquhart says he was hampered in planning the operation for his division by scanty intelligence filtered through the Second Army to Corps to Division.[16] This situation was not helped by lack of agreement on intelligence at higher headquarters. Montgomery's 21st Army Group staff were optimistic and thought little resistance would be encountered. Eisenhower's staff at SHAEF believed the 2nd S. S. Panzer Corps would be in the area, where the 9th and 10th S. S. Panzer Divisions were resting and refitting. But the next lower headquarters, 21st Army Group, did not agree; the Corps said the Germans had few infantry reserves and not more than fifty to one hundred tanks. Lieutenant General F. A. M. Browning told Urquhart he was not likely to meet more than a brigade group supported by a few tanks.[17] This put division planning in an awkward spot. Whom were they to believe? "More and more we saw that German reactions had not been taken into account at all."[18]

It must have been frustrating for the division commander to receive such a variety of views on the enemy, filtering down through the complex inter-Allied command system: from SHAEF to 21st British Army Group to Second British Army to British Airborne Corps to the British First Parachute Division. If there was one common belief that was shared by all of the higher headquarters, it was that the Germans were not capable of serious resistance. The attack was to leapfrog nearly 70 miles into enemy-held territory and to land not far from major centers of German population, but there was no analysis of the advantages this might provide the defenders.

Part of the intelligence failure can be explained. There was inadequate hard information on German strength. In the one week between the decision to mount the operation and the attack there was not time to collect additional information on the enemy forces in the area. The information already available was insufficient.

The failure to have accurate information about the geographic features is inexplicable. The intelligence service of the Netherland government-in-exile in London was good and it had direct contact with Holland. Surely there were Dutchmen in England who could have confirmed the feasibility of dropping paratroopers and landing gliders on the polder immediately south of the bridge. If this had been done the entire 1st Parachute Regiment might have seized the bridge and held it. There is no evidence that this question was put to the Dutch.

Even more inexplicable is the assumption that XXX Corps could make speed advancing along the very limited road network between the Belgian border and Arnhem. A look at the road map would have given one clear indication: traffic jam. There was one main highway and very few secondary roads. If the polder country was unsuitable for air landings, how could it be used for the tanks and trucks of XXX Corps? If these vehicles were confined to the roads, then would not the advantage be with the defenders? A few determined defenders could slow or block the movement of vastly superior forces.

General Montgomery had a reputation for conservative and cautious operations: attack only when the situation is "tidy," and then with overwhelmingly superior forces. In this instance the superior forces were available; failure to give adequate attention to the terrain contributed to the failure to reach Arnhem in time.

Market Garden was conceived of as an airdrop on a dispirited and disorganized enemy who would not offer much resistance and who would probably welcome the opportunity to surrender. The Germans were therefore not really adequately considered in preparing the plan, and that, together with other errors—about the weather, about the terrain near the Arnhem bridge, about moving troops with speed across the polder country—led to failure. The viper in the *Market* at Arnhem was poor intelligence.

Arnhem was finally liberated April 15, 1945, less than a month before the war in Europe ended.

6.
The Bulge in the
Ardennes:
Hitler's Last Threat

DECEMBER 16, 1944

ALTHOUGH OPERATION *Market Garden* failed
to open a way across the Rhine toward the Ruhr and
Berlin, the western Allies continued their push to the east
along the entire front.

The first order of business was to clear the Scheldt
Estuary of Germans so that the great inland Belgian port of
Antwerp could be used as the major supply port. The German forces were well entrenched on the Dutch islands of
South Beveland and Walcheren, forming more than twenty
miles of the northern shores of the Scheldt. These troops
were under orders to hold on as long as possible in order to
slow the Allied supply buildup. It required an assault by the
Canadian 2nd Division westward along the Isthmus to

South Beveland, combined with an amphibious landing by the British 52nd Division on the south shore, to clear that island. By the end of October 1944, after severe fighting often in waist-deep water caused by the flooding of the sea where the dikes had been breached, South Beveland had been secured by the Allies. On November 1 an amphibious landing was made on Walcheren Island where the dikes had been bombed to flood the defenses. It took nine days to liberate this island.

The cost of opening the port of Antwerp was high, amounting to 27,633 Canadian and British casualties, and even after the Dutch islands were cleared of Germans, another two weeks were required to clear the Scheldt Estuary of mines. The first ships began unloading in Antwerp on November 26, but since mid-October the Germans had launched rocket attacks on Antwerp, using one of Hitler's "secret weapons"—the V-2—with a range of 200 miles.

By mid-November, with German ground troops cleared from the Scheldt Estuary, 21st Army Group was able to launch an attack to drive the Germans from west of the Maas, an operation completed by December 4.

To the south, troops of the American First Army surrounded Aachen on October 12 and after a bitter battle of nine days captured the city. On November 16 the First U. S. Army and the newly activated Ninth U. S. Army launched an offensive east of Aachen toward the Rhine in what the Germans called the Third Battle of Aachen, but what is better known in American military history as the Battle of the Hurtgen Forest. Here in bitter fighting in a heavily wooded area, the American 4th, 9th and 28th Infantry divisions battled strongly entrenched Germans for access to the Rhine plain. By December 3 the Ninth Army had reached the banks of the Roer River. This barrier could not be crossed until control of the great earthen dams at Schmidt was secured. In German hands the water behind these dams could be used to flood the lower reaches of the river and sweep away any bridges in American hands. Aerial bombing of the dams had failed to breach the great earthworks so the V Corps of the First Army launched an attack on December 13 to secure control of the dams.

The southern army in the 12th U. S. Army Group, General George S. Patton's Third U. S. Army, launched an attack on November 8 in the area of Metz. The city was liberated on November 22, but it was nearly mid-December before all of its surrounding forts were captured.

Still farther south the 6th Army Group, after landing on the Mediterranean Coast of France on August 15, had advanced up the Rhone Valley and by September 11 had linked up with the northern forces near Dijon. On November 14 it launched an offensive toward the Alsace plains. The First French Army, attacking on the right, forced the Germans out of the Belfort gap and reached the Rhine near Mulhouse. A large portion of the German Nineteenth Army was surrounded in a pocket near Colmar. By November 22 the French 2nd Armored Division had liberated Strasbourg and on December 12 the Seventh U. S. Army captured Hagenau.

This fighting along the western boundaries of Germany exacted heavy losses among the infantry and created an acute replacement problem for both sides. The Allies combed line of communication and air corps units for men who could be used as infantry. The Supreme Commander, General Dwight D. Eisenhower, secured the agreement of the U. S. Army Chief of Staff, General George C. Marshall, to send new units to Europe without equipment so that they could be used promptly to bolster weakened divisions in the line. Battle losses were equally difficult for the Germans to replace; they were now caught in an ever-tightening vice between the western Allies and the armies of the Soviet Union coming from the east.

On the eastern front, by the end of October 1944 the Russians had isolated a German Army Group in Latvia; advanced into East Prussia; reached the Vistula in Poland; crossed the Danube on a wide front isolating the Germans in Budapest; and captured Belgrade in Yugoslavia together with Marshal Josip Tito's partisans. But like the Allies in the west, so too the Russians had reached the extreme limit of their supply lines. They were forced to pause to rest and regroup.

Despite the threat from both east and west to the "sacred soil" of the Reich, Adolf Hitler had decided on a bold course of action. He would launch a counteroffensive against the western Allies, deliver a knock-out blow, and force them to terms.

Hitler decided to make his major effort against the west at the time that the German armies were being driven out of France. On August 19 he directed Walter Buhle, Chief of the Army Staff at OKW, and Reich Minister Albert Speer to allocate large quantities of men and materiel to the forces in the west and announced that he planned to take the initiative at the beginning of November when poor flying weather would handicap Allied use of its overwhelming superiority in the air.

As the German armies were driven back toward the Reich, Hitler ordered that every effort be made to hold to the west of the Siegfried Line, despite the skepticism of most of the generals that that system of fortification could even be manned, let alone held.

On September 13, Hitler directed that the S. S. panzer

divisions be withdrawn from combat in the west, rested and regrouped, an order that was frustrated in part at least by the airdrop at Arnhem and the commitment of the 9th and 10th S. S. Panzer divisions to that battle. He also indicated an intention to form an S. S. panzer army of some of the S. S. divisions, a plan that caused concern if not alarm among the army generals, who did not view the elite party troops as an unmixed blessing.

On September 16 (the day before the airdrop at Arnhem) Hitler held a special meeting following the daily Fuehrer conference in the military headquarters in East Prussia. Present were Generals Wilhelm Keitel and Alfred Jodl from OKW, General Heinz Guderian, the Acting Chief of Staff of the Army, which at that time had direct responsibility for the Russian front, and Luftwaffe General Werner Kreipe, representing the absent Field Marshal Hermann Goering. Kreipe's diary (kept in violation of Hitler's orders forbidding the taking of notes at his meetings) recorded that Hitler cut the usual briefing short to announce to a special group his decision to counterattack in the west, launching an offensive from the Ardennes directed at Antwerp.* Hitler said a German victory in the west could bring an end to the war, and explained why he was convinced this was possible. He directed that the OKW staff under General Jodl prepare a detailed plan for the operation and warned that nobody should be told of the plan without his personal approval.

By October 11 the OKW had produced its detailed plan and on October 22 the Chief of Staff of the Western

---

* Much has been made of the fact that the German attack was against thinly held American lines in the Ardennes. The records clearly indicate that Hitler chose the Ardennes three months before the date the offensive took place, so the disposition and strength of the American forces could not have been the decisive factor in his decision.

Command, General Siegfried Westphal, and General Hans Krebs of Army Group "B," were summoned to the East Prussia headquarters. They were immediately asked to sign a secrecy agreement on an operation entitled *Wacht am Rhein* and were informed that if there were leaks about the plan they would be shot.

Again following the usual morning conference, Hitler convened a smaller meeting and personally briefed the assembled officers on *Wacht Am Rhein*. The plan was to attack from the Schnee Eifel through the Ardennes to secure crossings over the Meuse River and then to drive past Brussels to Antwerp. This would cut off all of the American, British and Canadian forces north of a line from Luxembourg-Brussels-Antwerp with the possible destruction of thirty to forty Allied divisions. In Hitler's opinion such a disaster would result in either England or the United States or both seeking terms to end the war.

Hitler told the generals that the attack would be carried out by Army Group "B," to which three armies would be assigned: the Sixth Panzer Army to spearhead the northern drive; the Fifth Panzer Army in the center; and the Seventh Army to protect the southern flank of the offensive against a counterattack by General Patton's Third U. S. Army. He told the generals that for planning purposes they could count on thirty divisions (eighteen infantry and twelve armored) of which nine (three infantry and six panzer) would have to be withdrawn from combat in the west to be reequipped for the attack.

Hitler gave his personal word that the reinforcements would be available and that the attack would be supported by 1,500 fighter aircraft. General Keitel added that there would be 4,250,000 gallons of motor fuel available as well as a special ammunition reserve of fifty trainloads. Finally, it was ordered that the existing forces in the west, less the nine divisions to be withdrawn, would have to hold the front for the next month (the date of the attack was set for November 25). The units earmarked for *Wacht am Rhein* and held in reserve were not to be committed to battle prior to the attack.

When General Westphal returned to Ziegenberg to the headquarters of the Commander in Chief West, Field Marshal Karl Rudolf Gerd von Rundstedt, there was an opportunity to analyze Hitler's design for victory out of the hearing of listening toadies who might criticize them as defeatists for daring to disagree with the master's plan. Rundstedt, one of the most respected of the elder field marshals, said, "All, absolutely all conditions for possible success of such an offensive were lacking."[1]

During the next several days a limited number of senior officers at Oberbefehlshaber West and at Army Group "B" studied Hitler's proposed offensive. The weaknesses appeared obvious to them. The plan was overly ambitious. There were not sufficient forces allocated to reach Antwerp, even if all of those promised became available. It seemed most likely that some of the units designated for the attack would become embroiled in the defensive battle then raging along the West Wall and would not be able to rest and refit for an offensive.

The generals were much more fearful of the American ability to react than was Hitler. They estimated that the U. S. forces had at least a two-to-one superiority and might launch an offensive prior to the scheduled German attack, thus disrupting the plan. They were also concerned lest the flanks of the offensive spearhead be dangerously exposed and vulnerable to counterattack.

Perhaps most important of all, the generals were skeptical that the attack would produce any decisive result. They were concerned that it would serve only to expend irreplaceable German units and result in nothing but a bulge in the line. As an alternative they proposed to envelop the American forces east of the Meuse, an objective they believed possible with the forces available.

On October 27, Rundstedt, Siegfried Westphal, Walther Model* and Hans Krebs presented the plan to the generals designated to command the attacking armies: General Hasso-Eccard von Manteuffel of the Fifth Panzer Army; S. S. General Sepp Dietrich of the Sixth Panzer Army; and General Erich Brandenberger of the Seventh Army.

On November 2, General Jodl of the OKW staff sent further instructions on the attack to Oberbefehlshaber West. Hitler had rejected any lesser objective than Antwerp, despite the suggestions of the generals. On November 10 the operations directive signed by Hitler was issued. A request by the generals for a simultaneous holding attack in the north at Geilenkirchen was also refused by Hitler as providing a dangerous warning for the enemy. The objective remained the same grandiose one: destroy the Allied forces north of the Luxembourg-Brussels-Antwerp line.

Repeated requests to modify the plan were refused by OKW. On November 18, Rundstedt asked for a free hand in determining when the attack should be made. On November 20, at Model's request, he proposed a double envelopment to destroy the fourteen Allied divisions in the Aachen area. On November 22, Jodl bluntly advised that no changes in the plan would be made.

On November 26, Jodl visited Oberbefehlshaber West and directed that the attack take place on December 10. At

---

* Field Marshal Model, Commander Army Group "B." He was junior to Field Marshal Rundstedt, but as a devoted Nazi he had special influence with Hitler.

this time there were further arguments against the Hitler plan, again bluntly rejected.

On December 2, Hitler called a conference in Berlin and the Commander of Army Group "B," Field Marshal Model, brought in the S. S. General Sepp Dietrich and General von Manteuffel, who had a brilliant record as an armored commander, to argue for a more modest operation. Hitler listened but made no concessions. On December 6 the final draft of the operations order prepared by Oberbefehlshaber West called for a secondary thrust. Despite all the efforts of the generals, Hitler refused to modify his plans in any respect and the final operations order as issued on December 9 was exactly as presented by Hitler on October 22.

Two days later Hitler went to the command post of Oberbefehlshaber West at Ziegenberg and in two sessions, on December 11 and 12, personally briefed the commanding generals of all of the corps and divisions that were to be used in the attack. On December 12 he ordered that the attack take place at dawn on December 16. The postponements for the attack had been necessitated by the time required for preparation.

Hitler was convinced that the offensive in the Ardennes would succeed and his explanation was impressive to the generals. Again it was a combination of military theory, history and intuition that seemed to govern his views. Hitler had already demonstrated his fanatical belief in the theory of Carl von Clausewitz, the dean of German military theorists, that offensive was the key to victory. So it must be: attack, attack, attack. The strength of the enemy was not really an important consideration in his decision. If the Germans attacked with fanatical determination they would be able to crush any opposition. The OKW estimate of Allied potential for resistance was encouraging: "The enemy for the moment was at the end of his strength." Hitler knew of the Allies' supply and replacement problems. American communications security was lax and the German monitoring service picked up ample information from line units about their needs for infantry replacements. The German leader was well aware of the severe losses the U. S. forces had been taking around Aachen and in the Hurtgen Forest.

Adolf Hitler was convinced that the final decision must come in the west. He regarded an enemy on the Rhine as more dangerous than one in East Prussia. The Ruhr industrial area threatened by the Allies in the west was more important to the German war effort than was Silesia, then not too far distant from the attacking Russians in the east.

Hitler also believed that terms could be reached with the western Allies, while with the Soviet Union it was a fight to the death. (His treatment of the Russians in the captured areas and of the prisoners of war from the eastern front assured that.) His hope still remained that one day he could come to terms with the British and again the achievements of his idol, Frederick the Great, came to mind. Had not Frederick defeated coalition armies with double the strength of his forces at the battles of Rossbach and Leuthen during the Seven-Year War, and had not the alliance against Germany split? Hitler believed it could be done again.

Hitler also reminded his generals that the Schnee Eifel and the Ardennes had been the sites for the start of previous great offensives by Germany. In 1914 three of the Imperial armies had swept through the Ardennes without a fight until they had reached the Belgian-French border. This had been repeated in 1940, and this time with mechanized forces. There would be a successful third time, in 1944, according to the Fuehrer.

As he briefed his generals on December 11 and 12, Hitler noted how thinly manned the American front was in the Schnee Eifel—four divisions holding an eighty-five-mile front; two of these, the 4th and 28th Infantry divisions, battered veterans of the Hurtgen Forest battle; one of the units, the 106th Infantry Division, a total newcomer to battle in the line for the first time; and only the 99th Infantry Division an apparently formidable foe.

Hitler noted that a drive from the Schnee Eifel through the Ardennes to the Meuse between Dinant and Liege would split the British, to the north, from the Americans to the south, and in addition the inevitable problems caused by a breakthrough at a juncture of military commands could create political differences between the Allies.

Hitler placed great emphasis on the advantages of the terrain for such an attack, actually listing some obstacles as assets, and it was true that in some respects he was right.

The Eifel is an area of forested hills in Germany bordered by the Rhine, Roer and Moselle rivers, in many respects an ideal area for a military buildup. An extensive rail network from Koblenz in the south and Cologne in the north, especially developed for the 1914 offensive, provided facilities for the hundreds of troop trains needed for the projected offensives. True, there were no large cities or towns in which to billet the troops, so that units would have to be scattered and widely dispersed in the small villages and crossroad hamlets throughout the area, or would have to make do with typical soldier-made pine-bough huts in the heavily wooded areas. But the very lack of large populated areas was in itself an advantage, for it did not present any concentration of attractive targets for Allied bombers, which were inclined to pass the obviously rural and non-industrial villages. The forests provided dispersal areas with good camouflage and proper vehicle discipline could hide the troops from the persistent aerial reconnaissance of the Allies. Hitler admonished the generals not to move troops into the forward areas until immediately before the attack and promised many security-investigation teams to check that everything was camouflaged and that all vehicles followed the same roads, paths or trails so that a multitude of telltale tracks, particularly revealing in snow, did not betray troop activity.

Hitler must surely have been less persuasive with the generals about the terrain to be fought over. The Eifel offered a fine assembly area. The Schnee Eifel—a tree-covered ridge lined with West Wall fortifications running from the southeast toward the northwest—was a good launching position for the attack. But the terrain to the west where the Eifel merged with the Ardennes in Luxembourg and Belgium was not soldiers' country, regardless of the experiences of 1914 and 1940. There was an adequate network of hard-surface roads, but no single main east-west route. The nearest was the road from Luxembourg to Namur, but neither this nor any of the other roads were broad, sweeping highways like the Autobahn built across Germany by Hitler. The ten all-weather roads leading west from Germany into Luxembourg and Belgium followed narrow and twisting valleys, crossed many winding rivers and streams, passed through alternate wooded areas and open fields and formed the main streets of innumerable small villages and crossroad settlements. Military movement off the roads, especially if the ground was soft or deeply snow-covered, was out of the question for all but men on foot.

(To the non-soldier, the best way to describe the

Ardennes is to note that Echternach has been called the Luxembourg-Switzerland and that the well-paved roads in the area are intended to attract tourists.) Hitler's soldiers would find the chopped-up nature of the ground, alternate dense forests and clearings, narrow valleys, deep draws and ravines most difficult terrain.

If there were any resistance, the alternate woods and fields created limited fields-of-fire. The road system channelized vehicular movement and created targets for Allied aircraft. There could be miles of rugged fighting if the Americans chose to utilize the numerous natural defensive positions.

Hitler had one additional bonus to offer his generals as an added incentive for victory: the weather. Beyond question, one of the most feared defensive weapons available to the Allies was their overwhelming superiority in the air. In good weather this meant that any visible German could become a target. German troops in Normandy had complained that not even a single soldier could walk across an open field during the day without being chased by an Allied fighter-bomber. Thus the attack must take place when the weather would be a German ally and neutralize the air-power advantage of the Allies. Goering had promised 2,000 fighters for the attack, but Hitler, who was usually willing to accept unquestionably the inflated estimates of his subordinates, cut the figure to 1,500 and even then realized that this number of fighters over the Ardennes would be no match for the Allies in good weather.

When he had first begun to talk in August of a counter-offensive in the west, Hitler had set a target date of late November. The rains in the Ardennes were heaviest in November and December and ground fog was frequent and apt to persist. His meteorologists assured him that there could be prolonged periods of bad weather to handicap if not completely to ground the Allied aircraft. Hitler wanted a long-enough period of bad weather before the attack to complete the troop movements without aerial reconnaissance, even though most of the troop and supply trains were to move at night only. He also wanted sufficient bad weather after the opening of the offensive to achieve a decisive victory before the airplanes could intervene and turn the tide of battle.

Hitler's meteorologists may not have told their Fuehrer that weather in the Ardennes was difficult to predict: that it was a boundary where weather sweeping in from the British Isles met that moving westward out of Russia, and that sudden changes could take place. Hitler assured the generals in that second week of December that the poor weather which had persisted thus far during the month would continue until victory!

There were two final ingredients for success on which the generals were briefed: security and deception. During the planning phase all informed personnel were required to sign a secrecy pledge forbidding them to share the information about the offensive with others and advising them that if there were leaks there would be executions. Special precautions had already been taken to prevent desertions across the lines which might enable the Americans to identify any of the new units moving into the area. Patrols had been limited to prevent personnel from being captured. Orders were now given that the subordinate unit commanders were not to be briefed on the objectives of the attack until a few hours before it began.

A plan was also drawn up to deceive the Americans. The Sixth Panzer Army had moved from Westphalia to an area on the west bank of the Rhine near Cologne. No effort had been made to hide its presence from the Americans.

This was the concentration area to which the Germans wished to draw attention. While the forces in the Eifel concentration area were on a strictly enforced radio silence, the units near Cologne continued their normal traffic, confident that the American monitoring services would hear and note their presence. The Fifth Panzer Army to the south was given a cover name in a further effort to disguise its presence: the "Field Rifle Command for Special Employment."

By moving new divisions into the Eifel and then later committing them to the battle in the Aachen area, the Germans succeeded in giving the impression that they were using the Eifel sector for the same purpose as the Americans: to rest weary units and to break in new ones. The shifting of new units into the area seemed to be balanced by the transfer out of old ones.

The statistics on combat forces available to Germany were still impressive and Hitler had an obsessive faith in numbers. During July and August of 1944, despite the defeat in France and the loss of further territory on the eastern front, there had been further increases in the number of combat units listed by the Wehrmacht: 18 new divisions, 10 new panzer brigades, and 100 separate infantry battalions had been organized. In September the Wehrmacht had available—on paper at least—327 divisions and brigades. These were impressive figures. What was not apparent was that many of the listed units existed mostly on paper, and that *all* were under strength.

In September Hitler had ordered the creation of an operational reserve of another 25 new divisions. To provide the necessary manpower the draft age was lowered to sixteen and raised to fifty.

The situation along the West Wall was not good despite the convincing statistics. The German forces were taking many casualties in the intensive fighting—100,000 during November and December. On November 23, Field Marshal Model reported that with the exception of four S. S. and one army panzer division, every unit earmarked for the offensive had already been committed to the defensive battle.

These discouraging statistics did not deter Hitler, if indeed they were known to him. He was convinced that an offensive in the west might succeed. He was determined on the grandiose concept: a drive to Antwerp. He would not accept any modifications by the generals. This was to be the blow to win the war.

U. S. APPRECIATION OF GERMAN INTENTIONS

During the months of October and November the American estimates of possible German courses of action on the western front were unusually perceptive in many respects.

At the time that Aachen was captured, Weekly Intelligence Summary No. 11 of the 12th U.S. Army Group made the following observations:

The enemy continued on the defensive during the week ended 21 October along the entire Western Front from Breskens to the Swiss border. Counterattacks on an important scale were mounted only in the Aachen area. . . . There is some evidence of enemy concern over the breach of the West Wall at Aachen. . . . There is also further evidence of withdrawal of panzer divisions from the line for rest and refitting and of enemy intentions to build up a strategic reserve of armored forces in the general area of Munster and Paderborn.

The enemy's effort to build up a strong panzer force as a strategic reserve is indicative of the use the enemy makes of the time granted him by inevitable Allied delay. With the exception of the penetration at Aachen, the enemy holds the West Wall virtually intact. . . .

The enemy has so far been able to seal off or, at least, to

prevent exploitation of each Allied penetration of the West Wall by switching armor from one sector to another. He is now apparently endeavoring to build up an armored reserve and given sufficient time, say until 1 December, he could probably scrape together a powerful striking force of panzer divisions . . .[2]

The following week, after commenting on a German counterattack against the British southeast flank in the vicinity of Weert and Liesel, the 12th Army Group devoted the bulk of its General Summary to the German rebuilding effort:

During the first three weeks of October the enemy brought only one new division to the Western front, but during the week ended 28 October three new divisions appeared on the Western front and in addition two divisions that had been held in reserve were committed. It is now apparent, however, that the reorganization of the German forces during the past two months has been fully as significant as the actual rate of reinforcements and indeed more important in restoring the fighting value of enemy forces in the West.

The summary then reviewed how the Germans had initially manned the West Wall with hastily formed battle groups from units retreating from France, from fortress battalions and from training units tranferred from the interior of Germany. In the second phase, during October, the summary said, these units were formed into formal combat divisions. The third phase had been the withdrawal from the line of a large part of the panzer force for complete resting and refitting.

The report went on: ". . . The enemy's most likely and serious capability would now appear to be a counterattack with strong forces of Panzer reserves against any Allied breakthrough in the Ninth or First Army sectors which threatens to push our advance to the Rhine. . . ."

On November 4, 12th U. S. Army Group intelligence commented on the Germans' continual building up of mobile tactical reserves and on the formation of an armored strategic reserve: "Tactical reconnaissance late in the week showed what appeared to be heavy troop movements into the Northern part of First U. S. Army's sector." The Germans, it speculated, were not likely to commit the last reserve of armor in the west until vital areas were threatened, and were fully capable of increasing the rate of reinforcement to the west.

The next week the report for November 11 commented in detail on the German reaction to the offensive of the Third U. S. Army that had begun in the Metz area on November 8. It said: "The key to the enemy's essential capabilities and intentions must be found in the disposition of his Panzer and Panzer Grenadier divisions. There is none opposing the Sixth Army Group, and there are but three opposing the Third Army's advance which has already made substantial progress." After analyzing the location of the German armored units in the west and especially those associated with the Sixth Panzer Army in the Paderborn area, the General Summary of the weekly report observed:

> The enemy's most important capabilities relate to his employment of this substantial panzer reserve on which he must base his chief hope of averting defeat this year. . . . The enemy's most likely capability is believed to be the strong reinforcement of the areas Northwest, West, or Southwest of Cologne with all available panzer reserves for attack on the Northern flank of the Ninth Army or the Southern flank of the VII Corps or for counterattack against any further Eastward advance toward Cologne.

The summary for November 18 analyzed in depth the German commitments to the increasingly fierce fighting in the west and noted that all of the tactical reserve of armor had been sent into the battles on the First and Third U. S.

Army fronts, except for the Sixth Panzer Army and possibly the 9th S. S. Panzer and 2nd Panzer divisions. (On November 23, Model made an almost identical observation.) The report indicated that three new infantry divisions had arrived on the front during the week and a reformed division had been recommitted. It observed that the Germans had sent eighteen divisions to the west in September, four in October, and eight thus far in November. The 12th U. S. Army Group intelligence staff then made this assessment:

> The most important enemy capability relates to the employment of Sixth Panzer Army particularly as it may be supported by a large fighter force. German fighters have not put in a large-scale appearance since the Merseberg raid by the Eighth Air Force and their recent inactivity may perhaps be explained by preparation for heavy support of ground forces. . . .
> If our attacks can be contained by the infantry and the tactical reserves that have been committed, it is obvious that the enemy will have no necessity for employing his strategic panzer reserve in an essentially defensive counterattack. He will then be in a position to launch a major counteroffensive. . . .

On November 25, Army Group again analyzed the increasing involvement of new German units in attempting to contain what were now three Allied offensives: by the first Army in the Aachen area, by the Third Army in the Saar Basin, and by the 6th Army Group in the Vosges. (These were the types of attacks that had worried Rundstedt's staff when they first reviewed Hitler's plan on October 12.) Again, the location and possible use of the German Sixth Panzer Army was a major consideration. The report said:

> The fact that the Sixth Panzer Army is concentrated in the Cologne Corridor necessitated placing major emphasis on the enemy capabilities of using these forces in either a counterattacking or a counteroffensive role in the First and Ninth US Army sectors. . . . This counteroffensive use of the Sixth Panzer

Army is a capability that appears less probable now than it did a week ago. . . . Enemy action in this respect cannot be predicted at this time. . . .

Then on December 2, 12th U. S. Army Group Intelligence Summary dropped all mention of a possible counteroffensive. The Germans seemed to be so heavily committed to the defensive battles along the West Wall and appeared to be taking such heavy losses that it now seemed mainly a question of whether they could hold the line. The summary estimated German casualties in the 12th U. S. Army Group area alone at 100,000 for November. In the all-out defense at the line of the Roer River, the Germans had put in sixteen divisions on a front of thirty miles. The attrition of manpower in this area was producing "an acute situation" and "at no time since September has such a critical dilemma confronted the enemy."

The last intelligence summary of the 12th U. S. Army Group before the German offensive in the Ardennes is worth quoting in full. It was issued December 12 for the week ending December 9.

1. *General Summary*

It is now certain that attrition is steadily sapping the strength of German forces on the Western Front and that the crust of defenses is thinner, more brittle and more vulnerable than it appears on our G-2 maps or to the troops in the line.

Two outstanding facts support this unqualified statement:

a. The first is that there is ample evidence that the strength of the infantry divisions that have been in the line on active sectors since the beginning of our offensives has been cut at least 50% and several other divisions are known to have been virtually destroyed. It is true that these emaciated divisions are supported by ten battered Panzer or Panzer Grenadier type divisions which make up the tactical reserves and by the fattening and still untouched Sixth SS Panzer Army. It is also evident, however, that to keep these infantry divisions alive at all the enemy has had to give them almost daily transfusions from the fortress troops which were once counted as a separate source of strength.

b. The second fact is that while the enemy's minimum replacement need in the face of our offensive is twenty divisions a month, the estimated total available to him from all sources, for the foreseeable future, is fifteen a month. Recently the enemy has not been even able to keep up this rate—his replacement rate for several weeks being only two or three a week.

These two basic facts—the deathly weakness of the individual infantry division in the line, plus the inevitability of the enemy falling still further in replacement arrears—make it certain that before long he will not only fail in his current attempt to withdraw and rest his tactical reserve but he will be forced to commit at least part of his Panzer Army to the line.

The enemy's primary capabilities continue to relate to the employment of the Sixth Panzer Army but it may not be possible for the enemy to have complete freedom of choice as to the time and place of its employment. The situation is becoming similar to that which existed at Caen and St. Lo. In the Normandy situation the enemy committed his armor at Caen with the result that when he needed it to control the St. Lo breakthrough he had difficulty in disengaging it. It was badly battered by the time it could be brought against the American forces. A break-through by the Third and Seventh U. S. Armies could easily develop into a similarly disastrous "end run" and Rundstedt appears to be determined to avoid the Normandy mistake. The decision to commit it will be forced upon him, however, by Allied pressure and his inability to supply adequate infantry reinforcements to the line. The enemy, furthermore, may have little discretion as to whether he will commit this armor in the North or in the South. Rundstedt must appreciate that a break-through in the Cologne-Dusseldorf area spells disaster. This is amply demonstrated by the fact that he immediately located this armor behind the line in that area. He must also realize that a break-through of the West Wall in the Strasbourg-Saar area would also have the gravest consequences. If the situation deteriorates seriously in the South, he will be forced to transfer some of the armor quickly to that area. At the same time, he must keep a strong reserve in the North to deal with a potential break-through in that area.

If lack of adequate infantry reinforcements requires the commitment of his strategic reserves, the enemy's capability of counterattacking any bridgeheads established East of the Roer is greatly diminished. Similarly the capability of mounting a major counteroffensive would be virtually destroyed if his armor is already engaged. All of the enemy's major capabilities, therefore, depend on the balance between the rate of attrition imposed by the Allied offensives and the rate of infantry reinforcements. The balance at present is in favor of the Allies. With continued Allied pressure in the South and in the North the breaking point may develop suddenly and without warning.

If the 12th U. S. Army Group estimate was optimistic, there was an equally optimistic appreciation of enemy strength in the operations order for an attack southeast from the Nijmegen area to destroy the German forces remaining between the Meuse and Rhine Rivers, signed by B. L. Montgomery, Field Marshal, C-in-C, 21st Army Group, dated December 16. It stated in part:

3. The enemy is at present fighting a defensive campaign on all fronts; his situation is such that he cannot stage major offensive operations. Furthermore, at all costs he has not the transport or the petrol that would be necessary for mobile operations, nor could his tanks compete with ours in the mobile battle.

4. The enemy is in a bad way; he has had a tremendous battering and has lost heavily in men and equipment. On no account can we relax, or have a "stand still," so as not to allow him time to recover and so as to wear down his strength still further. There will be difficulties caused by mud, cold, lack of air support during periods of bad weather, and so on. But we must continue to fight the enemy hard during the winter months.

THE ATTACK

At dawn on December 16 the Germans launched simultaneous attacks at five places along a seventy-mile sector,

THE BATTLE OF THE BULGE

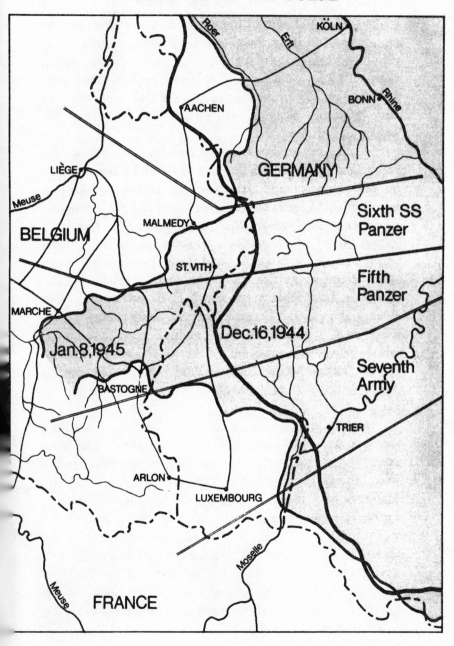

striking the VIII Corps of the First U. S. Army. The element of surprise was great, heightened by a disregard of the terrain in selecting points for the attack, particularly in using armored forces in areas not considered good for tank warfare. The attacks in many areas initially appeared light and were originally viewed by the Americans as possibly reconnaissance in force.

It was not until the second day that the attack was recognized by U. S. Headquarters to be an all-out counteroffensive and not just a raid. German airborne troops had been dropped behind the American lines and the Luftwaffe was making its greatest effort since Normandy. The Sixth Panzer Army was identified as spearheading a northern drive directed at Malmedy and Liège. Its principal units were identified as the 1st S. S. Panzer Division (Liebstandarte Adolf Hitler), the 2nd S. S. Panzer Division (Das Reich), the 9th S. S. Panzer Division (Hohenstaufen), and the 12th S. S. Panzer Division (Hitler Jugend). The southern spearhead was the Fifth Panzer Army, directed at crossing the Meuse between Dinant and Namur. The Seventh Army attacked into Luxembourg in the Echternach region.

Hitler's plan for a quick victory and dream of reaching the Meuse in twenty-four hours was frustrated from the start. The northern offensive encountered stubborn resistance. All efforts of the 12th S. S. Panzer Division to capture Malmedy were frustrated. The 7th U. S. Armored Division, hurriedly rushed into key defensive positions around the vital road junction of St. Vith, held that position until December 22 against the 2nd S. S. and 9th S. S. Panzer divisions. To the south the Fifth Panzer Army failed to capture Bastogne, although surrounding it and at one point, on December 24, using nine divisions in a futile effort to overrun the Americans holding the city.

On December 23 the weather cleared and Allied fighter-bombers began to take heavy casualties of German units. Good weather enabled Bastogne to be resupplied from the air until the city was relieved on December 26 by the 4th U. S. Armored Division of General Patton's Third Army driving up from the south.

The deepest penetration achieved by the attack was that of the 2nd Panzer Division, which on December 24 had cut the Ciney-Dinant road. It was four miles short of the Meuse River. But the 2nd Panzer Division paid a high price for its advanced position. The bulk of the division was caught at Celles out of gas and was wiped out by counterattacking American troops.

Hitler's bold gamble had failed. For the next two weeks the German units in the bulge fought desperately to prevent themselves from being crushed between the American armies to the north and south of them. By the second week in January it was a salvage operation, with the German infantry divisions trying to hold while the remnants of the panzer armies were withdrawn, led by the S. S. By January 23 the First U. S. Army had driven into St. Vith and the Germans were back to their starting line.

The bulge in the Ardennes had been a costly battle for both sides. It cost the Americans 70,000 casualties, but they had fought a brilliant defensive battle and had beaten the Germans decisively. Hitler's armies had suffered irreplaceable losses and gained only a momentary bulge or salient in the American lines, just as Field Marshal Rundstedt had predicted.

The Germans lost 100,000 men—one-third of the attacking force. Gone were 800 of the 2,000 tanks and assault guns that had taken part, 1,000 aircraft had been lost. In its intelligence summary of December 9 the 12th U. S. Army Group's use of the analogy of the German situation at Caen and Saint-Lô with that along the West Wall had not been so far wrong, although it had evolved differently. Just as the use of German armor at Caen had made it impossible to stop the breakout at Saint-Lô, so the use of German armor in the Ardennes had expended a force that could have been available later to contest the inevitable attacks from west and east.

On January 12 the Russians launched their winter offensive. There were no German reserves to oppose them. In the west, on March 7 the 9th U. S. Armored Division captured intact the railway bridge over the Rhine River at Remagen and American troops poured across to the east bank. A little over two weeks later, on March 23, elements of the Third U. S. Army crossed the Rhine south of Mainz. On the same day in the Wesel area north of the Ruhr, British, Canadian and U. S. forces, with the aid of an airdrop, landed on the east bank of the Rhine. Three days later the encirclement of the Ruhr commenced. It took just one week. The great industrial area was lost to Hitler and 325,000 prisoners were captured.

General von Manteuffel, commander of the Fifth Panzer Army, summarized it succinctly:

"The defensive power of the German forces in the West has been decisively impaired and the last strategic possibility of holding the decisive Rhine front has vanished."[3]

HOW IT HAPPENED

It is not too difficult to understand why Hitler ordered an offensive in the Ardennes.

He really believed that a third victory could be launched from the Eifel through the Ardennes. He was not oblivious to the hazards of such an effort, as is indicated by his respect for the Allied air superiority. He recognized the necessity for surprise and a strong and decisive blow to crack the thin line of U. S. forces holding the VIII Corps front. He knew his forces had to reach the Meuse in twenty-four to forty-eight hours or risk disaster.

But this time Hitler made a mistake fatal to most commanders. He completely underestimated the enemy. The attacks in the Ardennes in 1914 and 1940 had been in good weather, against little resistance, and by forces with an overwhelming superiority. The roadnet had been adequate and the terrain had not been an obstacle to the attackers.

This time, however, few of these factors were helpful. The weather was bad, which at first did provide cover and protection against Allied air, but it also made vehicular travel difficult on slippery and narrow roads and cross-country movement a well-nigh impossibility.

Hitler's forces not only did not have superiority, except in the first hours of the attack, but they were to face an enemy who would ultimately have a decisive superiority. Even more important, the initial resistance of the Americans could not be brushed aside lightly except in isolated instances. The Americans fought tenaciously as individuals, in isolated squads and platoons, by company and battalion, and used all of the natural defensive features of the terrain to greatest advantage.

Hitler's estimate that the Americans lacked reserves in the immediate area of the attack was correct. German intelligence had accurate information on the U. S. order of battle. What Hitler did not appreciate was the speed with which the Americans could and would move forces to meet the attack, or that they would display tactical brilliance in recognizing and holding those positions most calculated to delay or defeat the German offensive: Malmedy, St. Vith, Bastogne.

Hitler counted on creating frictions between the Allies

by attacking near the juncture of the British and American forces. The attack did create differences between the British and Americans. Momentary unhappiness and some permanent scars were created by the necessity to transfer the command of the U. S. First and Ninth armies from General Bradley's 12th U. S. Army Group to Field Marshal Montgomery's 21st Army Group. The German spearhead through the First U. S. Army lines made command of the northern forces from Bradley's headquarters in Luxembourg difficult. A great deal was made of this by the British and American press, but there was never much possibility of a permanent break between the Allies. In fact, it was remarkable how little friction developed between allies with such a disparity in assets, based together initially in the narrow confines of the British Islands, and under the command of strong-willed men of differing views on how to win the war.

If Hitler had counted on the capture of any appreciable amount of American supplies to support the offensive, this failed to materialize. The U. S. forces stubbornly held in the north, blocking the path to Liège where there were vast supply dumps. In most instances where supplies had to be abandoned in the initial assault, every effort was made to destroy or render the equipment useless.

But how could the American forces have been caught so completely by surprise?

The most precise answer is that of an intelligence failure in all respects. There was no hard intelligence information available indicating either the intention of the Germans to launch a counteroffensive, or the time and place of the attack. Without this information there could be no command decision to move forces into position to meet the enemy offensive or to launch a spoiling attack. Thus there was no reason to do more than was done, which was to recognize that the VIII Corps area was held by a dangerously thin line of troops and could be the target for an enemy counterattack.

On the basis of the information available, which was a fairly accurate order of battle of the German forces including those out of the line and not in contact with the American front units, the Allied intelligence estimates as reflected by the 12th U. S. Army Group Weekly Intelligence Summaries were a reasonably accurate reflection of the situation. There was no precise information available on German intentions other than what could be produced by analyzing what the enemy was doing and projecting on the basis of this what he might do in the future. This analysis consistently produced the reflection of the German intention to hold the line of the West Wall at all costs; to do everything possible to block the Allies from reaching the Rhine, or even more important, to prevent them from crossing it; and to hold the great industrial area of the Ruhr.

The withdrawal of German armor from the line had been carefully watched. Special attention was paid to the location and activities of the Sixth Panzer Army. It was correctly estimated that the German effort to get the armor out of the line and to hold the Sixth Panzer Army in reserve was for the purpose of counterattacking against the most severe Allied threat. During November the Army Group intelligence estimates even spoke of the possibility of a counteroffensive, and only dropped this plan for the Germans after the battles at Aachen, in the Saar and in Alsace had forced the commitment of more and more of the armor deemed necessary for any successful offensive. It is interesting to compare this development with Hitler's injunction that the units earmarked for the offensive should not be committed prematurely in the defensive battles, and with Field Marshal Model's observation on November 23 that only five of the twelve panzer divisions designated for the attack were still out of line.

The close parallel in the views of American intelligence and those of the German commands are noteworthy, and therein lies the basis for the major mistake on the part of U. S. intelligence. For it was not the German generals who were making the decisions or determining the strategy. It was Adolf Hitler. Field marshals Rundstedt and Model had urged a "small solution" on Hitler. Model persisted in this effort until December 2, just two weeks before the offensive was launched. It was the "small solution" which American intelligence was predicting: a spoiling counterattack by the Sixth Panzer Army against the most dangerous of the Allied threats, whether on the Cologne plain, in the Saar or in Alsace.

No general in his right mind would have made a decision to thrust a narrow armored spearhead deep into the American lines in an area where rapid withdrawal was impossible and where the sole protection against air attack was the most unpredictable of contingencies: the weather. Nor would a professional military man have chosen the terrain of the Eifel and Ardennes for an attack in the winter. And the commitment of the last of the possible reserves in a desperate gamble was not among the acceptable solutions at any military staff college.

Thus, failure to be constantly aware that Adolf Hitler alone made the strategic decisions, led Allied intelligence to place their commanders in a position where they could be surprised. So little was an offensive in the Ardennes considered to be a proper course for the German armies in the west, that Field Marshal von Rundstedt after the war made it clear to interrogators that he resented the tendency of some commentators to describe it as "the Rundstedt offensive."

The failure of Allied intelligence officers to anticipate the German offensive in the Ardennes, because they estimated what the enemy would do on the basis of what skilled professional generals would do under such circumstances, and not what Adolf Hitler might do, was a direct result of the failure of intelligence collection. No intelligence source produced information about Hitler's planned offensive. There were several bits and pieces of information which could be taken as indications of the coming attack. But none of these came from sufficiently credible sources or were conclusive evidence under the circumstances.

A look at those sources and other information available indicates some of the pitfalls of combat intelligence.

One of the most prolific sources of intelligence in warfare is the prisoner of war. Soldiers of every army are enjoined to tell their captors only their name, rank and military number and to remind the enemy interrogators that no more is required under the Geneva Conventions on the treatment of prisoners. But capture is a traumatic experience; when a man suddenly finds himself in the hands of people who have been doing their best to kill him and who have been described to him in the most horrifying terms, the vow of silence may well seem much less important than placating a captor who has him completely under his control. Soldiers do talk, and when they discover that their captors know as much or more about their own units than they themselves do, they see even less reason to keep silent.

During periods of intense combat, prisoners are taken by both sides. When a battle line is stable fewer prisoners are taken, and these almost always as a result of the patrolling undertaken to determine what the enemy is doing. Prior to the German attack out of the Eifel the battle line was relatively stable throughout the area. Few prisoners were taken and most of these knew only what was happening in their immediate area. As was noted, special precautions had been employed by the Germans to prevent desertions—security units watched the troops—and patrolling had been restricted to prevent prisoners from falling into American hands. In several areas the front was along river lines, which tended to reduce patrolling and line-crossing. Thus prior to December 16 very few German prisoners were taken who could report on the troop buildup in the Eifel, and none had specific details of the attack.

Another source of intelligence—captured documents—also declined with the drop-off in battle action. Again, even though soldiers are ordered not to carry papers which will give the enemy information, most soldiers usually carry a pay book or record which not only identifies their unit but will often provide a complete history of their military career. Officers, as has been noted, are sometimes foolish enough to carry orders or battle plans. Prior to the German attack no revealing documents were captured.

One of the prolific and revealing sources available to Allied intelligence was aerial reconnaissance, either pilot observations or photographs. The photographs were very useful for study and analysis over a period of time. Visual observations were useful too, but were subject to possible error as aircraft traveling at hundreds of miles an hour are not the best possible platform from which to count tanks or trucks on a road or guns in an emplacement. Hitler's choice of the poor weather period in late November and December for the buildup, combined with the restriction of most movement to night hours, limited this source.

Communications intelligence was also a valuable and

prolific source and one on which the Allies placed great—
perhaps too great—dependence. It is almost an axiom that
the security of military communications must of necessity
decrease in direct relation to the proximity to the battle line
and to the time available to get the message through. The
squad or platoon leader must shout his orders to his men,
and the enemy can hear him if within hearing range. The
company commander will use a runner if a man can move
around the battlefield and live. The company commander
will use a field telephone if the lines can be kept unbroken.
The battalion commander must of necessity use a field telephone or radio to his companies, and if it is an armored or
flying unit the tanks and planes will use radios. From that
echelon up, electronic communications are almost a necessity under conditions of modern warfare, and these can be
heard by any listener on the proper wave length unless they
are on a landline. Landlines are difficult to maintain in a
battle zone. Wires are cut by shellfire and bullets, and units
are constantly on the move. Landlines can also be tapped by
enemy patrols.

As a consequence the bulk of military communications
in battle are by radio, encoded or disguised to the extent
possible under the circumstances. In action there is no time
to spend encrypting or decoding messages, so generally the
best possible security depends on a few code words, which
usually become quickly known to the enemy.

"Lucky Forward" (Third U. S. Army Forward Headquarters) "this is Eagle Tac" (12th U. S. Army Group Tactical Headquarters) was a salutation which was probably as
well known to the German monitors as it was to the American operators during the battles on the western front. And
the American monitors were equally familiar with the call
signs of the German units.

It was for this reason that Hitler forbade any use of

electronic communications to handle messages related to the December 16 attack. All operational plans and orders were carried by messengers and couriers—usually officers— and unless the messengers strayed into the Allied lines, the information was secure. Thus, looking for clues concerning enemy action from communications intelligence can lead to serious error. This source produced no specific information on the impending attack in the Ardennes.

A final source of intelligence that might have produced information on the German attack was espionage. This was usually the most limited source of all. The spy had to be a very senior officer in one of the headquarters planning for the attack or assigned to one of the units designated to take part in the operation. In the case of the Ardennes offensive this meant the OKW staff, C-in-C West and Army Group "B" before October 22; the staffs of the commanders of the Fifth Panzer Army, Sixth Panzer Army and Seventh Army after October 22; and the division and brigade commanders after December 11 and 12. The odds were almost overwhelming against one of these men being an Allied agent.

Other possibilities existed for Allied espionage to obtain some advance information about the attack. Allen Dulles, representing the United States Office of Strategic Services in Switzerland, had top-level penetrations of the German Foreign Ministry and military headquarters in Berlin. But there was no information on Hitler's plan available there. Nothing was forthcoming from these sources. The Soviet intelligence services still had agents in Germany, but if Moscow received any information of a possible attack, no warning was sent to the western Allies. The Russians in fact did not even provide the Allied forces in western Europe with the German order of battle on the eastern front.

There were few other possibilities for intelligence from

espionage on the Ardennes offensive. Opportunities to place agents behind the German lines became fewer and fewer when the western forces reached the German border. The Allies were assisted in France, Belgium and Holland by the intelligence services of those countries and by very active Resistance forces behind the German lines. Intelligence provided by these patriots was exceptionally good in most instances.

Concerned lest German security measures block Resistance groups from collecting needed information when the liberating forces landed in France in June 1944, Allied intelligence working together—Americans, British and French—had parachuted more than fifty teams into the German-occupied countries of western Europe prior to the landing in Normandy. These teams, each with an observer and radio operator, were dropped near key transportation centers and other military targets to collect essential intelligence. They provided a great deal of important information, and German security did not succeed in putting the Resistance out of action; so it too continued to be an important source of information for the Allies.

All this ended at the German border. What resistance to Hitler and his Nazis that had existed inside Germany had been crushed after the abortive effort of July 20, 1944, on the Fuehrer's life. Despite the fact that most Germans wanted the war over, they were not ready to betray relatives and friends fighting in their nation's armed forces. There were slave laborers in Germany, conscripted from the occupied countries, but few of these made their way to the border area, and what information they had was generally of a low level. Quite frequently the Germans evacuated all civilians from the battle area. This not only lessened the number of possible informants, but it made it even more difficult for strangers to move around without attracting the attention of the security forces.

It was general procedure for each of the American armies in the field in Europe to have assigned to it field units of the Office of Strategic Services, one of which was charged with collecting intelligence through contact with the Resistance or from agents put through the German lines. The First U. S. Army did not have an OSS—secret intelligence—unit. The unit which had landed with the army in Normandy had been reassigned to the 12th U. S. Army Group at the request of the G-2 of the First Army. From Army Group this unit still attempted to collect intelligence on German activity along the First Army front, but the results were not terribly valuable.

There were two ways in which the OSS field units were able to put agents behind the German lines. The most practical method was to send the agent across the line on foot. If the line was thinly held an agent could slip across at night. But once across, the agent, if in civilian clothes, would have great difficulty moving around any evacuated area. If in German uniform, he would face questioning by Feldpolizei and have to answer a multitude of questions. In either case the result could be a quick execution, or perhaps even worse in the long run, being turned over to the Gestapo—Hitler's dread Geheime Staats Polizei.

In view of the difficulty of putting agents on foot through the front-line area, the OSS sometimes dropped agents by parachute not far behind the front. These men had to be dropped at a low altitude from planes sufficiently fast to move in and out of the antiaircraft areas. This was not ideal for agent-dropping. The usual technique was to drop agents from slow planes at low altitudes—slow so the agent had a chance to get his parachute open and to land near his target, and low so that he was not hanging suspended in the sky for any longer than was necessary, with the possibility of being seen or shot. But agent-dropping planes are not supposed to fly in areas of antiaircraft.

In the winter of 1944 there were not many agents getting into the Eifel area, and even fewer returning with any information of use.

These were the combined ingredients of the intelligence failure in the battle of the bulge in the Ardennes: an esimate based on what the German generals would be expected to do; inadequate hard intelligence on the enemy because of German communications security; weather preventing aerial reconnaissance; no spies; and few prisoners.

It could happen again. In fact, it has happened again: in Vietnam. Even with the great advance in the development of intelligence techniques, the organization of a competent national intelligence system, and the ever-increasing awareness of military commanders of the necessity of knowing about the enemy. If there is inadequate advance preparations and planning there will be failures.

7.
The Brilliance of
Hindsight

IN THE BRILLIANCE of hindsight it might be argued that in these five battles the failure of intelligence to provide the captains with the information necessary for victory could have been avoided. Or perhaps if the leaders had used their forces with greater skill the battles could have been won despite the lack of adequate advance information about the enemy.

In the case of each battle, much has been printed claiming how the disaster could have been averted if the leader had listened to this intelligence officer or to that advisor, or if he had made a different decision from the one he did.

1. In the German attack on Russia it could be argued

that if Hitler had listened to the brilliant armored expert General Heinz Guderian and his estimate of Russian tank strength, or to the high-ranking military men who did not believe it wise to launch a war on two-fronts, he would not have attacked Russia when he did. As noted, Hitler told Italian Foreign Minister Galeazzo Ciano several months after the attack that had he realized the strength of the Soviet Union he might not have started the war. This was a relatively brief moment of clarity and candor, for Hitler compounded the error many times before the end of nearly four years of bitter fighting between Russia and Germany. He refused consistently to listen to the generals' advice or to allow the military to fight the war.

Hitler's ruthless effort to destroy the Soviet Union was matched only by his total failure to estimate the war capacity of Russia. His unfounded optimism was fed by the early victories of the German troops in the summer of 1941, and he failed to weigh any evidence or hear any view that did not agree with his conviction of early and complete success.

No preparations were made for adversity. Bad news was greeted not by rational and sensible preparations, but by blind stubbornness and determination. Hitler may have engaged in self-reiterated assurances that he had always been right and would forever continue to be so. Rather than permit his generals to withdraw the forces in Russia to shortened lines for the winter of 1941-42, he insisted that they hold every foot of conquered territory. While the Germans may have saved much heavy equipment that would have been lost in a withdrawal, they nevertheless spread thin irreplaceable and limited manpower and ignored the potential of the Russian reserve armies.

Hitler committed that error so frequently associated

with the careers of dictators. He rid himself of all advisors who did not agree with him, as well as those who were inclined to argue with him about his proposals, and even those whose grudging obedience caused him to worry about their loyalty. The result was mediocrity in the high levels of the German command.

By the time of the planning for the attack on Russia in the fall of 1940, there were few around Hitler who cared— or dared—to question the probability of success. That there were serious questions which should have been answered before the start of this phase of the war is beyond dispute. If after the visit of the Russian mission to the tank factories, any German officer was concerned that the Red Army might have better tanks, this question should have been answered before the attack took place.

2. Hitler's attack on Russia achieved initial success because his opponent possessed some of Hitler's fatal characteristics. If Joseph Stalin had listened to his intelligence service or to the warnings from the British or Americans, might not the Red Army have been more alert? Stalin was convinced he had more time, and he did not wish to alarm the Germans by making military moves which Hitler might consider provocative. Like Hitler, he had little faith or confidence in his intelligence service and preferred to rely on his own judgment and intuition rather than heed what seems to be, in retrospect, valuable evidence of danger.

In any society, communist or capitalist, the balance of authority and influence between the military and civilian leaders is an important issue. It was an issue which the Russians had not properly faced at the time of the German attack in 1941, and which has troubled the communist state both before and since that time.

Outside observers, unable to be present at policy meetings or to know the proposals by various elements of the government in the Kremlin, have to assess the relative influence of the civilian and military authorities by seemingly superficial indications until the tests of time and trial give a more accurate evaluation. The numbers of military members of the Central Committee of the Communist Party of the Soviet Union, or of its Politburo or Presidium, give one indication. The prominence given in the press to statements by the marshals or the generals give another. The influence of the political commissars in the military forces is yet a third, coupled with such a basic factor as the degree of distinction permitted between officers and other ranks in the forces.

But the true test of the balance of authority between the civilians and the military comes in the allocation of resources for national defense, in the development of national strategy and in the conduct of war.

The fact that the German attack on the Soviet Union in 1941 achieved outstanding initial success must in part be attributed to the overwhelming domination of the Russian military by civilian authorities at that time. There can be no questioning of the right of civilian authorities to exercise controls over the military in any form of government except that which is exclusively and totally military. But where civilian authorities dominate the decision-making process in matters exclusively military even for—or perhaps one should say *exclusively* for—political reasons, then national catastrophe may result.

The purges of the late 1930's reduced the competence of the Soviet military forces. If one can give any credibility to the alleged justification for this bloodbath—that the military were disloyal to the regime, then presumably it could be explained as the civilian authorities taking steps to assure military subordination to the government and the party. If the purge of the military was the result of a deception operation by Hitler, in which he planted false evidence that the Russian General Staff had been plotting with the Germans, then it was a brilliant pre-battle victory for the Nazis.

Regardless of the reasons for the purges in the Russian military forces in the 1930's, the result set up a chain reaction which created an even greater imbalance between the civilian and military authorities. Only a very brave or a very foolish Russian general would have opposed Stalin too vigorously on such a key matter of national strategy as the disposition of forces in the territories occupied by the Red Army after the partition of Poland in 1939. It seems apparent that the predominant view of the General Staff was to put only light forces in those areas and to keep the principal forces in reserve well inside the Soviet Union. (Such a strategy was too closely associated with the ill-fated Marshal Tukhachevsky, who had been executed in the purge, to have been expressed vehemently.) Yet it was the civilian Stalin whose view prevailed, with the result that the bulk of the Russian forces were in the newly occupied territories with incomplete fortifications and poor communications, and great numbers were lost in encirclements by fast-moving German armor.

Stalin's domination over all military matters in Russia, at least until the early disasters of 1941 forced him to bring more military advisors into the inner councils of the Soviet Union, has been testified to by such authorities as Professor Vasily S. Yemelyanov. Yemelyanov was in weapons production during the Second World War (and later helped develop the Soviet atom bomb). In his memoirs in *Novy Mir* he describes how Stalin intervened in a technical debate on armor and directed the construction of tanks with two-ply armor which were worthless and had to be abandoned. If the Russian leader's influence dipped to this level of technical decision, then his views on national strategy must have been unassailable.

Any final judgment on Stalin's role in strategy could only be made with full knowledge of the courses of action presented to Stalin by his advisors, how much weight he gave to the advice, and why he finally selected the course that he took. It seems obvious that on such a fundamental issue of national strategy as the disposition of defensive forces against the obvious and growing German threat, Stalin the civilian overrode the military on two political grounds. The first was Stalin's conviction that having the forces forward in what had been the eastern areas of Poland gave him greater bargaining power in his competition with Germany for influence in the Balkans. The second was that strong forces in the forward area would prove a greater deterrence than if held in reserve. In both cases Stalin was wrong.

3. The senior American officers in Hawaii had received a message on November 27, which opened with the words, "This is a war warning." On the basis of this, why was the fleet surprised in Pearl Harbor? Why were the battleships caught at anchor in port? Why were there no air patrols to the north and northwest? If there was an alert, why was there surprise?

It can be argued that the alert at Pearl Harbor—and the degree of readiness of the fleet (and the army)—was appropriate for what was expected to happen in that part of the Pacific at the end of November 1941. There were few Americans who did not expect Japan to enter the war; a Japanese move had long been anticipated. Sometimes the longer one waits for something to happen, the less one is prepared when it does happen.

There was also a multiple choice as to where Japan might strike. In December 1941 the choices were in this order of priority: (1) Thailand; (2) Malaya; (3) The Netherlands Indies; (4) The Philippines; (5) The Maritime Provinces of the Soviet Union. One could add a sixth choice: Pearl Harbor. An attack on the base had been mentioned and speculated about as a possibility.

Again in retrospect, what was being said in so many words by American officials was, "We have no hard evidence as to specific Japanese intentions, but based on what information we do have, these seem to be the most likely courses of action."

There are few nursery tales more familiar to Americans than the fable about crying "wolf." And one cannot but have the feeling that the commanders in Hawaii were the victims of repeated wolf warnings: the Japanese are going to attack to the west, to the south, to the north, to the east!

True, the man on the spot must take the ultimate responsibility, but they, like their peers in Washington, and indeed the Commander in Chief, were all captains without eyes. The United States government had not considered a modern intelligence service essential in peace time.

4. The Japanese attacking Pearl Harbor benefitted from *almost* flawless intelligence. They knew from agent reports where the battleships would be anchored. Agents had advised that the fleet would probably be in port on Sunday, as this seemed to be the American custom. The Japanese had studied the British torpedo-plane attack on the Italian fleet in Taranto. The pilots trained intensively on how to launch torpedoes in shallow water. They attacked the airfields simultaneously to block a counterattack, and were wary and apprehensive about the location of the American carriers. The Japanese counted on surprise, and achieved it.

The only Japanese intelligence failure was an underestimate of the ability of the Americans to recover from disaster and to retaliate. Tactically this resulted in the Pearl Harbor attackers neglecting the ship-repair facilities and the petroleum storage areas. The repair facilities contributed to a rapid return to action of the U. S. Pacific Fleet. The loss of the fuel oil would have immobilized the fleet until more could have been brought from the mainland.

Japanese intelligence failed to properly assess the American reaction to the attack. Some believed the United States might seek terms after the loss at Pearl Harbor. Others were convinced the United States would devote such a portion of its resources to the war with Germany that it would be unable to interfere with the establishment of Japanese control in south Asia.

5. Would the raid on Dieppe have been made if the attackers had known the strength of the defenses? The answer is "probably." The British high command was insistent that a force of roughly division strength be landed on the German-held coast of France before an all-out invasion was attempted. The British believed that additional combat experience was needed before a major amphibious assault was attempted. The raid on Dieppe proved the validity of this view. Based upon the intelligence failure at Dieppe, every effort was made to insure that everything was known about the enemy to be faced in Normandy.

What is more difficult to answer is whether precisely the same forces would have been used in the Dieppe raid if there had been accurate intelligence on the pillboxes along the beach, the tank traps on the Promenade, the gun emplacements on the cliffs overlooking the harbor, and the other defenses to be encountered. Would the Royal Navy have permitted cruisers or battleships to move into shore waters to provide direct-fire support? Would paratroopers have been dropped behind the port to flank the defenders? Would direct assault have been made on the port? Normandy may help to answer: there, the Navy provided direct naval fire-support; there, airborne forces were dropped inland; and there was no direct assault on a fortified port.

6. The Germans at Dieppe were surprised, but they had been alerted to danger periods for British raids and August 18–19 fell in one of those alerts. The defenders reacted quickly. They were not certain whether it was a raid or the Second Front until captured prisoners and documents provided the answers.

The raid on Dieppe may have cost the Germans more than the losses on that day. It created the erroneous impression in some areas of the German High Command to the effect that with good coastal fortifications an Allied landing could be defeated on the beaches. This may have led to hesitancy in committing armor in Normandy, until it was too late to dislodge the Allies.

7. Would the British 1st Airborne Division have dropped north of the Rhine River at Arnhem if intelligence had been able to provide the location and strength of the S. S. Panzer Corps in the area? Here the answer must be "probably not." There were high ranking officers in the attacking force who felt they were going one bridge too far.

It would have taken intelligence of an extremely persuasive nature to have convinced the planners of *Market Garden* that the operation was not feasible. Agent reports on divisional shoulder patches were not enough to convince anyone that there were dangerous numbers of S. S. Panzer troops in the area. Communications intelligence reports identifying most of the major units of the two divisions would have been more useful. A captured German document giving a status report on the divisions would have been most persuasive, especially if it listed the location of the units, the number of combat effectives, the equipment available and the rate at which replacements were arriving from Germany. Such *hard* intelligence was not to be had.

8. The Germans at Arnhem took advantage of such intelligence as they had. Field Marshal Model's initial reactions were those of an experienced commander, and to him must go most of the credit for thwarting the seizure of the Arnhem bridge. After the operational plan for the Allied attack reached General Student, in the early hours of the battle, all that remained was to try to contain the offensives with the limited German forces available.

9. If American intelligence had been able to predict accurately the time and the place of the German offensive in the Ardennes, would the disposition of U. S. forces have been different? Or if General Bradley had placed more divisions in the line in the Ardennes, would the Germans then have attacked there?

Neither of these questions can be answered with any certainty. The intelligence staff of every senior allied headquarters concerned at one time or another had indicated the possibility of a German offensive in the Ardennes: the First Army,* 12th Army Group and SHAEF. All of these staffs had discussed the possibilities with the commanding generals. The decisions had been made to attack in the Aachen and Saar, and there were not enough troops to make these two attacks and still maintain a strong force in the Ardennes. If intelligence had been able to present conclusive evidence of the forthcoming German attack, the decisions of the commanders might have been different.

---

* Some authors have insisted that the First Army G-2 predicted the offensive. An examination of the estimate in question shows that it was a multiple-choice estimate, which also suggested the Germans could collapse and surrender or resort to unorthodox warfare.

10. The German attack in the Ardennes could well have taken place even if the line had been strongly held. When Hitler decided in September to launch a counter-offensive in the Ardennes, American dispositions played little or no role in his decision. He counted on doing the unexpected and achieving decisive surprise. His generals failed to persuade him to mount a more modest operation. The effect of possible losses in the Ardennes on the future of the war was ignored. Hitler apparently was not even concerned—if indeed he knew—that seven of the twelve panzer divisions assigned to the attacking force had been committed to the defensive battles along the West Wall.

An examination of these information failures raises the question of the role of intelligence in the decision-making process of the nations concerned.

The most effective national intelligence system at the start of the Second World War was that of the Soviet Union. It had remarkably accurate information on both Germany and Japan. Stalin chose to ignore the warnings of the German attack, but he must have placed some reliance on Richard Sorge's reports from Japan that there would be no attack on Russia in the Far East because he moved troops from there to protect Moscow. Just how good the Russian combat intelligence was during the war is not the subject of this study, but the successes of the partisans fighting behind the German lines in western Russia suggest that it was good.

German military intelligence concerned itself with potential enemies: principally France, Russia and Great Britain. The competing services of the Foreign Office and the Sicherheitsdienst did their best to undermine each other and the military. Hitler received and believed only what was acceptable to him.

The United States was trying to develop an intelligence system at the time of Pearl Harbor. Both the late start and the organizational difficulties certainly contributed to the disaster in Hawaii.

Japan had an extensive intelligence and security service concentrating on Asia and the Anglo-Saxon naval forces. It attempted to use Japanese all over the world to collect information. The amount of information collected was considerable, but save that reported by the embassies, most of it was low-level reporting on ship movements and the like rather than on potential of future enemies.

The British had one of the oldest of the secret intelligence services. They had suffered heavy losses when the Germans conquered western Europe, but with considerable skill and exceptional bravery were able to rebuild intelligence networks in enemy-held territory. The British also benefited by playing host in London to the intelligence services of the European governments-in-exile, particularly the French, Norwegian, Dutch and Belgian.

One general conclusion is in order about all of these national intelligence services: none was as good as the security of its country required. When the collection of information was extensive and successful, then the evaluation and analysis tended to be casual or even non-existent. If the intelligence system was supported by the central government—especially with money, facilities and cover—then the relationship with the decision makers was poor. In practically no case, with the possible exception of the British, were all of the various intelligence branches closely coordinated and tightly controlled. These intelligence branches included army, navy, air, economic, political, scientific, technical and internal security organizations.

It should be recognized that adequate intelligence, despite its ancient antecedents, has only recently been recognized by the United States as a necessity for national security and as an important career in the military profession.

In the United States prior to World War II a military officer who attempted to make a career in intelligence could well jeopardize his chances of promotion. If he wished to stay in the service he had to take the usual rotation of command, staff and training assignments. If he indicated preference for intelligence in the staff assignments, to the exclusion of operations or plans, he might be viewed by the promotion boards not as an officer trying to make himself expert in a vital element of the military profession, but as an eccentric or specialist who should not be considered for highest rank.

In peace time military intelligence was equated solely with attaché work, and this was all too frequently regarded as solely for the socialites and "cookie pushers." Military attachés are assigned to diplomatic missions by most nations to be in liaison with the armed services of the host country. In the conduct of this liaison the attaché is charged with discovering as much about the host service as he possibly can. As those in nearly every other profession can attest, the most effective liaison can frequently be achieved on a social basis. Military attachés discover that they can accomplish much more if they are on good social terms with officers in the host country's service. The military intelligence service of the host country will meanwhile be cultivating the military attachés in order to gain information about their service. This is not espionage, nor is it clandestine. It is a basic form of military intelligence collection which provides important information, and prior to World War II was one of the few attractive assignments available

in the U. S. intelligence system. An assignment as an attaché, however, was not considered as an essential step to
promotion.

The military intelligence staffs in Washington or with a
command had for some a slightly higher preference over the
attaché assignment. These were generally for one tour of
duty. Very few officers asked for a second assignment in
intelligence.

The intelligence staffs themselves were regarded as
subordinate to the War Plans Staff in both the Army and the
Navy, and this was reflected not only in the rank of the
officers but in the weight given the recommendations of the
respective organizations. These were but two of a multitude
of organizational problems that beset the intelligence services of the United States.

There was little or no coordination between the information services. The Department of State carefully guarded
cables and dispatches from its posts overseas and was reluc-
tant to distribute them to other departments and agencies.
Yet the American Foreign Service was the principal source
of information about other nations.

There was no clandestine collection agency for the
United States. The individual services tried to secure information as best they could, occasionally using agents, but
there was no professional service. A State Department official approached by the OSS during the war with a request
to place a man under cover in an American embassy in a
neutral country replied in shocked dismay that such was not
in keeping with diplomatic practices. The kindest thing that
can be said about this State Department officer is that he
probably had not had the opportunity to view at close hand
the work of the embassies of other nations, particularly the
Russian, German, British and French.

The communications intelligence effort of the United States was conducted by the military services, and for this they deserve great credit. A former Secretary of State had disbanded the so-called Black Chamber—cryptographic bureau—of that department with the classic remark: "Gentlemen do not read each other's mail!"

This accurately reflected the American attitude prior to World War II. Why should much attention be paid to intelligence, or much effort devoted either to its collection or analysis? Had not the country resolved to stay out of the affairs of other nations—let Europe solve its own problems and fight its own wars? America was protected by two vast oceans and could live by itself. Accurate knowledge about other nations' plans was not a national necessity.

There was little possibility that the United States would act to establish a national service prior to Pearl Harbor. The extension of the draft came within one vote of defeat in 1940. A proposal to create an intelligence service would have been voted down decisively and would have created a Congressional uproar of unbelievable dimensions.

President Roosevelt had sufficient authority under emergency legislation to act, and in 1940 he created the Office of the Coordinator of Information, predecessor of the Office of Strategic Services and to the Central Intelligence Agency.

The OSS could not accomplish in war time what must require decades to do properly—to develop a national intelligence service. Nor could the military services create overnight an experienced cadre of expert intelligence officers to man the staffs in Washington and of all the combat commands.

The price of national negligence was paid in battle.

References

Chapter 2

1. Walter Goerlitz, *History of the German General Staff, 1657 to 1945*, p. 389.
2. Isaac Deutscher, *Stalin: A Political Biography*, p. 418.
3. *Ibid.*, p. 435.
4. Speech to the Labor Front at Nuremberg, September 12, 1936.
5. Alan Clark, "25 Years After: The Day Hitler Attacked Russia," *The New York Times*, 6:19:66, VI, p. 12.
6. Deutscher, *op. cit.*, p. 427.
7. Franz von Papen, *Memoirs*, p. 473.
8. Waverley Root, *The Secret History of the War*, p. 506.
9. Joseph Clark Grew, *My Ten Years in Japan*, p. 383.
10. Walter Warlimont, *Inside Hitler's Headquarters, 1939–45*, p. 145.
11. Gregoire Gafencu, *Prelude to the Russian Campaign*, p. 189.
12. Franz Halder, *Diary*, p. 607.

13. Warlimont, *op. cit.*, p. 111.
14. William W. Kaufman, *Case Barbarossa: 1949–1950*, p. 50.
15. Goerlitz, *op. cit.*, p. 379.
16. Trumbull Higgins, *Hitler and Russia: The Third Reich in a Two–Front War, 1937–1943*, p. 68.
17. Kaufman, *op. cit.*, p. 52.
18. Warlimont, *op. cit.*, p. 138.
19. Donald McLachlin, *Room 39*, p. 242.
20. General Augustin Guilliame, *Soviet Arms and Soviet Power*, p. 16.
21. Von Papen, *op. cit.*, p. 418.
22. Walter Schellenberg, *The Labyrinth*, p. 114.
23. David Kahn, *The Codebreakers*, p. 455.
24. *Ibid.*, p. 454.
25. *Ibid.*, p. 465.
26. *Ibid.*, p. 461.
27. *Ibid.*, p. 438.
28. Schellenberg, *op. cit.*, p. 198.
29. *Ibid.*, p. 191.
30. *Ibid.*, p. 198.
31. *Ibid.*, p. 27.
32. *Ibid.*, p. 362.
33. *Ibid.*, p. 364.
34. *Ibid.*, p. 271.
35. *Ibid.*, p. 262.
36. Kahn, *op. cit.*, p. 645.
37. Halder, *op. cit.*, August 11, 1941.
38. Goerlitz, *op. cit.*, p. 385.
39. Heinz Guderian, *Panzer Leader*, p. 190.
40. *Ibid.*, p. 144.
41. *Ibid.*, p. 190.
42. Halder, *op. cit.*, June 7, 1941.
43. Schellenberg, *op. cit.*, p. 140.
44. Alexander Foote, *Handbook for Spies*, p. 91.
45. F. W. Deakin and G. R. Storry, *The Case of Richard Sorge*, p. 230.
46. *Ibid.*, p. 229.
47. *Ibid.*, p. 230.
48. Guderian, *op. cit.*, p. 143.
49. William Shirer, *Berlin Diary*, p. 842.
50. Kaufman, *op. cit.*, p. 53.

51. Shirer, *op. cit.*, p. 843.
52. Winston Churchill, *The Second World War*, p. 270.
53. Higgins, *op. cit.*, pp. 103–105.
54. Kaufman, *op. cit.*, p. 53.
55. McLachlin, *op. cit.*, p. 243.
56. Robert Sherwood, *Roosevelt and Hopkins*, p. 299.
57. Shirer, *op. cit.*, p. 843.
58. *Ibid.*, p. 844.
59. Deakin and Storry, *op. cit.*, p. 228.
60. Von Papen, *op. cit.*, p. 479.
61. Ian Colvin, *Master Spy*, p. 162.
62. Clark, *op. cit.*, p. 12.
63. Adolf Hitler, *Mein Kampf*, pp. 947-50.
64. Hugh Trevor-Roper, *Hitler's Generals*, p. 137.
65. Guderian, *op. cit.*, p. 180.
66. Galeazzo Ciano, *Diaries*, p. 455.
67. Deakin and Storry, *op. cit.*, p. 231.

Chapter 3

(Basic source material on the attack at Pearl Harbor is provided in the hearings and report of the Joint Committee on the Investigation of the Pearl Harbor Attack of the Seventy-ninth Congress published by the United States Government Printing Office, Washington, D.C., 1946. The hearings were published in eleven parts paged seriatum, and the exhibits, including the proceedings and reports of seven previous investigations, were published in another twenty-eight parts. The report of the Joint Committee was published separately.)

1. Pearl Harbor Attack Hearings, Part 12, Exhibit 1, p. 1.
2. *Ibid.*, pp. 8–10.
3. *Ibid.*, pp. 12–14.
4. *Ibid.*, pp. 15–16.
5. *Ibid.*, p. 16.
6. *Ibid.*, pp. 18–19.
7. *Ibid.*, p. 30.
8. *Ibid.*, p. 37.
9. *Ibid.*, p. 41.
10. *Ibid.*, p. 43.

11. *Ibid.*, p. 138.
12. *Ibid.*, p. 138.
13. *Ibid.*, p. 209.
14. *Ibid.*, p. 1.
15. *Ibid.*, p. 2.
16. *Ibid.*, p. 9.
17. *Ibid.*, p. 24.
18. *Ibid.*, p. 122.
19. *Ibid.*, p. 174.
20. *Ibid.*, p. 224.
21. *Ibid.*, p. 175.
22. *Ibid.*, p. 224.
23. *Ibid.*, p. 2.
24. *Ibid.*, p. 12.
25. *Ibid.*, p. 34.
26. *Ibid.*, p. 71.
27. *Ibid.*, p. 71.
28. *Ibid.*, p. 81.
29. *Ibid.*, p. 90.
30. *Ibid.*, p. 165.
31. *Ibid.*, p. 166.
32. *Ibid.*, p. 199.
33. *Ibid.*, p. 64.
34. *Ibid.*, p. 81.
35. *Ibid.*, p. 99.
36. *Ibid.*, p. 100.
37. *Ibid.*, p. 116.
38. *Ibid.*, p. 159.
39. *Ibid.*, p. 137.
40. *Ibid.*, p. 133.
41. *Ibid.*, p. 153.
42. *Ibid.*, p. 154.
43. *Ibid.*, p. 155.
44. *Ibid.*, p. 178.
45. *Ibid.*, pp. 200–02.
46. *Ibid.*, p. 204.
47. *Ibid.*, p. 208.
48. *Ibid.*, p. 209.
49. *Ibid.*, p. 215.
50. *Ibid.*, p. 234.
51. *Ibid.*, p. 236.

52. *Ibid.*, pp. 239–44.
53. *Ibid.*, p. 248.
54. *Ibid.*, p. 245.
55. *Ibid.*, pp. 13–14.
56. *Ibid.*, pp. 14–15.
57. *Ibid.*, p. 17.
58. *Ibid.*, p. 28.
59. *Ibid.*, pp. 29–30.
60. *Ibid.*, p. 41.
61. *Ibid.*, p. 45.
62. *Ibid.*, pp. 52–53.
63. *Ibid.*, p. 69.
64. *Ibid.*, pp. 80–81.
65. *Ibid.*, p. 85.
66. *Ibid.*, p. 87.
67. *Ibid.*, p. 88.
68. *Ibid.*, pp. 111–12.
69. *Ibid.*, pp. 127–28.
70. *Ibid.*, p. 154.
71. *Ibid.*, p. 192.
72. *Ibid.*, p. 197.
73. *Ibid.*, pp. 214–15.
74. *Ibid.*, p. 227.
75. Pearl Harbor Attack Hearings, Part 17, Exhibit 128, pp. 2870–74.
76. Pearl Harbor Attack Hearings, Part 2, p. 794.
77. Pearl Harbor Attack Hearings, Part 12, Exhibit 2, p. 254.
78. *Ibid.*, p. 261.
79. *Ibid.*, p. 262.
80. *Ibid.*, p. 263.
81. *Ibid.*, p. 270.
82. *Ibid.*, pp. 271–72.
83. *Ibid.*, p. 271.
84. *Ibid.*, p. 274.
85. *Ibid.*, p. 280.
86. *Ibid.*, p. 288.
87. *Ibid.*, p. 298.
88. Joseph Clark Grew, *My Ten Years in Japan*, p. 295.
89. *Ibid.*, p. 301.
90. *Ibid.*, p. 315.
91. *Ibid.*, p. 325.

92. *Ibid.*, p. 339.
93. *Ibid.*, p. 354.
94. *Ibid.*, p. 359.
95. *Ibid.*, p. 366.
96. *Ibid.*, p. 409.
97. *Ibid.*, p. 441.
98. *Ibid.*, p. 462.
99. *Ibid.*, p. 418.
100. Pearl Harbor Attack Hearings, Part 15, Exhibit 81, p. 1852.
101. *Ibid.*, Part 14, Exhibit 33, p. 1344.
102. *Ibid.*, p. 1349.
103. *Ibid.*, Part 15, Exhibit 81, p. 1848.
104. *Ibid.*, Part 14, Exhibit 33, p. 1357.
105. *Ibid.*, Part 15, Exhibit 81, p. 1845.
106. *Ibid.*, Part 14, Exhibit 33, p. 1366.
107. *Ibid.*, Part 15, Exhibit 81, p. 1839.
108. *Ibid.*, Exhibit 80, p. 1774.
109. *Ibid.*, Part 14, Exhibit 33, p. 1373.
110. *Ibid.*, Part 29, p. 2070.
111. *Ibid.*, p. 2070.
112. *Ibid.*, p. 2084.
113. *Ibid.*, Part 16, Exhibit 106, p. 2144.
114. *Ibid.*, Part 14, Exhibit 10, p. 1000.
115. Investigation of the Pearl Harbor Attack, Report, p. 77.
116. Pearl Harbor Attack Hearings, Part 16, Exhibit 106, p. 2227.
117. *Ibid.*, Part 15, Exhibit 44, p. 1452.
118. *Ibid.*, Part 16, Exhibit 106, p. 2149.
119. *Ibid.*, Part 14, Exhibit 14, p. 1395.
120. *Ibid.*, Part 16, Exhibit 106, p. 2160.
121. *Ibid.*, p. 2167.
122. *Ibid.*, p. 2170.
123. *Ibid.*, p. 2171.
124. *Ibid.*, p. 2175.
125. *Ibid.*, p. 2182.
126. *Ibid.*, p. 2213.
127. *Ibid.*, Part 14, Exhibit 37, p. 1402.
128. *Ibid.*, p. 1405.
129. *Ibid.*, Part 16, Exhibit 106, p. 2214.
130. *Ibid.*, p. 2223.

131. *Ibid.*, Part 14, Exhibit 37, p. 1406.
132. *Ibid.*, p. 1407.
133. *Ibid.*, Part 15, Exhibit 84, p. 1867.
134. Pearl Harbor Attack Report, p. 135.
135. Robert Sherwood, *Roosevelt and Hopkins*, p. 316.

Chapter 4

1. R. W. Thompson, *Dieppe at Dawn*, p. 175.
2. Terence Robertson, *Dieppe: The Shame and the Glory*, p. 152.
3. *Ibid.*, p. 154.
4. Bernard L. Montgomery, *Memoirs*, p. 75.
5. Winston Churchill, *The Second World War*, p. 272.
6. Robertson, *op. cit.*, p. 176.
7. *Ibid.*, p. 124.
8. Colonel C. P. Stacey, *Official History of the Canadian Army in the Second World War*, p. 397.
9. Robertson, *op. cit.*, p. 174.
10. J. R. M. Butler, *History of the Second World War*, p. 643.
11. *Ibid.*, p. 643.
12. Stacey, *op. cit.*, p. 350.
13. Jacques Mordal, *Dieppe: The Dawn of Decision*, p. 111.
14. Robertson, *op. cit.*, p. 172.
15. *Ibid.*, p. 173.
16. *Ibid.*, p. 182.
17. *Ibid.*, p. 173.
18. Stacey, *op. cit.*, p. 356.
19. Mordal, *op. cit.*, p. 160.
20. *Ibid.*, p. 161.
21. *Ibid.*, p. 162.
22. *Ibid.*, p. 113.
23. Stacey, *op. cit.*, p. 390.
24. Butler, *op. cit.*, p. 643.

Chapter 5

1. First United States Army, *G-2 Estimate 24*, 3 September 1944.

2. Charles B. MacDonald, "The Decision to Launch Operation Market Garden," in *Command Decisions*, p. 434.
3. Chester Wilmot, *The Struggle for Europe*, p. 501.
4. MacDonald, *op. cit.*, p. 437.
5. SHAEF, *Weekly Intelligence Summary No. 26*, September 16, 1944.
6. Cornelius Bauer, *The Battle of Arnhem*, p. 78.
7. R. E. Urquhart, *Arnhem*, p. 9.
8. Bauer, *op. cit.*, p. 78.
9. MacDonald, *op. cit.*, p. 437.
10. Urquhart, *op. cit.*, p. 42.
11. Winston Churchill, *The Second World War*, p. 519.
12. Omar Bradley, *A Soldier's Story*, pp. 416–18.
13. Sir Brian Horrocks, *A Full Life*, p. 231.
14. Bernard L. Montgomery, *The Memoirs*, p. 296.
15. Urquhart, *op. cit.*, pp. 198–99.
16. *Ibid.*, p. 7.
17. *Ibid.*, p. 9.
18. *Ibid.*, p. 17.

Chapter 6

1. Rundstedt Testimony, Trial of the Major War Criminals Before the International Military Tribunal, Nuremberg, August 12, 1946, Vol. XXXI, p. 29.
2. All of the intelligence reports relating to the battle of the Ardennes have been assembled by the U. S. Army's Historical Section.
3. General Hasso von Manteuffel, "The Ardennes," in *The Fatal Decision*, p. 270.

Bibliography

There is a great deal written about any battle of importance. With most modern military forces, after-action reports are prepared by the units engaged. After the war, official histories are prepared. The generals and admirals involved frequently write memoirs. Lesser participants write their accounts. If a disaster is involved, a court of inquiry may be held or a governmental investigation may take place.

In all of this documentation the role of intelligence is the least adequately treated. Few armies follow the practice of the United States where every division, corps, army and army group in action prepares a daily intelligence report and a weekly intelligence summary. When these are on file one can glean some of the details as to how much intelligence was available before the battle.

Chapter 2

General coverage of the German attack on Russia:
Clark, Alan, *Barbarossa: The Russian-German Conflict, 1941–45*, New York, 1965.

Higgins, Trumbull, *Hitler and Russia: The Third Reich in a Two-Front War, 1937–1943*, New York, 1966.

International Military Tribunal Proceedings: Trial of the Major War Criminals, Nuremberg, 1947.

Kaufman, William W., *Case Barbarossa: 1949–1950* (Unpublished manuscript), Cambridge, 1962.

Root, Waverley, *The Secret History of the War*, New York, 1945.

Warlimont, Walter, *Inside Hitler's Headquarters, 1939–45*, London, 1964.

The German side of the attack:

GENERAL:

Mann, Golo, *The History of Germany Since 1789*, New York, 1968.

Shirer, William L., *The Rise and Fall of the Third Reich*, New York, 1960.

Shirer, William L., *Berlin Diary*, New York, 1960.

INTELLIGENCE:

Abshagen, Karl Heinz, *Canaris*, London, 1956.

Ciano's Diplomatic Papers, London, 1948.

Colvin, Ian, *Master Spy*, New York, 1951.

Hitler's Secret Conversations, 1941–1944, New York, 1953.

Papen, Franz von, *Memoirs*, London, 1952.

Schellenberg, Walter, *The Labyrinth*, New York, 1956.

The von Hassell Diaries, London, 1948.

MILITARY:

Goerlitz, Walter, *History of the German General Staff, 1657–1945*, New York, 1955.

Guderian, General Heinz, *Panzer Leader*, London, 1952.

Halder, Franz, *Hitler as War Lord*, London, 1950.

Jacobsen, H. A. (ed.), *Decisive Battles of World War II*, New York, 1965.

Keitel, Wilhelm, *Memoirs*, New York, 1966.

Manstein, Field Marshal Erich von, *Lost Victories*, Chicago, 1958.

The Russian side of the attack:

INTELLIGENCE:

Dallin, David J., *Soviet Espionage*, New Haven, 1955.

Deakin, F. W., and Storry, G. R., *The Case of Richard Sorge*, New York, 1966.

Foote, Alexander, *Handbook for Spies*, London, 1949.

MILITARY:

Deutscher, Isaac, *Stalin: A Political Biography*, New York, 1967.

Gafencu, Gregoire, *Prelude to the Russian Campaign*, London, 1945.

Guilliame, General Augustin, *Soviet Arms and Secret Power*, Washington, D.C., 1949.

Liddell Hart, B. H., *The Red Army*, New York, 1956.

Chapter 3

A great deal of the source material for the study of the Japanese attack on Pearl Harbor is contained in the thirty-nine volumes of hearings and exhibits of the Joint Committee on the Investigation of the Pearl Harbor Attack of the Seventy-ninth Congress, Washington, D.C., 1946. These should be supplemented by the three volumes of Foreign Relations of the United States: Japan 1931–1941, Department of State, Washington, D.C.

Grew, Joseph C., *Ten Years in Japan*, New York, 1944.

Langer, William L., and Gleason, S. Everett, *The Undeclared War*, New York, 1953.

Morton, Louis, "Japan's Decision for War," in *Command Decisions*, Department of Army, Washington, D. C., 1960.

Sherwood, Robert, *Roosevelt and Hopkins*, New York, 1948.

Wohlstetter, Roberta, *Pearl Harbor: Warning and Decision*, Stanford, 1962.

Chapter 4

Austin, Alexander B., *We Landed at Dawn*, London, 1943.

Buckley, Christopher, *Norway: The Commandos: Dieppe*, London, 1951.

Butler, J. R. M., *History of the Second World War*, London, 1964.

Lepoitier, Rear Admiral Adolphe, *Raiders from the Sea*, London, 1954.

Mordal, Jacques, *Dieppe: The Dawn of Decision*, London, 1963.

Robertson, Terence, *Dieppe: The Shame and the Glory*, Boston, 1962.

Stacey, Colonel C. P., *Official History of the Canadian Army in the Second World War*, Ottawa, 1955.

Thompson, R. W., *Dieppe at Dawn*, London, 1957

Chapter 5

Bauer, Cornelius, *The Battle at Arnhem*, London, 1966.

History of the 2nd Battalion, The Parachute Regiment, Aldershot, 1946.

Horrocks, Sir Brian, *A Full Life*, London, Collins, 1960.

MacDonald, Charles B., "The Decision to Launch Operation Market Garden, in *Command Decisions*, Washington, D. C., 1960.

Montgomery, Bernard L., *Memoirs*, London, 1958.

Urquhart, Major General R. E., *Arnhem*, London, 1958.

Wilmot, Chester, *The Struggle for Europe*, London, 1952.

Chapter 6

Baldwin, Hanson, *Battles Lost and Won*, New York, 1966.

Bradley, Omar N., *A Soldier's Story*, New York, 1951.

Cole, Hugh M., *The Ardennes: Battle of the Bulge*, Washington, D.C., 1965.

Manteufell, Hasso von, "The Battle of the Ardennes, 1944–45," *Decisive Battles of World War II*, edited by H. A. Jacobsen, and J. Rohwer, New York, 1965.

Manteuffel, Hasso von, "The Ardennes," in *The Fatal Decisions*, edited by Seymour Freidin, and William Richardson, New York, 1956.

Merriam, Robert E., *Dark December*, New York, 1947.

Warlimont, Walter, *Inside Hitler's Headquarters, 1939–1945*, London, 1964.

Chapter 7

The most authoritative books on the development of the modern American intelligence system are:

Dulles, Allen W., *The Craft of Intelligence*, New York, 1963.
Kahn, David, *The Code Breakers*, New York, 1967.
Kent, Sherman, *Strategic Intelligence*, Princeton, 1949.
Kirkpatrick, Lyman B., Jr., *The Real CIA*, New York, 1968.

Index

Aachen, Third Battle of, 230
Abwehr (military intelligence service), 21, 42, 46, 47-48, 50, 52, 64, 66, 176, 222
Achtung, Panzer! (Gunderian), 51
Alanbrooke, Lord, 166, 223
  See also Brooke, General Sir Alan
Albania, 44
Aleutians, 160
Anglo-Soviet Alliance of May 26th, 163
Anti-Comintern Agreement, 79, 105
Anti-Comintern Pact, 28, 78
Antonescu, General Ion, 43
Ardennes, xii, 2, 9, 229-265, 276-277
Arizona (ship), 149
Armed Forces Signal Communications (WNV), 47
Army Signal Intelligence Service, 85
Arnhem, 2, 3, 9, 198-227, 275-276
Auslandsorganisation, 46
Austria, 20, 23, 29

Barbarossa, Case, 17-74
Bataan Peninsula, 160

Battle of Britain, 40, 42
Battles, 1-16
  See also names of battles
Beardall, Captain John R., 85
Beck, General Ludwig von, 51
Becker, Colonel, 61
Belgium, 22, 23, 39, 60, 205-206, 304
Bellinger, Rear Admiral Patrick, 146-147
Beneš, Eduard, 27
Beobactung-Dienst (Observation Service), 47
Berge, Wendell, 127, 129
Berkeley (destroyer), 187
Bessarabia, 27, 32
Best, S. Payne, 58
Blitzkrieg, 21
Bohemia, 20
Borneo, 146
Bradley, General Omar N., 207, 223, 256, 276
Brandenberger, General Erich, 236
Brauchitsch, General Walther von, 24

British Broadcasting Company, 161-162
British counterespionage service (MI-5), 168
British Expeditionary Force, 22, 40
Brooke, General Sir Alan, 166, 223
  See also Alanbrooke, Lord
Browning, Lieutenant General Sir Frederick, 215, 216
Buhle, Walter, 232
Bukovina, 34
Bulgaria, 32, 34, 36, 37, 203
Bulge in the Ardennes, xii, 2, 9, 229-265, 276-277

California (ship), 149
Calpe (ship), 179, 186, 195, 197
Canada, 2, 3, 14, 162, 164, 166, 167, 168, 173, 183, 184, 206, 229, 230
Canaris, Admiral Wilhelm, 21, 42, 48, 49, 66, 176
Cannae, Battle of, 1
Caroline Islands, 203
Casablanca Conference, 201
Castle, 120
Catto, Lieutenant Colonel Douglas, 184
Cavendish-Bentick, Victor, 65
Central Intelligence Agency (CIA), xi-xiv, 281
Charlemagne, 24
CHEKA, 52, 53
Chiang Kai-shek, 124, 126
China, 76, 77, 78, 80, 91, 93, 120-121, 124, 137, 139, 154, 155, 160, 201
Churchill, Winston, 65, 155, 162, 166, 171, 193, 199-200, 223
CIA (Central Intelligence Agency), xi-xiv, 281
Ciano, Count Galeazzo, 15, 71, 72, 268
Clausewitz, Carl von, 237
Colvin, Ian, 66
Combined Operations Intelligence, 170
Comintern, 53-54, 60, 201
Constantine, 24
Control (office), 56, 57, 62, 63
Cooke, Admiral Charles M., 144

Corregidor, 160
Cripps, Sir Stafford, 65, 66
Cuban missile crisis, 11
Czechoslovakia, 20, 23, 27, 29, 48

Daily News, 123
D-Day, 205, 220
De Caulaincourt, Armand, 24
De Gaulle, Charles, 22
Dekanozov, V. G., 39
Denmark, 21, 23, 192
Dieppe, xii, 2, 3, 14, 159-197, 199, 202, 274-275
  lessons learned at, 194-197
Dietrich, General Sepp, 236, 237
Drang Nach Osten, 67
Dulles, Allen, 262
Dunkirk, Battle of, 1
Dzerzhinsky, Feliks, 52

Eden, Anthony, 27, 65
Egypt, 200, 201
Eisenhower, General Dwight D., 195, 202, 206, 207, 223-224, 231-232
Elliot, George E., Jr., 153
Espionage Act of June 15, 1917, 129
Estonia, 27, 32
Etorofu Island, 83

Federal Bureau of Investigation (FBI), 147
Fernie (ship), 179
Finland, 32-35, 36, 43-44, 49, 50, 59
Forschungsamt (Research Office), 47, 61
Fourth Department of the General Staff, 55, 63
France, 3, 4, 20, 22, 23, 27, 29, 30, 31, 32, 48, 57, 60, 79, 81, 159-197, 199, 202, 203, 204, 206, 208, 210, 214, 263, 274-275, 277, 280
  collapse of, 22
  declares war, 21
Franco, General Francisco, 28
Frederick I, 23-24
Fremde Heeres Ost (Foreign Armies East), 45, 46, 49
French Indo-China, 100-101, 127

Frost, Lieutenant Colonel J. D., 218-219, 220
Funkaufklärungsdienst (Radio Reconnaissance Service), 47

G-2 Staff (Intelligence), 86, 136-137, 139, 204-205, 248, 276
Geheime Staats Polizei (Gestapo), 13, 264
Geneva Conventions, 259
German Military Intelligence Service, 66
German Workers' Party, 26
Germany, 2, 3-4, 5, 6-16, 26, 75, 78, 79, 81, 84, 92, 93-94, 96, 98, 100, 104, 117, 119, 267-281
    Arnhem, 2, 3, 9, 198-227, 275-276
    Barbarossa case, 17-74
    Bulge in the Ardennes, xii, 2, 9, 229-265, 276-277
    Dieppe, xii, 2, 3, 14, 159-197, 199, 202, 274-275
    intelligence services of, 44-52, 174-178
Gestapo, 13, 264
Gettysburg, Battle of, 1
Gibson, Hugh, 120
Gilbert Islands, 201
Goering, Hermann, 40, 41, 47, 61, 233, 241
Great Britain, 2, 3, 9, 12, 14, 20, 22, 23, 29, 30, 31, 32, 33, 40-42, 48, 54, 57, 58, 75-77, 79, 82, 83, 98, 101, 104, 121, 125-128, 134, 137, 155, 159-197, 201, 207, 208, 210, 214, 216, 218-219, 220-221, 223-227, 234, 238, 242, 245, 256, 273, 275-280
    declares war, 21
    intelligence services of, 169-174
Greece, 43, 44, 81
Grew, Joseph Clark, 90, 103, 132-134, 142, 150
Guam, 75, 160, 203
Guderian, General Heinz, 51, 63, 70, 71, 233, 268

Haase, General Conrad von, 183, 189, 194

Hainan Island, 101
Halder, General Franz, 174, 193
Halem, Nicholas von, 66
Hamaguchi, Premier Yuko, 78
Hamilton, Lord, 39
Hara, Prime Minister Takashi, 77
Harnack, Arvid, 61
Hawaii, 75-157, 272-273
Hayashi, General Senjuro, 78
Heeresnachrichten Wesens (Army Communications System), 47
Heinrichs, General, 43
Helena (ship), 149
Hess, Rudolf, 18, 39-40
Himmler, Heinrich, 7, 21, 47-48
Hindenburg, Paul von, 17, 19
Hirade, Captain Hodeo, 83
Hitler, Adolf, 5-7, 10-12, 15, 30, 32-52, 61-64, 67-68, 71-73, 79, 81, 115, 133, 143, 155-156, 165, 174-175, 190-193, 202-204, 208, 232-244, 253-263, 268-271, 277
    denounces disarmament clause of Versailles Treaty, 20
    initial success of, 18
Ho Chi Minh, 54
Holland, 3, 5, 22, 23, 60, 79, 82, 134, 155, 171, 263
    Arnhem, 2, 3, 9, 198-227, 275-276
    Resistance in, 212-213
Hong Kong, 75, 137, 159
Honolulu (ship), 149
Hoover, Herbert, 120
Hopkins, Harry, 85, 88, 151
Horota, Koki, 78
Horrocks, General Sir Brian, 223
Hull, Cordell, 85, 88, 90-91, 110, 111, 120, 126, 127, 138-139, 146
Hungary, 34, 37, 43, 44, 59
Hurtgen Forest, Battle of, 230

Iguchi, Councillor Sadao, 97, 116, 119
Indochina, 80, 81, 93, 101-102, 121
Inukai, Prime Minister Ki, 78
Iraq, 38
Italy, 15, 28, 35, 36-37, 44, 59, 60, 79, 95, 96, 117, 161, 200-201, 273

Japan, 2, 3, 9, 12, 13, 28, 31, 32, 35, 38, 58, 66, 71, 73, 159-161, 201, 203, 272-274, 278
    Pearl Harbor, 3, 14, 75-157, 159, 272-273, 274, 278
Japanese Imperial Conference, 81
Jasperson, Lieutenant Colonel, 185
Java Sea, Battle of, 160
Jews, 19, 26, 50
Jodl, General Alfred, 23, 41, 42, 43, 233, 236-237
Johnson, General Hugh, 133
Justinian, 24

Kanlkuests, Admiral, 184
Karelian Isthmus, 33
Kasai, 121
Kaya, 127
Keitel, Field Marshal Wilhelm, 49, 233, 234
Kennedy, John F., 11
Kimmel, Admiral, 142-146, 147
Kiplinger, 120
Knox, Frank, 88, 137-138, 140
Koestring, General Ernst, 12, 51
Kokumin (publication), 133
Konoye, Fumimaro, 71, 79-80, 81, 83, 103, 134
Korea, 157
Koulicheff, Alexander, 61, 62
Krafts, Major, 218
Krebs, Colonel Hans, 39, 234, 236
Kreipe, General Werner, 233
Kurusu, Ambassador Saburo, 88-89, 109-114, 123

Labatt, Colonel Robert R., 185
Latin America, 92
Latvia, 27, 32, 232
Laval, Pierre, 27
Layton, Captain Edwin, 147-148
League of Nations, 27, 77
Lenin, Vladimir, 52, 53, 54
Libya, 200
Lithuania, 20, 32, 65
Litvinov, Maxim, 29, 30
Locarno Pact of 1925, 27
Lockhard, Joseph L., 153
Lovat, Lord S. C. J. P., 180-182
Lucy, see Roessler, Rudolf

Luxembourg, 22, 240, 241, 256
Luzon, 131

MI-5 (British counterespionage service), 168
Macassar Straits, 159
McNaughton, Lieutenant General A. G. L., 165, 166, 173
Magic messages, 85, 89, 90, 152
Maginot Line, 22, 48
Maisky, Ivan, 65
Malaya, 82, 137, 139, 273
Manchuria, 28, 76, 99
Manteuffel, General Hasso-Eccard von, 236, 237, 254
Maritime Provinces, 273
Market Garden, 3, 207-227, 229, 275-276
Marne, Battle of, 1
Marshall, General George C., 138, 151, 163, 164, 231
Marshall Islands, 203
Maryland (ship), 149
Matsuoka, Yosuke, 38, 80-81, 93-96, 133, 143
Mein Kampf (Hitler), 18, 67
Memel, 20, 23
Menard, Lieutenant Colonel, 186
Merritt, Lieutenant Colonel Charles C. I., 183
Midway Islands, 160-161
Military Intelligence Department (U.S.S.R.), 55
Mills-Robert, Major Derek, 182
Model, Field Marshal Walther, 218, 236, 237, 244, 247, 258, 276
Molotov, Vyacheslav M., 30, 31, 32, 33, 34, 35-36, 70, 163, 164, 174
Montgomery, Lieutenant General Bernard, 165, 168, 206-207, 208-210, 213, 217, 223-224, 227, 250, 256
Moore, Frederick, 120, 122
Moravia, 20
Mori, 147
Mountbatten, Lord Louis, 165, 166, 192
Mueller, Josef, 66
Mussolini, Benito, 36, 43

Narodnyi Komissariat Vnutrennikh Del (NKVD), 13, 15-16, 49, 52, 53, 55, 56, 57, 68
National Mobilization Bill, 79
National Socialist German Workers' Party, 19, 26, 27
Naval Communications Division, 85-86
Netherlands East Indies, 82, 101, 126, 137, 139, 155, 159, 160, 273
New Guinea, 160
New York Times, The, 122
Niedermeyer, Colonel Ritter von, 62
NKVD, 13, 15-16, 49, 52, 53, 55, 56, 57, 68
Noguma, Admiral Chuichi, 149, 156
Nomura, Kichisaburo, 91, 94, 97, 103-104, 105, 106, 111, 117-121, 122-127, 143, 156
Norway, 21-22, 23, 35, 39, 174
Novy Mir (Yemelyanov), 271

Oberkommando der Wehrmacht (OKW), 6, 30, 40, 43, 49, 175-176, 190, 232, 236, 237-238, 262
Office of the Coordinator of Information, 281
Office of Naval Intelligence (ONI), 85, 142
Office of Strategic Services (OSS), 264-265, 280, 281
Oklahoma (ship), 149
OKW (Oberkommando der Wehrmacht), 6, 30, 40, 43, 49, 175-176, 190, 232, 236, 237-238, 262
O'Laughlin, 122
Olympic Games, 39
ONI (Office of Naval Intelligence), 85, 142
Operation Overlord, 205
Operation Sea Lion, 23, 41, 42
OPNAV, 143
OSS (Office of Strategic Services), 264-265, 280, 281
Ostbau Ost, 41
Ott, General Eugen, 62, 73, 96
Oumansky, Constantine, 65
Outer Mongolia, 32, 79

Paget, General Sir Bernard, 168
Panama Canal, 128, 129
Panay (ship), 78
Papen, Franz von, 19, 37, 66
Parao, 101
Patton, General George S., 206, 231, 234, 253
Paul, Prince of Yugoslavia, 37, 43
Pearl Harbor, 3, 14, 75-157, 159, 272-273, 274, 278
Pennsylvania (ship), 149
Philippines, 75, 82, 85, 131, 137, 139-140, 146, 153, 159, 160, 273
Phillips, Lieutenant Colonel, 186-187
Photographic Interpretation Unit, 169
Pinto, Colonel Orestes N., 222
Poland, 21, 22, 23, 27, 29, 30, 31, 32, 41, 42-43, 48, 58, 65, 79, 232, 271
Portugal, 176
Portuguese Timor, 101
Pratt, Admiral William V., 121
Pravda, 39
Prince Albert (ship), 188
Prince of Wales (ship), 9, 159
Purple code, 85, 88, 89

Quebec Conference, 201

Racial prejudice, 19, 26, 30, 50, 67, 76
Radio Intelligence Unit, 160
Rado, Alexander, 61, 62
Raeder, Admiral Erich, 174
Raleigh (ship), 149
Rashid Ali, 38
Red Chapel, 49, 60-61
Reichstag, 38
Repulse (ship), 9, 159
Ribbentrop, Joachim von, 34, 37, 38, 45, 62, 70, 114-115
Roberts, Major General John Hamilton, 179, 186, 195, 196-197
Roehm, Ernst, 19
Roessler, Rudolf, 61, 62
Rokossovsky, Colonel-General Konstantin K., 50

Rommel, Field Marshal Erwin, 161, 202

Roosevelt, Franklin D., 82, 87-88, 103, 111, 112, 113, 133, 146, 151, 155, 156, 164, 281

Roosevelt, Theodore, 80, 156

Rote Kapelle, Die (Red Chapel), 49, 60-61

Rowehl, Colonel, 52

Rumania, 30, 32, 34, 36, 37, 59, 65, 203

Rundstedt, Gerd von, 162, 173, 177, 183-184, 188, 191, 193, 235, 236, 249, 253

Russo-Japanese War, 80

S. S. Troops, 18, 21, 48

Saar, the, 20, 23, 206

Saito, Viscount Hoboru, 78

Schelia, Legionsrat von, 61

Schellenberg, Walter, 48, 49

Schleicher, General Kurt von, 19

Scholl, Major, 62-63

Schulenburg, Werner von der, 31, 32, 33, 37, 38, 39, 70

Schulze-Boysen, Lieutenant Colonel Harry, 61

Scotland, 39-40, 185

SD (Sicherheitsdienst), 15-16, 21, 46, 48, 49, 50, 277

Secret Intelligence Service, 169-170

SHAEF (Supreme Headquarters Allied Expeditionary Forces), xiii, 204-205, 213, 214-215, 222, 225, 276

Shivers, R. L., 128-129

Shoho (ship), 160

Shokaku (ship), 160

Siberia, 28, 136-137

Sicherheitsdienst (SD), 15-16, 21, 46, 48, 49, 50, 277

Sicily, 200

Siegfried Line, 206, 208

Signal Intelligence Service of the Army, 85

Simović, General Dušan, 44

Slavs, 26, 50

Slovakia, 20

Smetanin, Ambassador, 94

Social Democratic Party, 26, 27

Sonderdienst Dahlem (Special Services at Dahlem), 47

Sonderkommando (special units), 72

Sorge, Richard, 13, 62-63, 66, 73, 277

Soviet-Japanese Neutrality Treaty, 98

Spain, 46, 192

Speer, Albert, 232

Spratley Islands, 101

Stacey, Colonel C. P., 173

Stalin, Joseph, 9, 15, 26-33, 37-40, 52-74, 161-164, 193, 199-201, 269-272, 277

Standley, William H., 121

Stark, Admiral Harold R., 119, 120, 138-140, 142-146

Stauffenberg, Count Claus S. von, 202

Steinhardt, Laurence, 38, 65

Stevens, Major R. H., 58

Stimson, Henry L., 88, 137-138, 139

Stohrer, Eberhard von, 46

Storm Troopers, 18, 21, 48

Student, General, 222, 276

Sudeten, 20

Supreme Headquarters Allied Expeditionary Forces (SHAEF), xi, 204-205, 213, 214-215, 222, 225, 276

Suzuki, 127

Sweden, 50

Switzerland, 57, 60, 204, 241, 262

Takahashi, Finance Minister Korekiyo, 78

Tass, 66

Taylor, Angus M., Jr., 127

Tennessee (ship), 149

Texas (ship), 129

Thaiese Singora, 101

Thailand, 100, 121, 128, 136, 137, 155, 273

Thermopylae, Battle of, 1

Thiele, Major General Fritz, 47

Thomas, General G. I., 215

Thomas, Senator, 120, 122

Three Power Pact, 103

Tito, Josip, 54, 201, 232

Togliatti, Palmiro, 54
Tojo, Hideki, 83, 103, 120, 127, 134
Toyoda, Teijiro, 81, 103
Treaty of 1911, 132
Trieste, 201
Tripartite Pact, 35-36, 37, 76, 84, 92, 96, 115, 122, 133
Trotsky, Leon, 52
Tukhachevsky, Marshal Mikhail, 28, 49, 67, 68, 271
Tunisia, 200
Turkey, 30, 31, 36-37, 50
Turner, Admiral Richmond Kelly, 120

Union of Soviet Socialist Republics, 2, 3, 5, 8-9, 11-13, 14, 15, 16, 75, 76, 79, 81, 95, 119, 135, 156, 161, 162, 163, 164, 175, 192, 193, 199-200, 203, 232, 238, 242, 254, 262, 267-272, 277, 280
   Barbarossa case, 17-74
   intelligence services of, 52-70
United States of America, 2, 3, 9, 11, 12, 14, 23, 33, 54, 64, 66, 159-161, 163, 164, 200, 202, 207, 223-224, 230, 231, 234, 244-250, 252, 254, 255-257, 261, 272-274, 276, 278-281
   intelligence services of, 84-117
   Pearl Harbor, 3, 14, 75-157, 159, 272-273, 274, 278
U.S.S. *Antares* (ship), 148
U.S.S. *Condor* (ship), 148
U.S.S. *Ward* (ship), 148
Untermenschen (inferior people), 67, 72
Unwin, Major Reginald, 173-174
Urquhart, Major General R. E., 214, 215, 217, 219, 222, 224
Utah (ship), 149

Veasey, Lieutenant A. S. S., 182
Versailles Treaty, 18, 20
Vietnam, 265
Vinogradov, S., 37
Von Bentivegni, Colonel, 61

Wacht am Rhein, 234, 235
Wakasugi, Kaname, 105, 121
Wake Island, 75, 160
Walcheren Islands, 230
Washington Naval Conference, 77
Washington Naval Treaty, 77
Waterloo, Battle of, 2
Wehrmachtnachrichtenvergingun-gen (WNV), 47
Welles, Sumner, 65, 103
Wenneker, Admiral, 73
West Virginia (ship), 149
Westphal, General Siegfried, 234, 235, 236
With Napoleon in Russia (de Caulaincourt), 24
Witzleben, Field Marshal Erwin von, 202
WNV (Wehrmachtnachrichten-vergingungen), 47
Workers' Party, 18

Yamamoto, Admiral Isoroku, 80, 82, 83, 84, 108, 142, 155, 161
Yamamoto, Kumaicho, 108, 109-114
Yemelyanov, Vasily S., 271-272
Yezhov, Nikolai, 49
Yorktown (ship), 161
Young, Major Peter, 180, 197
Yugoslavia, 37, 39, 43, 44, 65, 81, 232

Zeitler, Colonel-General Kurt, 193